International Political Theory

Series Editor

Gary Browning
Department of International Relations, Politics,
and Sociology
Oxford Brookes University
Oxford, United Kingdom

The International Political Theory Series provides students and scholars with cutting-edge scholarship that explores the ways in which we theorise the international. Political theory has by tradition implicitly accepted the bounds of the state, and this series of intellectually rigorous and innovative monographs and edited volumes takes the discipline forward, reflecting both the burgeoning of IR as a discipline and the concurrent internationalisation of traditional political theory issues and concepts. Offering a wide-ranging examination of how International Politics is to be interpreted, the titles in the series thus bridge the IR-political theory divide. The aim of the series is to explore international issues in analytic, historical and radical ways that complement and extend common forms of conceiving international relations such as realism, liberalism and constructivism.

More information about this series at
http://www.springer.com/series/14842

Allyn Fives • Keith Breen
Editors

Philosophy and Political Engagement

Reflection in the Public Sphere

Editors
Allyn Fives
National University of Ireland
Galway, Republic of Ireland

Keith Breen
Queen's University, Belfast
Northern Ireland

International Political Theory
ISBN 978-1-137-44586-5   ISBN 978-1-137-44587-2   (eBook)
DOI 10.1057/978-1-137-44587-2

Library of Congress Control Number: 2016938241

Cover illustration: © PAINTING / Alamy Stock Photo

Printed on acid-free paper

This Palgrave Macmillan imprint is published by Springer Nature
The registered company is Macmillan Publishers Ltd. London

This volume of essays is dedicated to Joseph Mahon, to mark his retirement from the National University of Ireland, Galway, where he taught philosophy from 1968 to 2013.

ACKNOWLEDGEMENTS

As editors, we would like to thank the people who have helped to make this book possible. We would first like to acknowledge our shared debt to the person to whom the book is dedicated, Joseph Mahon. As undergraduate students of philosophy in the early 1990s in what was then known as University College Galway, we had the immense good fortune to participate in a number of Joseph's highly engaging classes, ranging from applied ethics, through metaethics and existentialism, to Marxism and contemporary political theory. Like all our fellow students at that time and many others before us, we were deeply impressed by Joseph as a teacher of philosophy, as a thinker unafraid to address the thorniest of moral problems, and as a man of subtle wit and clear decency. It is no exaggeration to say that the example he set played an important role in kindling and in subsequently maintaining our interest in ethics and political philosophy.

We also want to thank various colleagues who kindly provided their time and expertise in a variety of capacities. Our thanks here to Gary Browning, David Carroll, Ruth Fletcher, Alan Kearns, Kelvin Knight, Ève Célia Morisi, Ann V. Murphy, Paddy McQueen, Fabian Schuppert, Jennifer Schweppe, Jeremy Watkins, and Tom Walker. We are grateful, as well, to the authors in this volume for their commitment, creativity, and patience.

We have benefitted from a very supportive relationship with the editorial team at Palgrave. Our thanks, in particular, to Sara Crowley Vigneau, Andrew Baird, Jemima Warren, and Imogen Gordon Clark.

An earlier version of Chap. 7 appeared as Pettit, P. (2015) 'Three Mistakes about Democracy', *Kilikya Felsefe Dergisi*, 2, 1–13. We would like to thank the editors of *Kilikya Felsefe Dergisi* for their permission to print that article in revised form.

CONTENTS

About the Authors

Keith Breen is Senior Lecturer in Political and Social Theory at Queen's University, Belfast, Northern Ireland. His general research areas are contemporary political and social theory, the current focus of his research being questions of political ethics and philosophies of work and economic organization. His other research interests include theories of modernity and intersubjectivity, in particular the socio-political thought of Max Weber, Hannah Arendt, Jürgen Habermas, and Alasdair MacIntyre. He has published widely in peer-reviewed journals and is the author of *Under Weber's Shadow: Modernity, Subjectivity and Politics in Habermas, Arendt and MacIntyre* (2012). He is also co-editor of *After the Nation? Critical Reflections on Nationalism and Postnationalism* (2010) and of *Freedom and Domination: Exploring Republican Freedom* (2016).

Allyn Fives is Lecturer in Political Theory in the School of Political Science and Sociology at the National University of Ireland, Galway, Republic of Ireland. He is the author of *Political Reason: Morality and the Public Sphere* (2013) and *Political and Philosophical Debates in Welfare* (2008). His newest book, *on the topic of power and childhood*, is forthcoming with Manchester University Press in 2016. He has published in peer-reviewed journals in the areas of political reason, welfare theory, the political thought of Rawls and MacIntyre, and civic education. He is also affiliated with the UNESCO Child and Family Research Centre and has been involved in numerous social science studies. His social science publications have been in the areas of children's reading self-beliefs and the methodological and ethical questions raised by Randomized Controlled

Trials (RCTs). He teaches in the areas of political theory and research ethics and is Chair of the University's Research Ethics Committee.

John Foley is the author of *From the Absurd to Revolt: The Coherence of Camus' Philosophical Thought* (2008). He completed his PhD in Philosophy at the National University of Ireland, Galway, in 2002, and between 2004 and 2006 was the recipient of a post-doctoral fellowship from the Irish Research Council for the Humanities and Social Sciences. He has taught in Galway, Carbondale (Illinois), Aix-en-Provence, and London. He lives in London.

Richard Hull is Lecturer in Philosophy at the National University of Ireland, Galway, Republic of Ireland. He is the author of *Deprivation and Freedom* (2007) and of numerous peer-reviewed journal articles on freedom, disability, parental responsibility, and the doctrine of double effect. He is Director of the Centre of Bioethical Research and Analysis (COBRA), Ireland's first bioethics centre, established in 2001 as part of the Department of Philosophy, and is also a member of the National Advisory Committee on Bioethics. He teaches in the areas of bioethics, medical ethics, political theory, and applied philosophy.

Russell Keat is Emeritus Professor of Political Theory in the School of Social and Political Studies at the University of Edinburgh, Scotland. His research interests are in political theory and market economies, including issues about the boundaries between market and non-market spheres, consumer sovereignty and cultural goods, and the ethical implications of market institutions and varieties of capitalism. Publications in this area include *Cultural Goods and the Limits of the Market* (2000) and two collections co-edited with Nick Abercrombie and Nigel Whiteley, *Enterprise Culture* (1991) and *The Authority of the Consumer* (1994). Earlier research included work on the philosophy of the social sciences (*Social Theory as Science*, with John Urry, 1975/1982), Habermas's critical theory (*The Politics of Social Theory*, 1981), and phenomenology (*Understanding Phenomenology*, with Michael Hammond and Jane Howarth, 1991).

Alasdair MacIntyre is the Rev. John A. O'Brien Senior Research Professor of Philosophy at the University of Notre Dame, USA. He is also a senior research fellow at the Centre for Contemporary Aristotelian Studies in Ethics and Politics, London Metropolitan University. His major publications include *Edith Stein: A Philosophical Prologue, 1913–22* (2006), two volumes of his selected essays, *The Tasks of Philosophy* and *Ethics and Politics* (2006), *Dependent Rational Animals* (1999), *Three Rival Versions of Moral Enquiry* (1990), *Whose Justice? Which Rationality?* (1988), *After Virtue* (1981), and *A Short History of Ethics* (1967). He has taught at a number of universities, including Oxford, Manchester, Essex, Princeton, Brandeis, Boston, Vanderbilt, Duke, and the University of Notre Dame.

James Edwin Mahon is Professor of Philosophy and Chair of the Department of Philosophy at CUNY-Lehman College, USA. He has taught at Washington and Lee University, Duke, and Yale. He was a visiting scholar in the Faculty of Philosophy at the University of Cambridge, a visiting fellow in the Department of Philosophy at Princeton University, and a visiting researcher at Yale Law School. His primary research interests are in moral philosophy, especially the nature and scope of moral duties, the history of moral philosophy, especially Kant, Mill, twentieth-century metaethics, and the intersection of law and applied ethics. He is the author of *Motivational Internalism and the Authority of Morality* (2011) and his essays have appeared in *What Happened in and to Moral Philosophy in the Twentieth Century?* (2013), *Contemporary Media Ethics* (2013), *The Philosophy of Deception* (2009), *Researching and Applying Metaphor* (1999), and *Metaphor and Rational Discourse* (1997). His articles have appeared in the *Encyclopedia of Lying and Deception*, *Stanford Encyclopedia of Philosophy*, *The Encyclopedia of Philosophy*, *The British Journal for the History of Philosophy*, *Kantian Review*, *Philosophy*, *The Journal of Value Inquiry*, *The International Journal of Applied Philosophy*, and *Studies in the History of Ethics*.

Joseph Mahon was Lecturer in Philosophy at the National University of Ireland, Galway, Republic of Ireland, from 1968 to 2013. His research and publications have concentrated on topics in Marxism, existentialism, feminism, applied ethics, and cultural policy. In addition to numerous journal articles, critical notices, and reviews, he has published three sole-authored books: *Simone de Beauvoir and Her Catholicism* (2002), *Existentialism, Feminism, and Simone de Beauvoir* (1997), and *An Introduction to Practical Ethics* (1984). His articles have appeared in *Journal of Moral Education*, *Understanding: A Journal of Ideas*, *Irish Medical Times*, *Philosophical Studies*, *History of European Ideas*, *Journal of*

Medical Ethics, Philosophy in Review, and *Politico.* He was also founding editor of *Understanding: A Journal of Ideas* (1972–75).

Felix Ó Murchadha is Professor of Philosophy at the National University of Ireland, Galway, Republic of Ireland. His areas of research include phenomenology (especially Heidegger, Merleau-Ponty, Ricoeur, Levinas, and Marion), philosophy of religion, and philosophy of time and of violence. He is the author of *A Phenomenology of Christian Life: Glory and Night* (2013), *The Time of Revolution: Kairos and Chronos in Heidegger* (2013), *Zeit des Handelns und Möglichkeit der Verwandlung: Kairologie und Chronologie bei Heidegger im Jahrzehnt nach 'Sein und Zeit'* (1999), and editor of *Violence, Victims, Justifications: Philosophical Approaches* (2006). He has also published numerous journal articles and book chapters on his various research interests.

Annie McKeown O'Donovan is a researcher at the National University of Ireland, Galway, Republic of Ireland, with trans-disciplinary research interests in the broad area of applied philosophy. She has research experience from studying on MA in Philosophy: Ethics, Culture, and Global Change in the National University of Ireland, Galway, and on the MSc in Equality Studies at the School of Social Justice in University College Dublin. Her research in those programmes was primarily concerned with the influence of political philosophy on real world issues, such as mechanisms of transitional justice and solidarity in nationalism and the welfare state. She has publications forthcoming in 2016.

Philip Pettit is Laurance S. Rockefeller University Professor of Politics and Human Values at Princeton University, USA, and the Distinguished Professor of Philosophy at the Australian National University, Canberra. He works in moral and political theory and on background issues in the philosophy of mind and metaphysics. His single-authored books include *The Robust Demands of the Good: Ethics with Attachment, Virtue, and Respect* (2015), *Just Freedom: A Moral Compass for a Complex World* (2014), *On the People's Terms: A Republican Theory and Model of Democracy* (2012), *Made with Words: Hobbes on Language, Mind, and Politics* (2008), *Examen a Zapatero* (2008), *Penser en société* (2004), *Rules, Reasons, and Norms* (2002), *A Theory of Freedom* (2001), *Republicanism* (1997), and *The Common Mind* (1996). His co-authored books include *Group Agency* (with Christian List, 2011), *A Political Philosophy in Public Life: Civic*

Republicanism in Zapatero's Spain (with José Martí, 2010), *The Economy of Esteem* (with Geoffrey Brennan, 2004), and *Mind, Morality, and Explanation* (with Frank Jackson and Michael Smith, 2004). He gave the Tanner Lectures on Human Values at Berkeley in April 2015 under the title *The Birth of Ethics*, which is currently in preparation for publication.

Allen W. Wood is Professor of Philosophy at Indiana University, USA. He is the author of many articles and chapters in philosophical journals and anthologies. His book-length publications include *Immanuel Kant's Groundwork for the Metaphysics of Morals: A Commentary* (with Dieter Schönecker, 2015), *The Free Development of Each: Studies in Reason, Right, and Ethics in Classical German Philosophy* (2014), *Kantian Ethics* (2008), *Kant* (2004), *Unsettling Obligations* (2002), *Kant's Ethical Thought* (1999), *Hegel's Ethical Thought* (1990), *Karl Marx* (1981, second expanded edition 2004), *Kant's Rational Theology* (1978, reissued 2009), and *Kant's Moral Religion* (1970, reissued 2009). He is general editor (with Paul Guyer) of the *Cambridge Edition of Kant's Writings in English Translation*, for which he has edited, translated, or otherwise contributed to six volumes. Among the other books he has edited are *The Cambridge History of Philosophy in the Nineteenth Century (1790–1870)* (with Songsuk Susan Hahn, 2012), *Fichte: Attempt at a Critique of All Revelation* (2010), *Kant: Groundwork for the Metaphysics of Morals* (2002), *Hegel: Elements of the Philosophy of Right* (1991), and *Self and Nature in Kant's Philosophy* (1984). He is currently working on a book on Fichte's ethical thought.

CHAPTER 1

Introduction

Allyn Fives and Keith Breen

Do philosophers have a responsibility to their society that is distinct from their responsibility to it as citizens? If so, what form does this responsibility take? It has been argued by many that philosophy has a specific contribution to make to the discussion and resolution of public matters. Such a philosophical enterprise concerns itself with issues that are of a public rather than a purely private nature, or issues that have political rather than simply intellectual or academic relevance. This was the conclusion of many philosophers who began to engage in practical ethics in the 1960s and 1970s. At that time, Joseph Mahon argued that, as moral language is used in appraising everyday practices—political, legal, religious, economic, educational, and domestic—then philosophers should 'concern themselves with these practices, and make that concern primary, pervasive and lasting in their professional practice. It is good philosophical sense to do so, and, ultimately, the only professional initiative that can be justified' (Mahon 1975, pp. 10–11). The main objective of this edited volume is

A. Fives (✉)
School of Political Science and Sociology, UNESCO Child and Family Research Centre, at the National University of Ireland, Galway, Republic of Ireland

K. Breen
Queen's University, Belfast, Northern Ireland

A. Fives, K. Breen (eds.), *Philosophy and Political Engagement*,
DOI 10.1057/978-1-137-44587-2_1

1

to explore both what type of contribution philosophy can make to public matters and what type of reasoning is appropriate when addressing public matters now. These questions are addressed by leading international scholars working in the fields of moral and political philosophy.

The essays in Part I of this book examine the role of philosophy in practical ethics. It is the case that many believe philosophy is ill-equipped to help address the fundamental challenges faced in contemporary democratic politics. In his introductory chapter to Part I, Allyn Fives asks whether we are caught on the horns of the following dilemma. On the one hand, to successfully engage in critical, rational analysis one must establish some distance with respect to the everyday world and its prevailing presuppositions and practices. Does it follow that philosophers will be too detached from political reality to have any appreciation of, and impact on, public matters? On the other hand, if philosophers do become engaged in practical matters, will they then lose the detachment necessary for truly general and abstract philosophical work? In the following three chapters, the role of philosophers in practical ethics is further explored. Joseph Mahon investigates the contributions of philosophers to public matters in the twentieth century and asks what this tells us about the proper role of philosophy now. He charts the course of a debate, spanning more than a century, concerning the role of philosophy in practical and applied issues, a debate marked by the prevailing influence of both J.S. Mill and Karl Marx. James E. Mahon extends this exploration, analysing the role of philosophers in debating the rights and wrongs of abortion. In particular, he considers the impact on the field of practical ethics of Judith Jarvis Thomson's seminal 1971 essay on abortion and then analyses the contrasting views of Thomson and Joseph Mahon on this important and pressing topic. In their essay, Richard Hull and Annie McKeown O'Donovan examine the case for assisted death in certain clearly defined circumstances. Through an analysis of the distinction between acts and omissions, they conclude that we should continue to question our traditional moral landscape and to encourage more action in the light of our humanitarian convictions.

The essays in Part II address the issues of ethical commitment and political engagement. Are philosophers entitled to let their ethical convictions influence their philosophical analyses of contemporary political issues? Indeed, is philosophy a barren and meaningless endeavour without such ethical commitment to provide its starting point and its parameters? Alasdair MacIntyre takes up this theme in his analysis of the works of

George Bernard Shaw and G.K. Chesterton and their public interventions on the social evil of poverty. MacIntyre asks what does it matter for society as a whole if philosophers—and, indeed, non-philosophers—no longer presuppose answers to fundamental philosophical questions, answers provided in part by Aristotelian and Thomist accounts of the human good? It is argued by many, in particular by liberals, that in our contemporary pluralist and individualist age, citizens are entitled to disagree about the bigger ethical questions that these philosophical accounts and traditions claim to answer. However, in their respective essays, Russell Keat and Keith Breen argue that ethical commitment to some account of the human good—or, more precisely, of a plurality of human goods—is unavoidable and that such ethical commitment is valuable when reflecting on the policy issues of meaningful work and the state's support for cultural goods. Returning again to the observation that we will encounter a plurality of such ethical commitments, Allyn Fives examines the role of philosophical analysis in situations where ethical principles come into conflict, focusing in particular on the longstanding debates about research ethics and the institutional review of research in universities. He argues that philosophy has a dual role, combining the abstract and general reasoning involved in theoretical analysis, on the one hand, with the practical reasoning required to work through moral conflicts, on the other.

Finally, we turn to the justification of power, as well as resistance, in Part III. What role can philosophy play in the normative justification of power relations, distinguishing legitimate from illegitimate power? Philip Pettit puts forward the case for a republican model of democracy. Pettit's argument is that such a regime is legitimate because it rests on power relations that preserve rather than hinder individual freedom, that is, relations of non-domination. However, throughout the modern period many philosophers, including Marx and his followers, have questioned the very possibility of making a distinction between legitimate and illegitimate power relations in societies structured in line with capitalist imperatives. In his essay, Allen W. Wood re-examines Karl Marx's writings on capitalism, ethics, and revolutionary activity and argues that these writings remain necessary reading for those who hope, however forlornly, for future human progress. In his contribution, John Foley adds to this theme by revisiting the debate between Albert Camus and his critics on the left, in particular Jean-Paul Sartre and Simone de Beauvoir, over whether there can ever be a justification for political violence. Exploring the phenomenon and lived experience of violence further, Felix Ó Murchadha then questions the very possibility of a philosophical examination of violence that is not itself implicated in the very violence it seeks to examine.

The themes and issues considered here are assuredly varied, highlighting different societal problems and concerns. But while varied, these highlighted problems and concerns are linked insofar as they are faced by all of us in our various roles, including our roles as (ideally) reflective persons and responsible citizens. We therefore hope that taken together the essays in this volume, in throwing light on what is required of us as reflective persons and responsible citizens, illustrate the continued relevance of philosophy as a discipline and of philosophical thought generally to everyday life and practice.

REFERENCE

Mahon, J. (1975). Philosophy and public matters. *Understanding*, 5, 5–11.

Practical Ethics

CHAPTER 2

The Role of Philosophy in Public Matters

Allyn Fives

This book explores the role of philosophy in public matters and poses the following question: does philosophical reflection have a public or political role and, if so, what is it? In posing this question, there are good reasons to believe we are, or appear to be, caught on the horns of a dilemma. The appearance of dilemma arises in the following way. On the one hand, the understanding that is 'distinctively philosophical' is 'general and abstract, rationally reflective, and concerned with what can be known through different kinds of inquiry' (Williams 1985, p. 1). So as to successfully engage in such critical rational analysis, one must establish some distance with respect to the everyday world and its prevailing presuppositions and practices. While there are various methodological approaches taken in philosophical reflection, common to them all is a process of disengaging from the everyday world so as to better pursue a critical rational analysis of what is taken for granted. However, to the extent that philosophy is disengaged, will it also be ill-suited to play a public or political role? Will philosophy be uninformed about practical matters or too distant from those who need to be convinced by philosophical argument, or will it lack credibility among those who are making decisions and implementing their programmes in the public sphere?

A. Fives
School of Political Science and Sociology and UNESCO Child and Family
Research Centre at the National University of Ireland, Galway, Republic of Ireland

© The Editor(s) (if applicable) and The Author(s) 2016
A. Fives, K. Breen (eds.), *Philosophy and Political Engagement*,
DOI 10.1057/978-1-137-44587-2_2

On the other hand, some philosophers have called for a direct engagement in public matters, if philosophy is ever to be successful in attempts to persuade or actively collaborate with those who hold office, fill public roles, or agitate for public reform (Wolff 2011). However, again this seems problematic, for such direct public involvement, it can be argued, is antithetical to the philosophical disengagement required for critical rational analysis in general and also, specifically, for the impartial and dispassionate analysis of social mores and social injustices, as well as for the critique of ideology and its distorting effects on human consciousness. Can we remove ourselves from the horns of this dilemma? Is it possible to combine philosophical reflection with political engagement? Can the type of philosophical disengagement required for critical reflection somehow be made compatible with active involvement in public matters?

The contributors to this volume endeavour to answer questions of this sort, and each attempts to demonstrate how philosophy can engage with public matters. In doing so, the contributors are continuing a tradition of philosophical engagement with public matters that is, in one sense, as old as philosophy itself. It is a tradition that can be traced from classical Athens right up to revolutionary and reformist writers of the nineteenth and twentieth centuries and beyond. However, we can only undertake politically engaged philosophy if we take into consideration why many philosophers rejected such a project during the last century. It was argued that while philosophical reflection can help improve the concepts used in public debate, it is singularly ill-suited to play any role in resolving the substantive issues raised in such debates. What is more, it was argued, when philosophers stray beyond these limits, they are prone to make meaningless statements (philosophical nonsense) and also to promote a political environment hostile to critical rational enquiry.

In this chapter, I will first outline the reasons why many philosophers argued that they had only a restricted role in public matters. I will then look at subsequent efforts to expand that role. First, many philosophers began to make substantive normative arguments, promoting a particular type of society or a particular resolution to one of society's problems. And, second, some philosophers left the campus behind, entered the public arena, and tried to sway and influence people and events, whether as public commentators or as members of committees. Two themes will be central to this discussion. Because of the diversity of philosophical doctrines, there is no one distinctively philosophical approach to public matters, and philosophers employ different and perhaps incompatible methodological approaches.

Second, there is a diversity of moral considerations appropriate to public matters, and it is possible for these to come into conflict in any one instance. Given the diversity of methods and the possibility for moral conflict, how can philosophers engage in public matters in a way that is meaningful?

1 PHILOSOPHY AS CONCEPTUAL IMPROVEMENT

As we have seen already, for one school of thought philosophy should play only a limited role in public matters. I want to draw attention to two versions of this argument. The first, and perhaps the more extreme, derives from the work of Ludwig Wittgenstein and A.J. Ayer. They make a distinction between ethics, on the one hand, and science and philosophy, on the other. In his *Tractatus Logico-Philosophicus* (1921), Wittgenstein concluded by stating that 'What we cannot speak about we must pass over in silence' (1921, § 7, p. 89). While the propositions of mathematics and the empirical sciences can convey definite cognitive information, ethical and moral statements cannot. Therefore, 'it is clear that ethics cannot be put into words' (1921, § 6.42, p. 86).

A similar distinction is made in A.J. Ayer's *Language, Truth and Logic* (1946). It was an overriding aim of that book to identify and reject what Ayer referred to as 'metaphysical nonsense':

> For we shall maintain that no statement which refers to a 'reality' transcending the limits of all sense-experience can possibly have any literal significance; from which it must follow that the labours of those who have striven to describe such a reality have all been devoted to the production of nonsense (Ayer 1946, p. 34).

Ayer argued that a proposition is meaningful, if and only if, it can be empirically *verified*, whether directly through observations or indirectly based in part on observations and also analytic statements (Ayer 1946, p. 13). In contrast, many statements made about moral and ethical issues cannot be empirically verified and therefore, he believed, are nonsense.

There are good reasons to question the assumptions of Ayer and other logical positivists, in particular the view that meaningful statements are those that can be empirically *verified*. For example, Karl Popper attempted to show that empirical science does not progress through efforts to verify statements, but rather through efforts to show that a null hypothesis can be *falsified* or *refuted* (Popper 1963, p. 51). Indeed, by

1959 Ayer conceded it was no longer possible to maintain his distinction between meaningful statements and metaphysical nonsense (Ayer 1959, pp. 15–16).

Others who are broadly sympathetic with the idea that philosophy should play a minor role in public matters do not rest this argument on an account of metaphysical nonsense. They believe philosophy can play a role in our reflection on ethical matters, although this is the limited role of conceptual improvement. This argument is based on a metaethical account of what we are doing when we make moral judgements. It is argued, the improvement of concepts is pursued 'in the interests of clarity and coherence ... Coherence means either consistency or, more strongly, positive logical connection; and clarity is an aid to understanding and to the avoidance of intellectual confusion' (Raphael 1970, p. 20). Philosophy cannot and therefore should not attempt to go on to play the further role of 'critical evaluation of beliefs'; that is, 'the attempt to give rational grounds for accepting or rejecting beliefs which we normally take for granted' (Raphael 1970, p. 4). Thus, philosophy can play a *negative* role with respect to our moral beliefs, as conceptual analysis can show if beliefs are based on logical incoherence and/or lack of clarity; but philosophy cannot go on to play a *positive* role and identify what moral beliefs are valid or should be accepted.

It is assumed that philosophy cannot play this second, broader, role because of a particular metaethical view of moral judgement. For emotivists, when we use moral language, we express attitudes (Stevenson 1944; Hudson 1983 [1970]). For instance, when people conclude that poverty is an injustice, they are expressing their disapproval of poverty and the social, economic, and political contexts in which it arises. Those who, in contrast, believe that poverty is unfortunate, but that its presence is not sufficient evidence of injustice, are also expressing an attitude. Because competing views in public debates are based in large part on different and incompatible attitudes, philosophy cannot tell us which of the competing ethical views is correct. Philosophy can tell us if a moral judgement is based on conceptual confusion, because this is a matter of philosophical analysis, but it cannot tell us if the attitudes expressed in a moral judgement are correct, because attitudes cannot be either correct or incorrect.

What are the considerations motivating this approach to philosophy? This approach goes back to David Hume's distinction between the two sources of knowledge, what is now referred to as 'Hume's fork' (Hudson 1983 [1970]). For Hume, we can have knowledge through empirical observation and experience and also through logical analysis, but we cannot have knowledge of what is, morally speaking, right and wrong, as this instead is a matter of the *passions*. In moral matters, reason does play a role, but it is a secondary, supportive role to the passions: 'Reason is and ought only to be the slave of the passions' (Hume 1969 [1739–1740], Book 2, Part III, § 3, p. 462). Morality does not consist *merely* in a matter of fact or in rational principles (Hume 1969 [1739–1740], Book 3, Part I, §1, p. 521). Rather, it is a matter of sentiment, disapprobation or approbation, and it is an object of feeling, not an object of thought.

What we have said so far about emotivists is based on a distinction between different facets of moral judgements, namely, the parts that are and are not susceptible to rational analysis. On the basis of this distinction, emotivists do not contend that normative judgements fall outside the category of statements that are meaningful, unlike Ayer and Wittgenstein. Rather, they argue that in making moral judgements there is some nonrational remainder, that is, the expression of an attitude that cannot itself be given a rational justification. We can rationally analyse the logical consistency of a judgement and we can rationally analyse the beliefs a person has about a state of affairs, but a person's attitudes cannot be either rational or irrational (Stevenson 1944). Many may agree there is a nonrational remainder in moral judgement, but the real issue here is where that line should be drawn. While some conclude that only a narrow sphere of moral judgement is susceptible to rational analysis, others conclude that the sphere of reason is broader, and the majority of the contributors to this volume take the latter view.

Ayer's distinction between meaningful statements and metaphysical nonsense is unhelpful now, as it simply categorizes normative judgements as meaningless. Nonetheless, rational argumentation presupposes a distinction between statements that can and cannot be rationally justified, and in practice, some normative judgements will fall on the wrong side of this dividing line. What we can say is that the statements of philosophy should be meaningful, including philosophical statements about substantive normative issues, and that philosophy is a rational enterprise, whatever way we construe the term *rational*. Therefore, in principle, it must be possible to offer rational considerations in support of philosophical statements, as well as rational considerations that could cast doubt on philosophical statements. If we accept these basic assumptions, then we can say that *statements are not meaningful when no rational considerations can be offered to support or to cast doubt on them*. We will return to this below.

2   POLITICAL LEGITIMACY

I turn now from the question of the proper limits of philosophy to the question of political legitimacy. I will not be able to address the very important question of what makes power legitimate, a question addressed in particular by republican theorists such as Philip Pettit (see Chap. 10). Instead, I want to explore whether there is a connection—and, if so, what type of connection—between the type of philosophical engagement in public matters, on the one hand, and the type of political regime in existence, on the other. The implication of what we have said so far is that some of the statements made by philosophers about moral issues may not be meaningful, and also that philosophers may be unaware that what they have stated cannot be supported by or called into question by rational considerations. Is there some necessary connection between such meaningless engagement by philosophers and a politics that suppresses, rather than fosters, critical engagement in public matters?

We could proceed here by way of examples, both that of Nazi Germany and the Soviet Union. Firstly, Jonathan Glover has drawn a connection between Martin Heidegger's approach to philosophical reflection and the totalitarian politics of the regime he gave support to. Heidegger's real crime, Glover concludes,

> is about undermining philosophy's role in developing a climate of critical thought. His books are an embodiment of the idea that philosophy is an impenetrable fog, in which ideas not clearly understood have to be taken on trust … Deference is encouraged by having to take it on trust that the obscure means something important (Glover 2001, pp. 375–376).

Glover quotes a long segment from Heidegger's *Being and Time* that, Glover argues, represents Heidegger's trademark 'inarticulate complexity' and 'blurred' thinking. Glover also believes that Heidegger's approach to philosophy had a parallel in the political statements he made. Just as Heidegger believed we should defer to tradition in our thought, in politics he called for deference to authority, rather than a rational justification of the authority of the state: 'Let not propositions and "ideas" be the rules of your Being. The Fuhrer alone is the present and the future German reality and its law' (Heidegger, quoted in Glover 2001, p. 369).

However, there is another way to interpret the example of Heidegger. His was an effort to rehabilitate prejudice, that is, to reject the supremacy of reason in Enlightenment thought and instead to affirm the supremacy of presuppositions that are not themselves justified by reason (Gadamer 1989 [1975]). In addition, his work can be seen as a radical or extreme form of scepticism and as an alternative to both totalitarian and liberal-democratic politics. While the Nazis were guilty of a form of violence that led to an aestheticization or eroticization of violence, violence as an end in itself, liberal democrats are guilty of a different type of violence, one that forces reality to conform to a universal conceptual system. What lies between these two extremes is a type of philosophical engagement, one derived from the work of Heidegger and others, including Derrida, 'in which boundaries are destroyed', as suggested by Ó Murchadha, 'in order to interrupt and suspend norms, set aside boundaries, and release self and other to the vulnerability of their own being' (see Chap. 13).

A second example is the justifications offered for various forms of Marxist communism. In many instances, they were not meaningful, in the sense I have used here, as no rational considerations could be offered to support or to cast doubt on them. For example, G.A. Cohen had once believed that Marxist communism was justified by any and all moral considerations, and therefore objections to socialism must be based on an undisclosed class interest of those making the objections (Cohen 1995, pp. 5–6). Although Cohen came to realize that he had been mistaken to take this view, his original position was that it was unnecessary and pointless to offer rational justifications for the Marxist view of communism. What are the political implications of such an approach to philosophy? One possible implication is a regime that forbids and crushes dissent because, it is claimed, all such dissent is based on overt or covert class interest. For instance, Aleksandr Solzhenitsyn was imprisoned in a labour camp (*Gulag*) for the reason that his private letters were found to contain statements critical of Stalin's rule. Although later, during the Khrushchev era, Solzhenitsyn did publish an account of his time in the Gulag in the November 1961 issue of *Novy Mir*, he was prevented from publishing further accounts of his experiences, in the *Gulag* and internal exile, and was forced into exile abroad as a dissident (Solzhenitsyn 1973; Thomas 1999).

Solzhenitsyn is rightly seen as an individual possessing many of the virtues required of a public intellectual, not least, commitment to disclosing the wrongs done on behalf of a regime. But the example leaves many questions unanswered. First, it does not establish definitively that revolutionary regimes lack legitimacy or that philosophers should not support revolutionary movements. Although Albert Camus, among others, highlighted the way revolutionary movements sacrificed individual freedom (see Chap. 12), there are strong grounds to argue that the ways in which power was exercised in the Soviet Union to limit criticism of its legitimacy entailed a gross misuse of Marx's own ideas and methodology (see Chap. 11). Second, the example does not tell us that publicly engaged philosophers must be democrats. Although the regime denied to Solzhenitsyn basic liberal-democratic rights, Solzhenitsyn was neither a liberal nor a democrat and was highly critical of the crassness of Western consumerist society. Finally, the example does not establish that publicly engaged philosophers must limit themselves to the tasks of conceptual improvement laid out by logical positivists. Indeed, Solzhenitsyn gave priority to religious faith and to individual conscience, and many philosophers now would question whether faith and conscience fall within the realm of a public sphere philosophy (Solzhenitsyn 1975, in Thomas 1999, p. 404).

3   The Public Role of Philosophy

Our theme is the dilemma we face whenever we try to apply philosophy to public matters. If disengagement is necessary for philosophical reflection, does it follow that philosophical reflection is ill-suited to public matters? What are the appropriate limits and standards that should be observed when philosophers engage in public matters? Based on what we have said so far about the limitations of logical positivism and also the dangers of some forms of philosophical engagement, we can propose the following: *when philosophers are involved in public matters, their statements should be meaningful and should be compatible with an approach to politics that fosters rather than suppresses critical engagement in public matters.*

In the remainder of this chapter, I will look briefly at two ways in which philosophers can play a public role along the lines outlined here. First, we can engage in substantive normative theory and try to resolve the misuse of concepts in everyday contexts, criticizing injustices, and phenomena such as domination, ideology, and compulsions that are responsible for the distortion of perception and understanding. Second, we can bring philosophy off the campus and into the public domain. That is, we can make an effort to apply our philosophical deliberations and conclusions to, in some way, influence the course taken in the wider society on public matters.

Substantive Normative Theory

Philosophical reflection now is regularly applied in an effort to provide answers, whether intended as partial or complete, to many questions of public concern. Seminal texts on social justice, animal ethics, terrorism, abortion, capital punishment, children's rights, and so on are all examples of philosophy playing a public role. The 'Statement of Purpose' that accompanied the first issue of the journal *Philosophy & Public Affairs* in 1971 outlined a public role for philosophy as follows:

> Issues of public concern often have an important philosophical dimension. *Philosophy & Public Affairs* is founded in the belief that a philosophical examination of these issues can contribute to their clarification and to their resolution ... *Philosophy & Public Affairs* is designed to fill the need for a periodical in which philosophers with different viewpoints and philosophically inclined writers from various disciplines – including law, political science, economics, and sociology – can bring their distinctive methods to bear on problems that concern everyone (Cohen 1971, front matter).

How can we justify any attempt to use philosophical reflection in this way so as to contribute to the clarification *and* to the resolution of issues of public concern? Clearly, such a standpoint gives philosophy a broad role. Philosophy can do more than merely analyse whether concepts such as justice and domination are used and defined coherently and clearly. It can also do more than merely highlight where judgements of value are not logically consistent or clear and/or not in accordance with the facts. Rather, it is now widely believed that philosophy can and should have a *normative* or *ideological* role, namely, that it can and should be used to put forward norms or ideals for the organization of society. *A Theory of Justice* (1971) is the book most closely associated with the renaissance of this type of political philosophy. In it, John Rawls did try to show that alternative norms or ideals should be rejected, and for a variety of reasons, including those of logical consistency and clarity. However, Rawls also drew on normative values, in particular the value that gave primacy to the rights protecting individual freedom. In so doing, he argued for a particular theory of justice, one which strove to guarantee individual liberty, but also fair equality of opportunity and a distribution of income and wealth that was to the greatest benefit of the least well off.

If philosophers are now entitled (and even obliged) to make such substantive prescriptions, how can we be sure that such philosophical engagements in public matters will be meaningful and compatible with an approach to politics that fosters rather than suppresses critical engagement in public matters? Many different answers have been given to this question, and many of these are represented by the contributors to this volume.

The approach I have taken in this chapter owes more to the analytical tradition in moral philosophy than it does to continental philosophy. According to one version of analytical philosophy, the role of the moral philosopher is to apply the analytical and critical skills of philosophy to help resolve issues of public concern. In this volume, for example, arguments are made for assisted suicide (see Chap. 5) and abortion (see Chap. 4). In each case, philosophers are arguing from theoretical premises to substantive normative conclusions. In contrast to this, continental philosophy represents a sceptical approach to theoretical reasoning. Hans-Georg Gadamer rejects what he calls the Enlightenment prejudice against prejudice, that is, the unquestioned rejection of the value or significance of unquestioned assumptions. Instead, his hermeneutics begins from a standpoint or horizon composed of such prejudices and seeks insight through a 'fusion of horizons' that involves an 'openness to experience' and an openness to 'the other' truly as a 'Thou' in an 'I-Thou' interaction (Gadamer 1989 [1975], pp. 357, 341). Others criticize the damage done by an overly rationalistic approach to philosophy, equating it with a form of violence (see Chap. 13).

A further question is whether philosophers must remain ethically neutral if they are to make statements that are meaningful. Perfectionists start from ethical ideas about what makes life valuable or good, and from that basis they then address public matters. For instance, while Joseph Raz acknowledges that there is a plurality of good ways of life and ethical values, he believes such substantive normative commitments should be included in public debates because the resulting agreements will have greater moral significance (Raz 1986). Some point out that all ways of life embody or express some ethical commitment, and therefore it is an illusion to think that we could engage in public matters and yet remain neutral regarding ethical values (see Chaps. 7 and 8). And, finally, it has also been argued that such substantive normative commitments are a feature of moral thinking generally for ordinary people or 'plain persons', and that some philosophical approaches, such as Aristotelianism and Thomism, are better placed to accommodate this human need for ethical commitment (see Chap. 6).

I have tried elsewhere to provide an argument for an approach that owes a lot to John Rawls and his account of reasonableness (Fives 2010, 2013).

Rawls starts by reminding us that in political philosophy, our concern is with the moral legitimacy of coercive institutions and that this restricted focus should bear on what we consider to be appropriate considerations in public debate (Rawls 1989, p. 244). Put simply, there are many moral issues about which we need not agree, and should not expect others to agree with us, when our concern is whether our coercive institutions have legitimacy. We need not agree on what the overarching purpose of human life is, on whether moral truth is revealed through religious faith, and so on. Instead, when we approach others as 'reasonable' fellow citizens, we accept that what we must agree on are the fair terms of social cooperation. We also accept that we are to offer 'public' considerations in defence of our proposals, that is, considerations that others, as our moral equals, can reasonably be expected to accept (Rawls 1999b [1997], p. 579).

This is not the place to defend Rawls's account of the public role for philosophy. Rather, it can be taken as an example, one of many, of how we can give philosophy a role that is much broader than the mere analysis of concepts, while at the same time believing with some confidence that such philosophical statements will be meaningful and also compatible with an approach to politics that fosters, rather than suppresses, critical engagement in public matters. For Rawls, the moral and ethical judgements of the public sphere cannot be based on what is claimed to be the truth of any one moral doctrine, at least not without accepting that coercive institutions should impose this moral doctrine on all those who feel they have good reasons to reject it (Rawls 1999a [1987], p. 425). Instead, public morals and ethics should be based on the reasonableness of fellow citizens.

I have argued elsewhere that this is highly defensible as an approach to moral justification, because at its core is the idea of moral equality. It assumes that in morally justifying ourselves to others we view those others as free and equal moral persons (Fives 2013, p. 131). Or to put the same point another way, the reasonable citizen is ready 'to politically address others of different persuasions in terms of public reasons' (Freeman 2000, p. 401). This would seem to be a plausible candidate for an approach to philosophy that is publicly engaged and in which philosophers make meaningful statements in a manner that fosters rather than suppresses critical engagement with public matters. Under this approach, we are required to offer public reasons for the justification of our proposals, that is, reasons it is reasonable to expect others to accept. We are also required, in the basic rights that we guarantee, to place the greatest possible importance on individual freedom.

Bringing Philosophy into the Public Domain

As mentioned above, the other way in which philosophy can play a public role is when we make an effort to apply its deliberations and conclusions to in some way influence the course taken in the wider society on public matters. It may be said that Rawls's publication of *A Theory of Justice* (1971) had such an impact on the wider society by virtue of its influence upon subsequent reflection on and writings about social justice, including the importance it had for those who were critical of his arguments (see Nozick 1974). But what is intended here is something quite different. The second way in which philosophy can play a public role is when those who put forward philosophical arguments, sometimes literally but always figuratively, leave the campus behind and enter the public domain.

Philosophy and Moral Dilemmas

I will look at two ways that philosophy can be brought into the public domain in this sense. First, it can happen when we engage with the wider public in a direct and explicit effort to *shape* how people think about a topic and also how they act, including what policies they implement. This explicit and direct effort to shape public opinion and public policy may be marked by persuasion, exhortation, or even public demonstration or protest. When we take philosophical reflection off the campus and into the public domain in this way, should we expect to experience some discontinuity between philosophical reflection and public life such that the standards of rational justification appropriate to philosophy are to some significant degree inappropriate to public life? Below, we explore this question by addressing the issue of *moral dilemmas* in public life.

One answer to this question comes from Noam Chomsky's 1967 essay on the responsibility of intellectuals, published in the *New York Review of Books*. The line of argument in Chomsky's essay suggests that philosophical reflection can and should strive after truth and that we can and should use philosophical truth to expose the lies and distortions of public life. Put simply, 'It is the responsibility of intellectuals to speak the truth and to expose lies' (Chomsky 1967). In addition, because of their access to the skills and resources needed to expose the lies of those with power, the responsibilities of *intellectuals* are greater than their fellow citizens, since they have 'the leisure, the facilities, and the training to seek the truth lying behind the veil of distortion and misrepresentation, ideology and class interest, through which the events of current history are presented to us' (Chomsky 1967).

Chomsky's position is that there is a sharp discontinuity between philosophy and the public realm in one sense: while the aim of the philosopher is to arrive at truth, in the main, the aim of those in power is to hide the truth of what they are doing and its consequences. However, in a more fundamental sense, there is no discontinuity, for Chomsky, between the two: we can and should apply the standards and ideals of philosophical reflection directly and without translation to the public realm, and so public actors—politicians, civil servants, and other office holders—are to be praised or condemned depending on whether or not they meet the standards and ideals of philosophical truth.

Chomsky represents what has been described by some as the 'public intellectual' who, because without power, is therefore without stain or compromise. The public intellectual in this guise is

necessarily defined by a posture of detachment, alienation, and nonconformity…
Not despite, but because of his overriding desire to help society, he must convince others and himself that what he really loves is truth and not society (Melzer 2003, p. 11).

In his 1967 essay, Chomsky highlights many of the occasions when various public figures in the US lied and misrepresented reality so as to disguise the role of the US government and its armed forces in the Vietnam War. To those in power, the lies may have seemed necessary so as to pursue their policies, which in turn may have seemed justified to them. In Chomsky's approach, the exposure of the lie is all that is required for passing moral judgement. However, what Chomsky does not consider is whether lies, those relating to the Vietnam War or to any other public matter, could ever have a moral justification.

Others have addressed the possibility that the moral standards that forbid lying (along with other moral principles and ideals) may not be applicable to public life in precisely the same way as they apply to other spheres of life. Those who occupy public offices and perform public roles take on new responsibilities, but they are also presented with new moral challenges and even moral dilemmas. This is the case when office holders are confident that, morally speaking, they must act in a particular way or authorize a type of action that they would consider morally objectionable if it were to occur in another context. If our moral principles and commitments do come into conflict, philosophy must do more than simply point out that one of these principles or commitments has been violated. Rather, philosophy must address whether there are any moral limits to what we may do when the responsibilities of our office seem to require that we get our *hands dirty*.

When we speak of getting hands dirty, for the purposes of this discussion, we will not only refer to gross violations of human rights such as torture, genocide, and ethnic cleansing. We are also referring to more prosaic, everyday instances of morally suboptimal behaviour in public office, including

> lying, or at least concealment and making of misleading statements; breaking promises; special pleading; temporary coalition with the distasteful; sacrifice of the interest of worthy persons to those of unworthy persons; and ... coercion up to blackmail (Williams 1978, p. 59).

Such action may sometimes seem to be required, in particular, so as to promote some objective that will be of benefit to many people. Nonetheless, even when dirty work like this has a justification based on consequentialist considerations, there may remain reasons why we should find it morally troublesome. This may be due to 'an overriding concern for a record of un-monstrous and respectworthy conduct, and of action that has never been mean or inhuman' (Hampshire 1978a, p. 10). Even if we know that some dirty deeds are morally justified by their likely good consequences, we are also right to believe that we would be, morally speaking, *stained* by having carried out those deeds ourselves. What the arguments of Stuart Hampshire and others point to is the presence of moral conflict and moral dilemma: 'We ordinarily encounter serious moral problems as conflicts between moral claims which, considered *a priori*, seem absolute and exceptionless and which are in fact irreconcilable in situations that present the problem' (Hampshire 1978b, p. 40).

The most important feature of public roles is the requirement of impersonality on behalf of the person who fills the role, and this has two important implications: 'it implies both a heightened concern for results and a stricter requirement of impartiality' (Nagel 1978, p. 82). Therefore, in contrast to private relations, such as friendship, marriage, parenthood, and so on, when it comes to the moral justification of an action within a public institution (e.g., a school, hospital, army, or government ministry), far greater significance should be given to its effects or consequences and to the requirement that public officials display no partiality in the way that these effects or consequences are distributed. Because of this heightened requirement of impartiality, sometimes ruthlessness is licensed. To return to the arena addressed by Chomsky—a situation of war—it *may* be necessary to conceal the truth of some military activity so as to improve the likelihood that those activities are successful, and it *may* be necessary for a public official to lie and to conceal the truth about these activities, even to those she or he has personal relationships with.

What does this tell us about the role philosophy can play when it leaves the campus and enters the public domain? While some insist that moral dilemmas are only apparent and not real—for the reason that, properly understood, morality could never require us to perform actions such as lying and special pleading (Donagan 1993; Foot 2002; de Haan 2001)—we have pointed to where public life in particular does generate moral conflicts. The first implication of this argument is that we should be slower to condemn those in power who, because of their public role, have been compelled to make difficult decisions and therefore to act ruthlessly. However, the second implication is that we should be more sensitive to and aware of the moral discomfort that should be felt whenever ruthless action is justified. While utilitarians will argue that if lying is required so as to best promote happiness, then there is no moral dilemma in this case, Bernard Williams argues that even when the dirty action has some moral justification in its favour that has outweighed the reasons against it, there is a 'moral remainder, ... [an] uncancelled moral disagreeableness'. This 'particularly arises in cases where the moral justification of the action is of a consequentialist or maximizing kind, while what has gone to the wall is a right' (Williams 1978, p. 63). Therefore, the second implication for philosophy's public role is that we need to ensure we do not ever become blind to the negative consequences of ruthless action, even when all things considered it is morally justified.

What this shows is the real possibility of moral conflict or dilemma. It follows that although Chomsky was right that US office holders had lied about what the US armed forces were doing in Vietnam, the role of the philosopher must be broader than bringing attention to lies such as these. The philosopher must be sensitive to moral dilemmas as well. If that is so, let us consider the example of Jean Paul Sartre. Was he justified when he lied about his personal experiences of the Soviet Union after visiting there in 1954, claiming there was total freedom of thought and expression (Johnson 1988, p. 244)? Sartre may have believed that he was faced with a dilemma and that, although he should be truthful, he should also support an allegedly socialist regime. However, his approach can be criticized for the ramifications it has for philosophy and politics. If we do not even acknowledge dilemmas when they arise, but rather try to hide them, is this compatible with open critical engagement? And if we do not acknowledge any 'uncancelled moral disagreeableness' when we work through a moral dilemma, are we more likely to take any means necessary to pursue our aims and do so without shame or guilt?

Philosophy on the Committee
The second way we can bring philosophy into the public domain is for those who are used to thinking philosophically to become involved in *committee work*. This involvement often will be premised on the assumption that the person in question is an expert concerning the philosophical dimension of a public matter. Examples include the work done by ethicists on committees established to provide ethical oversight and review of research proposals within universities and other institutions, via Research Ethics Committees and Institutional Review Boards (see Chap. 9), as well as state-authorized commissions of enquiry, such as *The Warnock Report into Human Fertilisation and Embryology* and *The Williams Report on Obscenity and Film Censorship* (see Chap. 3). Committee work is both more direct and more prosaic than efforts to shape public opinion and policy through persuasion, exhortation, and demonstration or protest. Participation on committees will involve playing some role in making decisions that will then be implemented (e.g., an ethical review of a research protocol, a policy recommendation made to a government, and so on). At the same time, it requires collaboration with others and adherence to the protocol or remit of a committee.

It may be the case that philosophers should not take part in committees of this kind, both for reasons to do with philosophy and politics. Is there an incompatibility between philosophy and this type of public action, such that philosophy has no credibility in public affairs and individuals will be discredited *qua* philosophers by this form of public engagement?

Dan Brock has commented on his involvement with the US President's Commission for the Study of Ethical Problems in Medicine during the years 1981–82. His experiences led him to conclude that philosophy lacked credibility in the public policy arena, in part because non-philosophers have little knowledge of what philosophers do and what the criteria are for having done well as a philosopher. In addition, because many philosophers accept that basic moral principles cannot ultimately be established as true or objectively correct, their 'grounds for using their expertise or title to press their own views on moral questions may in turn be uncertain' (Brock 1987, p. 790). Brock also concluded that there was a deep conflict between the aims of philosophical activity and the goals and constraints of the public policy process. While *truth* is the central virtue of scholarly work, requiring us to follow arguments and evidence where they lead without regard for the social consequences of doing so, for those engaged in policy formation, in contrast, it is irresponsible not to focus 'on how their actions will *affect* policy' (Brock 1987, p. 787, emphasis added).

Brock did believe there were benefits to philosophy from its engagement in public policy. It can lead to a more realistic understanding of the constraints of political reality and better-informed applied ethics (Brock 1987, p. 791). Nonetheless, when one's focus shifts from truth to the consequences of one's actions, as it must do, for instance, when engaged with others in an attempt to agree on the shared findings of a committee, this 'leads to manipulative attitudes toward others that I am not comfortable with and fosters playing a little fast and loose with the truth as best one understands it, in a way that is inimical to the scholarly academic enterprise' (Brock 1987, p. 789). The example he gives of playing fast and loose with the truth is illustrative. Brock notes the committee came to a shared view that stopping life-sustaining treatment at the request of a competent patient was morally permissible, but he also notes that the commissioners' reasons for reaching this conclusion 'were confused'. They were confused because they thought (wrongly, in Brock's view) that in stopping life support one was 'allowing' the patient to die, and that this was very different from 'killing' the patient (Brock 1987, p. 788).

An alternative view is that philosophy is perfectly compatible with committee work. To start with, it could be said that what Brock takes to be *true*, namely that there is no morally significant distinction between stopping life support and intentionally killing a patient, is a contentious and controversial claim concerning ultimate questions or general principles in morality (See Chap. 5). As Rawls would argue, Brock may have been expecting too much from himself and others, since in public life we need not and should not expect others to agree with us on such questions. In addition, we need not agree on such questions so as to make progress on less contentious issues. As Albert Jonsen and Stephen Toulmin found from their own experience of committee work, while debate over general principles ran on interminably, quick agreement greeted more specific cases (Jonsen and Toulmin 1988; Jonsen 1995, p. 239). What Jonsen and Toulmin discovered is that, in committee work, we will be ineffective if we insist on first securing a consensus on general moral principles, but in any case it is inappropriate to do so. In fact, committee work revealed to them the need to focus on *cases* and their properties when we debate public issues, and, thus, it revealed to them the appropriate approach philosophy should take when engaged in public matters.

When we engage in committee work, we need not agree on the fundamentals of morality so as to reach shared decisions on ethical issues; as pointed out by Jonathan Wolff, 'progress on the penultimate questions need not wait for solutions to the ultimate ones'. What matters is 'not convincing yourself that you have the best position, but carrying others with you' and also 'working out how people can get much of what they want without taking too much away from others' (Wolff 2011, p. 6). An example Wolff cites comes from the issue of road safety. Cars are dangerous, and while stopping all people from driving would bring the danger to an end, it would be a disproportionate response. The way to 'carry others with you' is to agree to allow people drive, but not in the most dangerous ways. This, he believes, provides a model of how to make progress more generally in public policy debates (Wolff 2011, p. 204). We can look for relatively small changes that amount to a large step forward for one group, but only minimal concessions for another.

But how can we carry others with us in ways that do not conflict with philosophical principles and, in Brock's terms, 'play fast and loose' with the truth? What Rawls tries to provide us with is a way to resolve moral issues through the giving of reasons and a way of doing so that is suited to public life in a free society. We should only require that others be reasonable, view each other as free and equal persons, and offer terms of social cooperation that it is reasonable to expect each to accept. Instead of believing that we may or should deceive others who disagree with our proposals because of deep moral commitments they have that, they believe, forbid agreement, we should simply put those deep moral disagreements to one side. Far from playing fast and loose with the truth, this simply entails refusing to pronounce on moral truth when such pronouncement is inappropriate in the public domain. Nonetheless, this remains a moral approach, since it is a search for agreement that has moral justification, that is, a search for moral agreement *suited* to the political realm of a free society.

4   Conclusions

Because of the diversity of philosophical doctrines, there is no one distinctively philosophical approach to public matters, and philosophers employ different and perhaps incompatible methodological approaches. In addition, there is a diversity of moral considerations appropriate to public matters, and it is possible for these to come into conflict in any one instance. Given the diversity of methods and the possibility for moral conflict, it may seem unlikely that philosophers can engage in public matters in a way that is meaningful.

Nonetheless, a number of tentative conclusions are suggested by this short introductory analysis. Sometimes the best we can do is agree on a course of action that all things considered is the right thing to do, but nonetheless we should feel uncomfortable with the moral sacrifices we have agreed to make. This requires us to be realistic and acknowledge that moral conflicts will arise. If philosophers can remain open to the possibility that they may be called on to justify their arguments to others in a situation of genuine moral conflict this should encourage philosophical modesty.

Some may be concerned that such work will corrupt the philosopher, who will be required to countenance the unthinkable when faced with moral dilemmas. Yet this need not be so. Rather, we as philosophers must be aware of what is lost when dirty deeds are performed in public office, and this awareness can be used as a moral check against the abuse of power and the excessive use of dirty deeds. Others may be concerned that even the more prosaic sphere of committee work will be corrupting, as it is an environment that prioritizes action and decision over reflection and nuanced distinctions. While philosophical reflection can be unhelpful in this environment if we think of it solely as an individualistic search for truth, nonetheless, it can be a means to help others come to an agreed position, especially if we understand this 'means' in Wolff's terms as trying to 'carry others with you'.

We have explored whether philosophy can play a role other than conceptual improvement. We should pause to remind ourselves that the philosophical skills of analysis and argument are needed in the public-policy domain to make distinctions and work out what follows from these. The example Jonathan Wolff (2011, p. 202) cites is Ronald Dworkin's attempt to show that both pro- and anti-abortion activists exhibit great concern for both the interests of the mother and those of the fetus. This observation, based on an analysis of the coherence and clarity of arguments in the public domain, could help to reduce the animosity between the opposing sides in the debate. Although we have been concerned to justify a role for philosophy that is broader than conceptual improvement, nonetheless, conceptual work is one area where philosophy has made important contributions to public life and should continue to do so.

Acknowledgments I would like to acknowledge the insightful comments made on an earlier draft of this chapter by Joseph Mahon and Keith Breen. I have also benefitted from discussing some of the issues raised in this chapter with David Archard, Mark Haugaard, Richard Hull, and Jonathan Wolff.

References

Ayer, A. J. (1946). *Language, truth and logic* (2nd ed.). London: Gollancz.

Ayer, A. J. (1959). Editor's introduction. In A. J. Ayer (Ed.), *Logical positivism*. New York: The Free Press.

Brock, D. W. (1987). Truth or consequences: The role of philosophers in policymaking. *Ethics*, 97(4), 786–791.

Chomsky, N. (1967). The responsibility of intellectuals. *The New York Review of Books*, 23 February. Retrieved July 20 2015, from http://www.nybooks.com/articles/archives/1967/feb/23/a-special-supplement-the-responsibility-of-intelle/.

Cohen, M. (1971). Statement of purpose. *Philosophy & Public Affairs*, 1(1).

Cohen, G. A. (1995). *Self-ownership, freedom, and equality*. Cambridge: Cambridge University Press.

de Haan, J. (2001). The definition of moral dilemmas: A logical problem. *Ethical Theory and Moral Practice*, 4(3), 267–284.

Donagan, A. (1993). Moral dilemmas, genuine and spurious: A comparative anatomy. *Ethics*, 104(1), 7–21.

Fives, A. (2010). Reasonableness, pluralism, and liberal moral doctrines. *The Journal of Value Inquiry*, 44(3), 321–339.

Fives, A. (2013). *Political reason: Morality and the public sphere*. Basingstoke: Palgrave.

Foot, P. (2002). Moral dilemmas revisited. In P. Foot (Ed.), *Moral dilemmas and other topics in moral philosophy* (pp. 175–188). Oxford: Clarendon Press.

Freeman, S. (2000). Deliberative democracy: A sympathetic comment. *Philosophy & Public Affairs*, 29(4), 371–418.

Gadamer, H.-G. (1989 [1975]). *Truth and method* (2nd ed., J. Weinsheimer & D. G. Marshall, Trans.). London: Sheed and Ward.

Glover, J. (2001). *Humanity: A moral history of the twentieth century*. London: Pimlico.

Hampshire, S. (1978a). Morality and pessimism. In S. Hampshire (Ed.), *Public and private morality* (pp. 1–22). Cambridge: Cambridge University Press.

Hampshire, S. (1978b). Public and private morality. In S. Hampshire (Ed.), *Public and private morality* (pp. 23–53). Cambridge: Cambridge University Press.

Hudson, W. D. (1983 [1970]). *Modern moral philosophy* (2nd ed.). London: Macmillan.

Hume, D. (1969 [1739–1740]). In E. C. Mossner (Ed.), *A treatise of human nature*. Harmondsworth: Penguin.

Johnson, P. (1988). *Intellectuals*. London: Weidenfeld and Nicholson.

Jonsen, A. R. (1995). Casuistry: An alternative or complement to principles? *Kennedy Institute of Ethics Journal*, 5(3), 237–251.

Jonsen, A. R., & Toulmin, S. (1988). *The abuse of casuistry: A history of moral reasoning*. Berkeley, CA: University of California Press.

Melzer, A. M. (2003). What is an intellectual? In A. M. Melzer, J. Weinberger, & M. R. Zinman (Eds.), *The public intellectual: Between philosophy and politics* (pp. 3–14). Oxford: Rowman and Littlefield.

Nagel, T. (1978). Ruthlessness in public life. In S. Hampshire (Ed.), *Public and private morality* (pp. 75–91). Cambridge: Cambridge University Press.

Nozick, R. (1974). *Anarchy, state, and utopia*. New York: Basic Books.

Popper, K. (2002 [1963]). *Conjectures and refutations: The growth of scientific knowledge*. London: Routledge.

Raphael, D. D. (1970). *Problems of political philosophy*. London: Macmillan.

Rawls, J. (1971). *A theory of justice*. Oxford: Oxford University Press.

Rawls, J. (1989). The domain of the political and the overlapping consensus. *New York University Law Review*, 64(2), 233–255.

Rawls, J. (1999a [1987]). The idea of an overlapping consensus. In S. Freeman (Ed.), John Rawls: Collected papers (pp. 421–448). Cambridge, MA: Harvard University Press.

Rawls, J. (1999b [1997]). The idea of public reason revisited. In S. Freeman (Ed.), John Rawls: Collected papers (pp. 573–615). Cambridge, MA: Harvard University Press.

Raz, J. (1986). *The morality of freedom*. Oxford: Clarendon.

Solzhenitsyn, A. (1975). *From under the rubble*. London: Collins.

Solzhenitsyn, A. (2003 [1973]). *The Gulag Archipelago, 1918–1956* (T. Whitney & H. Willets, Trans.). London: The Harvill Press.

Stevenson, C. L. (1944). *Ethics and language*. New Haven, CT: Yale University Press.

Thomas, D. M. (1999). *Alexander Solzhenitsyn: A century in his life*. London: Abacus.

Williams, B. (1978). Politics and moral character. In S. Hampshire (Ed.), *Public and private morality* (pp. 23–53). Cambridge: Cambridge University Press.

Williams, B. (1985). *Ethics and the limits of philosophy*. London: Fontana Press.

Wittgenstein, L. (2001 [1921]). *Tractatus Logico-Philosophicus* (D. F. Pears & B. F. McGuinness, Trans.). London: Routledge.

Wolff, J. (2011). *Ethics and public policy*. London: Routledge.

CHAPTER 3

On Philosophy's Contribution to Public Matters: Charting the Course of a Debate

Joseph Mahon

There are two rival views on the subject of philosophers and public matters. One is that philosophers are, if not uniquely equipped, then at least exceptionally well-equipped to analyze and pronounce on such matters; the opposing view is that philosophers are uniquely ill-equipped, and unsuited, to expatiate on what were called 'the big questions of life'. Noam Chomsky articulated the first of these views, in 1968, when he maintained that

> There is no profession that can claim with greater authenticity that its concern is the intellectual culture of the society or that it possesses the tools for the analysis of ideology and the critique of social knowledge and its use (Chomsky 1972 [1968], p. 208).

The rival view declared that philosophers, as philosophers, were not interested in the real world; their sole professional concern was to analyze the *talk* of those who were concerned about the real world. As such, professional philosophers were not remotely likely to have developed any special competence with which they could make a telling contribution to public debates.

J. Mahon
National University of Ireland, Galway, Republic of Ireland

© The Editor(s) (if applicable) and The Author(s) 2016   29
A. Fives, K. Breen (eds.), *Philosophy and Political Engagement*,
DOI 10.1057/978-1-137-44587-2_3

This apolitical view of philosophy received its most aggressive expression in W.D. Hudson's *Modern Moral Philosophy*, which opened with the following words: 'This book is not about what people ought to do. It is about what they are doing when they *talk* about what they ought to do' (Hudson 1970, p. 1). Hudson went on to illustrate his distinction between moral philosophers and moralists by way of the parliamentary debate at an all-night sitting of the House of Commons when the *Divorce Reform Bill* (1969) was receiving its second and third readings. This Bill recognized the breakdown of marriage as the sole ground for divorce. It raised the question: ought divorce law to be reformed along these lines? The moral philosopher, said Hudson, would not wish to participate in this 'first-order' debate, not as a moral philosopher at any rate. Rather, 'It is the logical features of the debate itself which would interest him, as a philosopher. What had these people been doing when they talked about what they ought to do?' (Hudson 1970, p. 2). Jonathan Wolff has given another twist to this side of the argument in his recently published *Ethics and Public Policy*, where he notes that philosophers are *temperamentally* ill-suited to participation in public-policy formation and committee work. This is because 'Philosophers don't have to compromise because they are under no pressure to agree to produce a practical outcome' (Wolff 2011, pp. 193–194).

Other philosophers have a foot in both camps, so to speak, mainly by virtue of their actual work. In 1971, for instance, in a review for *The Listener*, of Harold Wilson's memoirs, Alasdair MacIntyre published a scathing attack on the 1966–1970 Labour government, its record in office, and Wilson's self-serving account of his administration's achievements (MacIntyre 1971b). Yet in that very same year, *The Listener* published the text of a broadcast discussion between MacIntyre and Bryan Magee, in which MacIntyre envisages a mainly metatheoretical, or 'second-order', role for philosophy vis-à-vis the social sciences and laments the fact that

> Philosophy does tend to sterilise the mind and the imagination far too easily ...
> I think, to read Austin and Wittgenstein and Hart is for many sociologists
> an experience that is at once illuminating and dazzling. They see and they
> cannot see as a result (MacIntyre 1971a, p. 237).

In this short essay, I propose to chart the course of this debate in greater detail. Section 1 reviews the dominant tradition in post-war moral philosophy, when moral philosophers sought to become logicians of moral language and scrupulously refused to discuss the most serious moral and political issues of the day. It also documents and explains the backlash against the 1950s orthodoxy, leading to the emergence of a new branch of philosophy, to be variously called 'practical ethics', 'applied ethics', and 'applied philosophy'. Section 2 records the views of the later Wittgenstein, but especially the argument propounded by Chomsky, that philosophers should be social critics, devoting their time and analytical skills, in a time of crisis, to unmasking the pretensions and mystifications of dominant ideologies. I close this section with a reminder that the most illustrious continental philosophers of the post-war era—Sartre, Beauvoir, Camus, and Merleau-Ponty—had long since been politically engaged, especially Camus during his editorship at *Combat* (Camus 2006). In Section 3, I note the disconnect between MacIntyre's political writing for *The Listener* and his acid view of (analytic) philosophy as a second-order discipline which sterilizes the mind and weakens the imagination. This paradoxical position can be explained, I argue, by way of MacIntyre's (2013) acknowledgement, in a self-portrait penned in his eightieth year, of the formative influence of Sartrian existentialism and Marxism on his early thinking.

In Section 4, I document Stuart Hampshire's critique of American foreign policy, at the end of the 1960s, as 'a coarse, quantitative, calculative Benthamism' (Hampshire 1972, p. 264). I venture to explain Hampshire's crossing of the divide between philosophy and the public world by way of his familiarity with the Marxist canon, his war-time record in counterintelligence, and his involvement in 'teach-ins' while a professor at Princeton. In Section 5, I document Herbert Marcuse's argument that normative ethics has a *bona fide* place in Marxist theory and the claim—advanced by Hampshire and Marcuse alike—that normative ethics identifies the general norms which set standards for human progress toward greater freedom and happiness and, as such, is politically indispensable. In Section 6, I recall the immensity of the contributions made to public policy and public debate by Bernard Williams and Mary Warnock in their roles as chairpersons of government-commissioned committees of inquiry into pornography and the law, human fertilization and embryology, respectively. In Section 7, I review the crusading work done by J.S. Mill in the nineteenth century and by Peter Singer much more recently in two other areas of public policy: regulating the sale and availability of poisons and alcohol (Mill) and making provisions for animal welfare and safety (Singer). I conclude by siding with those who claim that philosophy can contribute significantly to matters of public importance, and I then attempt to identify the most propitious ways in which this can be done now.

1   MORAL PHILOSOPHY AS A SECOND-ORDER DISCIPLINE

'The 1950s', wrote Jonathan Rée, was to be 'the golden age of 20th-century English philosophy' (Rée 1989, p. 13). P.F. Strawson recalled how, as the numbness of wartime receded, 'a new idea' made itself felt, and 'gripped the imaginations' of young philosophers such as himself (Strawson, quoted in Rée 1989, p. 13). Their objective was to modernize the entire intellectual world: they would pull down worm-eaten old philosophical structures; they would flush out the last of the superstitions, including science worship itself; in short, they would make the world safe for sceptical, circumspect, down-to-earth common sense.

Drawn closer and closer to the view, by Wittgenstein and others, that philosophy was a relentless struggle against the bewitchment of our intelligence by language, moral philosophers of the post-war era responded by attempting to delineate the hidden features, or 'depth grammar', of moral language specifically. 'Ethics as I conceive it', said R.M. Hare in the Preface to his book *The Language of Morals*, 'is the logical study of the language of morals' (Hare 1952, p. v). 'When philosophers have written on the subject of "ethics"', wrote Paul Edwards,

> they have among other things discussed the question 'What (if any) is the meaning of the moral predicates (i.e., terms of the form "good" and "evil", "virtuous" and "sinful", "ought", "duty", etc.) ... [and] the moral judgements in which such terms occur (e.g., "You oughtn't to have done that")?', and the related question 'What is the nature of moral disagreement?' (Edwards, in Edwards and Pap 1973, p. 288).

The orthodoxy of the 'high tide' was that there were first-order moral problems (such as, 'Is the targeting of civilians in war ever justified?') and second-order moral topics (such as, 'Some Alleged Differences between Imperatives and Indicatives').[1] First-order moral problems were the province of the moralist, the novelist, the parliamentarian, and the popular press. Second-order moral problems, what the American ethicist C.L. Stevenson, called 'narrowly specialized' questions, were the province of the moral philosopher (Stevenson 1944, p. 1). He was a specialist in moral language, or moral logic (a thing of its own, according to the extremists). He stood to the moralist much as the accountant does to the businessman; he didn't actually do the work or make the money, but he explained some of the rules which had to be observed (Anonymous, *New Statesman*, 1973, p. 11).

This view of moral philosophy as a second-order discipline generating a kind of mental hygiene came under sustained assault during the 1960s, especially in the USA. This led to the emergence of a new branch of philosophy, known variously as 'practical ethics', 'applied ethics', and 'applied philosophy'. Four main reasons can be given for the emergence, or birth, of this 'practical' philosophy:

1. It was a hostile, embarrassed, and guilty reaction to the post-war orthodoxy, which was perceived as hopelessly abstract, technical, and detached (Mahon 1984, pp. 8–20; Zohar 1981).
2. The Vietnam War forced a great many academics and students to take sides on moral issues raised by that war, issues ranging from imperialism and the bombing of civilian targets on the one hand, to civil disobedience and draft-dodging on the other (Duncan 1980).
3. It was a response to a widespread call for *involvement*, for greater, more meaningful participation in public affairs. Philosophers, it was argued by Noam Chomsky and others, should make their subject 'relevant', and developing a new branch of ethics, to be called 'practical' or 'applied ethics', seemed an obvious way of doing so.
4. The influence of existentialist philosophers such as Jean-Paul Sartre, Simone de Beauvoir, and Albert Camus was also significant. Existentialism, itself a largely post-war European philosophy, raised questions about the most poignant and basic features of human existence, such as that we all die, that we have a responsibility for our own lives, and that we are susceptible to a kind of self-deception called 'bad faith'. Practical ethics, it is sometimes said, is part of the legacy of existentialism to later generations (Zohar 1981).

2 WITTGENSTEIN, CHOMSKY, AND SOCIAL CRITICISM

The campaign to make philosophy relevant to the everyday world had been gathering momentum ever since Wittgenstein wrote as follows to his pupil, Norman Malcolm, in 1944:

> What is the use of studying philosophy if all that it does for you is to enable you to talk with some plausibility about some abstruse questions of logic, etc., and if it does not improve your thinking about the important questions of everyday life ... You see, I know that it's difficult to think *well* about 'certainty', 'probability', 'perception', etc. But it is, if possible, still more difficult to think, or *try* to think, really honestly about your life and

other people's lives. And the trouble is that thinking about these things is *not thrilling*, but often downright nasty. And when it's nasty then it's *most* important (Wittgenstein, in Malcolm 1967, p. 58).

In 1968, Noam Chomsky—who since 1965 had been a national leader of opposition to the American war effort in Vietnam, and to American imperialism in general—lent his weight to the campaign to politicize philosophy with an essay in *Ethics*, October 1968, under the title 'Philosophers and Public Policy'. In this essay, Chomsky posed the following question: 'What is one's responsibility *as a philosopher?*' He acknowledges the reasonable answer that

> Integrity, both personal and scholarly, demands that we face the questions that arise internally in some particular domain of study ... It would be a sacrifice of such integrity to allow external factors to determine the course of research. This would represent a kind of "subversion of scholarship" (Chomsky 1972 [1968], p. 207).

Chomsky replied to this reasonable argument as follows:

> I do not doubt that those who pursued their work at the Goethe Institute, in the shadow of Dachau, justified themselves by such considerations as these. Two or three years ago, I would have accepted this line of argument as correct, and it still seems to be persuasive (Chomsky 1972 [1968], p. 208).

But now, two or three years later, Chomsky identifies a counterargument to the orthodox, reasonable one:

> namely, that in a time of crisis one should abandon, or at least restrict, professional concerns and activities that do not adapt themselves in a natural way toward the resolution of that crisis. This argument is actually consistent with the first; and it can, I think, be maintained that this is all there is to the matter (Chomsky 1972 [1968], p. 208).

Acceptance of the counterargument conduces to what he calls 'a schizophrenic existence', one whereby in times of peace and plenty, academics confine their work to purely professional matters, and in times of crisis, they don't.

At this juncture, Chomsky distinguishes between two types of intellectuals: (1) *the technical expert*, whose technical expertise elevates him to positions of power and influence; and (2) *the social critic*, whose most pressing function is that of unmasking ideology, not least the ideology of the technical experts, for 'it is natural to expect that any group with access to power will construct an ideology that justifies its dominance on grounds of the general welfare' (Chomsky 1972 [1968], p. 208). As Chomsky perceived it, the role of the social critic in post-industrial society had become more crucial than ever; and in this context the potential contribution of the discipline of philosophy deserved to be emphasized. Post-industrial society was likely to be 'marked by the access to power of an intellectual elite, basing its claim to power on a presumably "value free" technology of social management' (Chomsky 1972 [1968], p. 211). With this eventuality, the role of the social critic becomes that of 'analyzing the content of the claimed "expertise", its empirical justification, and its social use'. This becomes the point of entry for philosophers, since:

> These are typical questions of philosophy. The same analytical approach that seeks to explore the nature of scientific theories in general or the structure of some particular domain of knowledge, or to investigate the concept of a human action can be turned to the study of the technology of control and manipulation that goes under the name of "behavioural science" and that serves as the basis for the ideology of the "new mandarins" (Chomsky 1972 [1968], p. 211).

Chomsky's broad challenge to the philosophers—to apply their exceptional analytical skills to the analysis of public issues—reverberated throughout universities in the late 1960s, resonating with staff and students alike, during a period of unprecedented political ferment on the campuses. The decade or so following 1968 saw the publication of a cascade of anthologies in applied philosophy, with edited collections such as De George's *Ethics and Society* (1968), Kuykendall's *Philosophy in the Age of Crisis* (1970), Held, Nielsen, and Parsons's *Philosophy and Political Action* (1972), Beauchamp and Perlin's *Ethical Issues in Death and Dying* (1978), Weir's *Ethical Issues in Death and Dying* (1977), Rachels's *Moral Problems* (1979), and Regan's *Matters of Life and Death* (1980). In May 1969, the Society for Philosophy and Public Affairs (originally the Society for Philosophy and Public Policy) was founded by Sidney Morgenbesser, Thomas Nagel, and others, while a new journal, *Philosophy & Public Affairs*, edited by Marshall Cohen, began publication in 1971.

3   MacIntyre, Beauvoir, Camus, and Evangelical Theology

Needless to say, Chomsky himself seized the opportunity, in his essay, to address what he called 'questions of public policy [which] arise in the United States at this particular historical moment', very quickly retailing his trademark conclusion that 'Increasingly, the United States has become both the agent of repression and—to use Howard Zin's phrase— "the white-gloved financier of counter-revolution" throughout the world' (Chomsky 1972 [1968], p. 201). Another example of the kind of contribution a professional philosopher could make to public political debate was provided by Alasdair MacIntyre—then teaching at Brandeis University—in his review, in 1971, of Harold Wilson's memoirs, *The Labour Government 1966–70: A Personal Record.* Here MacIntyre excoriates that particular Labour government's response to the issue of the Kenyan Asians, its stance on the Vietnam and Biafran conflicts, and its approach to the sterling crisis and industrial relations. He criticizes what he calls Wilson's narrowness of vision as follows:

Hence, in the memoirs, so many features of the social landscape never come into sight at all, and so many others appear in truncated form. There is no serious attempt to identify the malaise of British industry; no discussion of the peculiar kind of importance that welfare had in the Sixties or how welfare priorities ought to have been identified; no recognition of the way in which in the Sixties the political self-identification of the working class began to change, and the struggle for wages became successful in quite a new way (MacIntyre 1971b, p. 150).

MacIntyre concludes his review as follows:

Mr Wilson once boasted that he had tried to read Marx, but had not succeeded in getting beyond the opening pages of *Capital.* I would recommend him to try *The 18th Brumaire of Louis Bonaparte* instead: for not only does Marx lay bare in that work the type of key relationship between politics and social forces which Mr Wilson ignores, but he also explains why it is the petty-bourgeois politicians who may well prove unable to understand the point that he is making (MacIntyre 1971b, p. 151).

It is, then, disappointing to learn—though not altogether surprising in the context of the post-war history of ideas—that MacIntyre himself envisaged a primarily metatheoretical or second-order role for philosophy in 1971, the very same year in which he had published his critique of Labour Party politics. In a formal discussion with Bryan Magee—broadcast on BBC Radio 3 on the subject of 'political philosophy and its emergence from the doldrums'—he noted that:

> How a society is is in large part a matter of how its members understand social reality, and how they understand social reality is in large part a matter of whether their understanding is rational or confused: of whether they have, to use another idiom, true or false consciousness, how far their vision is ideologically distorted, and the like. We could not deploy any of these notions of ideology or false consciousness unless we presupposed a concept of rationality, and we cannot deploy a concept of rationality in the social sciences unless we are prepared to do philosophical work on what constitutes rationality in different areas of human life (MacIntyre 1971a, p. 237).

MacIntyre went on to make two further points in his 'conversation' with Magee: (1) that doing philosophy tends to sterilize the mind and weaken the imagination, thereby weakening enthusiasm for programmes of scientific discovery (and, one might add, willingness to participate in set-piece political debate); (2) that students coming into the social sciences had expectations which were once fulfilled by 'evangelical theology', but that these expectations were unlikely to be satisfied by exposure to the social sciences, so that these same students would be better advised to remain with evangelical theology!

MacIntyre's position, at this juncture, might then be characterized, in Chomsky's sweet phrasing of it, as 'schizophrenic'—abandoning philosophy when sufficiently motivated to enter political debate, then returning to philosophy to resume conversation with one's professional colleagues. But I should like to put a different spin on it. It would, I think, be more accurate to say that MacIntyre saw a particular type of philosophy, or way of doing philosophy, as inimical to political engagement. At all events, the most illustrious of the post-war European intellectuals—about whom MacIntyre (1964) had written at length in his chapter on existentialism in D.J. O'Connor's magnificent *A Critical History of Western Philosophy*—had not been diminished by the rigid formalities of analytic philosophy.

Both Beauvoir and Camus, for instance, had written with distinction about the death penalty, taking different sides on the issue, and in doing so had blended philosophy, politics, jurisprudence, theology, and historical analysis without discomfort. To take just Beauvoir's contribution, very briefly: in her essay '*Oeil pour Oeil*' (in Beauvoir 1948, pp. 107–40), published in Sartre's campaigning journal, *Les Temps modernes*, in February 1946, she explains and attempts to justify her refusal to sign the petition seeking clemency for the collaborationist, fascist author Robert Brasillach. In doing so, she writes about the War Crimes Tribunal, Mussolini, 'Kharkov's executioners', the Occupation, the purge, the concept of punishment, the 'old *jus talionis*', the metaphysical source of the idea of justice, social justice, the restoration of a moral equilibrium, and the saving power of God's grace. Her argument, in a nutshell, is that the degradation of human beings into objects ('*la degradation de l'homme en chose*') is an absolute evil ('*un mal absolu*') and that an absolute evil deserves an absolute punishment:

> Society solemnly rejects those who are responsible for the crimes which society rejects, and when these crimes are particularly abominable only one punishment can restore the equilibrium, and that punishment is death (Beauvoir 1948, pp. 123–4; see also Mahon 2002, pp. 137–64).

Camus did sign the petition, albeit reluctantly. Years later, he argued with great power and sophistication against the death penalty, and the French government's retention of the guillotine, in his essay 'Reflections on the Guillotine' (Camus 1995 [1957]), and on this issue I side with him. But the point at issue here is that Camus and Beauvoir both had available to them, and made extensive use of, a vastly richer and more adaptable philosophical prose, as well as a more muscular vision of philosophy itself, than that available to their Anglo-American contemporaries.

4   Hampshire, Vietnam, and Reasonable Judgment in Politics

In 1967, Stuart Hampshire had articulated a view of (analytic) philosophy similar to that expressed by MacIntyre, in an article on R.D. Laing's fusion of existentialist philosophy and psychiatry. 'One thing at least seems certain', he wrote:

> claims about the effectiveness of methods of therapy have to be settled, if at all, only by slow empirical investigation in hospitals and consulting-rooms, where philosophy neither has, nor ever could have, anything to contribute. The contribution of philosophy, at best, can only be to criticise the clarity

and plausibility of the theories that are supposed to justify particular methods of treatment. A method might be shown to be effective in practice, even though the theory of mental functioning on which it was based was ill-founded, badly formulated, and not to be believed (Hampshire 1967, p. 290).

Yet we are informed by the editors of the collection *Philosophy and Political Action* (Held et al. 1972, p. vii) that 'Mr. Hampshire was the speaker at our first meeting in October 1969', the first meeting, that is, of the New York Group of the recently founded Society for Philosophy and Public Policy. The collection just cited includes a reprint of Hampshire's review of the third volume of Bertrand Russell's memoirs, a review first published in the *New York Review of Books* in October 1970.

Here Hampshire excoriates the American government's established model of reason, which he characterizes as

a coarse, quantitative, calculative Benthamism, refined by game theory, which adds and subtracts incentives and disincentives, volumes of firepower, and amounts of social services, and then arrives by computation at probable human responses distributed in a total population: which calculates the cost-effectiveness of alternative policies by the number of American lives to be dissipated in securing the sufficient compliance of foreigners to dominant American interests (Hampshire 1972, p. 264).

Only the radicals had unmasked this counterfeit model of rationality, continues Hampshire:

For liberals, the prolonged aerial terrorism, the ever new burnt villages, the resettlement camps, the free-fire zones, and the Harvard professors calmly assessing their efficiency were a surprise, and seemed an inexplicable collapse in national decency ... The radicals ... could, and did, say – "I told you so: why would you not believe that the American government, with its academic and military advisers, is ready to match atrocity with atrocity indefinitely in defense of American influence in Asian countries, no matter what the cost to local populations?" (Hampshire 1972, pp. 251, 262).

In opposition to calculative reason, Hampshire offers 'an amended criterion of practical reasonableness'. The amended criterion 'will single out for support those policies which are intrinsically reasonable, relative to standard and permanent common interests and sentiments' (Hampshire 1972, p. 267). It 'appeals to certain very general facts about standard, recurring human needs and sentiments, but it does not depend on any precise computation of remote consequences' (Hampshire 1972, p. 269). From this perspective:

> Some policies can be dismissed as contrary to reason, in spite of the conse-quential advantages that they may seem to bring in particular circumstances, because their successful execution would involve too great a coarsening of the sensibilities of their agents, and for this reason would make their lives subhuman, wretched, and shameful to themselves ... The Southeast Asian policies of the US government under three Presidents, with popular support and the advice of business managers and academic experts, have been con-trary to reason in this looser sense (Hampshire 1972, pp. 269–70).

So how did Hampshire come to adopt the 'schizophrenic' position on philosophy and the public world? I venture to offer two reasons. First, no less than MacIntyre, he was no stranger to Marxism; he could reconcile Marxism with a concern for a world in crisis, but not the apolitical ana-lytic philosophy in vogue at the time. In 1972, Hampshire led a discus-sion, broadcast on BBC Radio 3 and published in *The Listener*, on the topic 'Is Marxism Alive and Well?' The other two panellists were Leszek Kolakowski and Charles Taylor. Hampshire's Marxist sympathies and his familiarity with Marxist scholarship are evident throughout. Much of the discussion centred on Lukács, focussing first of all on his contribution to the debate between the determinist and the neo-Kantian interpretations of the relation between consciousness and the so-called objective movement of historical events. Then Hampshire moved the discussion on to a con-sideration of Lukács's 'literary criticism', where he perceived 'a curiously closed and authoritarian mind at work' (Hampshire et al. 1972, p. 584). Taylor's take on Lukács as a literary critic was that 'His rejection of so much that happened in European literature after 1910 is that he sees it simply as an attack on reason—and of course in a way it is, in Joyce or in Proust' (Hampshire et al. 1972, p. 584). Hampshire replied that Lukács's 'picture of reason' is the nineteenth-century picture of mastery, rather than the sceptical, mocking one that is found in Hegel. Hampshire's clos-ing remarks on Marxism in the West, finally, read almost like an alterna-tive, more nuanced phrasing of Chomsky's vision of the philosopher as a social critic:

> Surely it's a fact that, in the advanced industrial countries of the West, Marxism is largely used as a weapon ... of criticism of culture ... because it's certainly the case that in the United States, and also in Western Europe,

this form of criticism of contemporary society is a prevailing one among the young, among people in universities: that is to say, cultural criticism which applies equally to capitalist culture and to Soviet culture, criticism of high technology, of highly disciplined, highly conforming, modern societies (Hampshire et al. 1972, p. 585).

Hampshire also had, in abundance, what MacIntyre calls 'a prior and continuing engagement with a variety of practices and a reflective grasp of what is involved in such engagement' (MacIntyre 2013, p. 31). I refer, of course, to his war record: he worked in counterintelligence, crossed paths with Kim Philby (probably at Bletchley Park), and interrogated French collaborators and Nazi officers, most notably the Gestapo commander, Ernst Kaltenbrunner, which led to his insistence—rare among twentieth-century analytic philosophers—'on the reality of evil' (O'Grady 2004, p. 2).

5 MARCUSE, HAMPSHIRE, COHEN, AND THE GOOD SOCIETY

The Marxist philosopher Herbert Marcuse had no hesitation in joining this discussion and, moreover, did so unequivocally on the side of those who claim a commanding place for moral and political philosophy in debates on matters of public importance. The subtext of his 1968 paper, 'Ethics and Revolution', is that ethics has a *bona fide* place within Marxist theory and should not be seen—as it was by the neo-Kantian Marxists—as a (mere) Kantian supplement to Marxist science and the Marxist political project, still less as an anachronistic, doomed attempt at reconciling class enemies—the view expressed by Karl Kautsky (1906) in his *Ethics and the Materialistic Conception of History*.[2]

Marcuse's paper itself—his main contribution to this whole debate—may be summarized as follows: (1) philosophy has much to say about the real world and the great periods of historical change; (2) this contribution comes via ethics and political philosophy; (3) ethics—or, to be precise, normative ethics—identifies the general norms which set the standards for human progress towards greater freedom and happiness; (4) these standards emerge *historically* via the great revolutions, wars of independence, and civil rights struggles and then become fixed features of subsequent moral reasoning; (5) later struggles for liberation and progress come inescapably to be evaluated by these same standards; (6) from this normative perspective, it is clear that there are forms of violence and suppression which no revolutionary situation can justify, because they negate the very end for which the revolution is a means. Such are arbitrary violence, cruelty, and indiscriminate terror (Marcuse 1968, p. 141).

And (7), with reference to the Bolshevik Revolution in particular, a moral justification can be found for

accelerated industrialization, the elimination of non-cooperative layers of management from the economy, the enforcement of work discipline, sacrifices in the satisfaction of needs imposed by the priority of heavy industry in the first stages of industrialization, and suspension of civil liberties if they were used for sabotaging these objectives. And we can reject, without long discussion, as not justifiable, even in terms of the revolution, the Moscow trials, the permanent terror, the concentration camps, and the dictatorship of the Party over the working classes (Marcuse 1968, p. 146).

In an interview published in *Time* in 1977, Marcuse returned to the distinction between 'defensive' and 'aggressive violence', as he had originally called them (Marcuse 1968, p. 139). On this occasion, he repudiated the actions of the Baader-Meinhof terrorists in no uncertain manner, and in doing so drew a distinction between *resistance* and *terrorism*, explaining this distinction as follows:

If no other means of abolishing repression are available, people have the right to resist. But I speak of people and not individuals, and when I speak of repression I speak of dictatorship such as Hitler's Germany ... The victims of the current terrorism are by no stretch of the imagination responsible for capitalism, as Hitler and Himmler were responsible for the concentration camps and the extermination of six million Jews. I would indeed say that the assassination of Hitler and Himmler would have been justified. The present killings are not (Marcuse, in Knox 1977, p. 12).

It is surely more than mere coincidence that Hampshire had answered the same question—'Does a political cause ever give us the right to kill?'—in the same way just a year earlier:

[A] moral rule against all assassinations for political reasons is needed, even though there will be very unusual and extreme circumstances in which an assassination in peacetime is justified. For example, if a group of prominent Germans had arranged the assassination of Hitler in August, 1939, with a view to making peace, it is my opinion that they would have acted rightly (Hampshire 1976, p. 6).

Hampshire and Marcuse were both adamant about the importance of normative ethics. In Hampshire's case, it matters for the following two reasons: (1) normative ethics identifies underlying principles which may correct the confusions of ordinary moral opinion; and (2) moral principles have their origin in the control of killing and in the control of sexual activity, since the survival of the species depends on there being such controls. For Marcuse, normative ethics is crucial (1) because it identifies the general norms which set the standards for human progress towards greater freedom and happiness, and (2) because every political initiative— including the Bolshevik one—will be judged by these standards: does it promote and extend human freedom and happiness, that is, a life without fear and misery, and a life in peace?

Towards the end of the twentieth century, the analytical Marxist, Jerry Cohen, proposed a still more overtly political role for moral and political philosophy. In a formal interview with Mario Scanella of *The Philosophers' Magazine*, in 1997, Cohen first of all agreed that philosophy 'sharpens our analytic skill and enables us to be more honest as human beings'. But it can and must do a lot more, he insists:

> From a socialist political point of view, philosophy is invaluable because it assists in two essential tasks. The first is that it exposes the lies, the hypocrisy and the sophisms of those who defend inequality and injustice and capitalism ... Equally, in the more positive task of socialist construction, it is very important for philosophers to participate with economists, sociologists and others in addressing the problems of the design and functioning of a socialist society (Cohen 1997, p. 42).

Marx, he continues, had decided not to offer a blueprint for a future socialist society, a view shared by Eric Hobsbawm (2011) in his *How to Change the World: Tales of Marx and Marxism*.[3] Marx's omission, continues Cohen, was 'one of his biggest mistakes because unless socialists have a tolerably definite conception of the socialist society which they favour, they will not attract anyone else to their vision' (Cohen 1997, p. 42).

6   Williams, Warnock, and 'Everything that Constitutes a Culture'

In England, matters were taken a stage further when two leading professional philosophers—Bernard Williams and Mary Warnock—were appointed by the British Government of the day to chair committees of inquiry into obscenity and film censorship (Williams) and into human fertilization and embryology (Warnock). Their reports, now best known as *The Williams Report* (1979) and *The Warnock Report* (1984), have been immensely influential, not just in promoting and clarifying public debate on these issues, but in having several of their recommendations made into law. I shall be writing about *The Williams Report* later—when the discussion reverts to Mill—but for the present, this is how *The Guardian*, in an editorial, hailed its achievements:

> It avoids a paternalism by which one section of the community makes illegal what another section wants ... Those who want pornography can have it. Those who don't won't be obliged to run its gauntlet at the newsagent's or in the West End. The feeling remains, however, that the Provost of King's College and his associates, having been landed with porn, have started a grand inquiry into everything that constitutes a culture. Perhaps Mr Whitelaw could find them a pretext to continue? Carry on Williams! (Editor, *The Guardian*, 1979, p. 16).[4]

Making reasonable provisions in law for the sale and consumption of pornography may not exactly have been what Wittgenstein had in mind when he spoke of 'the important questions of everyday life'. And Chomsky, no doubt, was much more concerned about the 'culture' of power elites and the damage it caused, both nationally and internationally. Nonetheless, the work of Williams and his associates, I submit, gives tangible support to Chomsky's claim that 'the interpretation and analysis provided by the philosopher are essential ingredients in any serious attempt to change the world' (Chomsky 1972 [1968], p. 215).

The Warnock Report was published in 1984, making 64 recommendations in relation to assisted human reproduction. Its recommendations included the following:

> Legislation should provide that research may be carried out on any embryo resulting from in vitro fertilisation, whatever its provenance, up to the fourteenth day after fertilisation, but subject to all other restrictions as may be imposed by the licensing body.
>
> Legislation should be introduced to render criminal the creation or operation in the United Kingdom of agencies whose purposes include the recruitment of women for surrogate pregnancy or making arrangements for individuals or couples who wish to utilise the services of a carrying mother; such legislation should be wide enough to include both profit and non-profit making organisations (Warnock 1984, pp. 81, 86).

In August 1991, the British Government brought in the *Human Fertility and Embryology Act 1991*, which gave legal effect to many of the Warnock recommendations. It refused, however, to place a legal ban on surrogacy and on non-profit surrogacy arrangements. Indeed, by the late 1980s, Warnock herself had come to have second thoughts on the surrogacy issue (Grove 1989).

Then, in 1994, *The Observer* published a richly ironic, but virulent, response from Melanie Phillips to *The Warnock Report* and, as she saw it, its deleterious impact on public policy. Her response was richly ironic in view of the fact that British 'linguistic philosophy' had not long since been ridiculed as 'timid, complacent, pedantic, mandarin' (Anonymous, *New Statesman*, 1973, p. 8). Phillips deplored and lamented what she termed 'the moral vacuum' in which, as she perceived them, the disciplines of genetics and embryology were then operating. This vacuum, she contended, had been created by *The Warnock Report* because:

> This intellectually and morally bankrupt report, which devised the cynical expedient of the 14-day limit to permit research on embryos to go ahead, embodied the philosophy of consequentialism, which denies intrinsic right or wrong and judges actions solely by their consequences (Phillips 1994, p. 23).

Theologians alone, she added—in an unintended, but comic reprise of MacIntyre's paean to evangelical theology—were capable of properly engaging with these issues. Carelessly identifying consequentialism with 'a culture devoted to gratifying individualism', she hastily concluded that the idea that

> we should live by codes of conduct that may limit the pursuit of personal fulfilment in the interests of others who may be adversely affected, is rejected – as indeed all codes are by definition rejected – as illiberal and authoritarian. The issue is therefore ripe to be hijacked by Warnockian consequentialism. The result is designer babies (Phillips 1994, p.23).

It need hardly be said that Phillips exaggerates the consequentialist mentality of *The Warnock Report* to suit her own purposes. There is nothing consequentialist about such key sentences as 'Everyone agrees that it is completely unacceptable to make use of a child or an adult as a subject of a research procedure which may cause harm or death' (Warnock 1984, p. 61). Consequentialism comes into play only when the *Report* addresses the vexed question of the metaphysical status of the in vitro embryo, and what protection, if any, it should be offered in law. Be that as it may, it looked as if one strand of British moral philosophy had not been mandarin, apolitical, and irrelevant after all, or at least not entirely so. A philosophical theory—any philosophical theory—which could, with any reasonableness, be accused of creating a culture welcoming to designer babies was undeniably hands-on!

7   Mill, Singer, Wolff, and Public Policy

In general, however, professional philosophers are not called upon to head up committees of investigation into matters of public importance; this job—in Ireland as elsewhere—is delegated routinely to senior members of the legal and medical professions.[5] In his recent book, *Ethics and Public Policy*, Jonathan Wolff offers a number of reasons for concluding that philosophers, in any event, are not particularly well suited to this kind of work. 'Philosophers, on the whole, are individualists and controversialists, who prize originality over agreement, which they tend to find dull and uninteresting'. Philosophers tend to think that theory or abstract principle can be applied 'neat' to practical issues. But things don't work like that in the real world:

> So, for example, Peter Singer's argument that 'all animals are equal' has very radical consequences for how human beings should treat non-human animals. But it is a fantasy to think that policy makers might read Singer, realize that our practices are wrong, and then, on that basis, completely revise what we do … Similarly, John Stuart Mill's liberty principle, which states that the only justification for interfering with the liberty of any adult human being is to prevent harm, or risk of harm, to others, appears to recommend policies regarding the regulation of drugs and gambling that are far more liberal than any society has ever permitted, at least in the modern world (Wolff 2011, pp. 193–4).

The views of Singer and Mill help shape the debate on public policy issues, says Wolff, but 'they do not settle anything'.

But neither Mill nor Singer was as starry-eyed as Wolff seems to think. Chapter 5 of Mill's modern classic, *On Liberty*, is entitled 'Applications', and it includes detailed discussion of whether and to what extent a government is justified in placing restrictions on the sale of poisons and, in addition, 'whether … it should take measures to render the means of drunkenness more costly, or add to the difficulty of procuring them by limiting the number of places of sale' (Mill 1977 [1859], p. 170). His remarks on the sale of poisons and alcohol may easily and reasonably be extended to the debate concerning (other) recreational drugs (or 'stimulants', as Mill was pleased to call them).

Mill, for instance, favoured regulation rather than prohibition in the case of alcohol and poisons. In the case of poisons, he argued that 'If poisons were never bought or used for any purpose except the commission of murder, it would be right to prohibit their manufacture and sale' (Mill 1977 [1859], p. 165). But in point of fact, says Mill, poisons are also bought 'for innocent' as well as for 'useful purposes'. He thinks, then, that the sale of poisons should not be banned, but, rather, regulated. It is reasonable, he advises, to warn the prospective buyer of a poisonous substance of the danger of doing so, but not to forcibly prevent him from exposing himself to that danger. Warning him of the danger by, for example,

> labelling the drug with some word expressive of its dangerous character may be enforced without violation of liberty: the buyer cannot wish not to know that the thing he possesses has poisonous qualities (Mill 1977 [1859], p. 166).

The law, then, should permit the sale and purchase of poisonous substances subject to regulation: for example, the appendage of a label advertising the poisonous nature of each of these substances. This regulation would not impinge on the customer's liberty, since it can be presumed that he would not *want* to poison himself. The law would not be restricting his liberty because it would not be stopping him from doing something he wants to do.

Further regulation, such as 'requiring in all cases the certificate of a medical practitioner would make it sometimes impossible, always expensive, to obtain the article for legitimate use'. So, the only additional (but not negligible) regulation, besides labelling, that Mill would advise or countenance

> consists in providing what, in the apt language of Bentham, is called "preappointed evidence" ... The seller, for example, might be required to enter in a register the exact time of the transaction, the name and address of the buyer, the precise quality and quantity sold; to ask the purpose for which it was wanted, and record the answer he received ... Such regulations would in general be no material impediment to obtaining the article, but a very considerable one to making an improper use of it without detection (Mill 1977 [1859], p. 166).

Mill tries to strike a balance here between leaving people free to do what they want and keeping people safe from harming themselves, while also discouraging them from harming others when they exercise that same freedom. People can be protected from dangerous substances *either* by making it a criminal offence to sell and possess such substances—what Mill calls the 'punitive' approach—*or* by alerting them to the dangers of certain substances by way of labelling, age restriction, requiring retail premises to be licensed, and so on—what he calls the 'protective' approach. Governments take the latter approach when it comes to tobacco and alcohol; on Mill's argument, it seems they should adopt the same approach when it comes to (other) recreational drugs.

It is, I think, of some importance to note that Mill does not advocate regulation (rather than prohibition) for the sake of consistency. He is not scandalized by any lack of consistency in public policy, or at any rate not openly so. He advocates regulation because he believes it is workable and, more fundamentally, because he believes it strikes the best balance between protecting people's freedom and protecting these same people, and others, from certain uses of that freedom.

Mill's thinking, and in particular his harm principle—'the only purpose for which power can be rightfully exercised over any member of a civilized community, against his will, is to prevent harm to others' (Mill 1977 [1859], p. 68)—forms the main and acknowledged philosophical basis of *The Williams Report.*[6] Its central argument may be summarized as follows: (1) any conduct which cannot be proven to harm people should not be suppressed by law; (2) the sale and consumption of pornography has not been proven to harm people; and (3), therefore, the sale and consumption of pornography should not be suppressed by law. Its second, equally important, argument may be summarized as follows: (1) what is offensive to people may, justifiably, be restricted by law; (2) pornography is deeply offensive to many people; and (3), therefore, the sale and distribution of pornography may, justifiably, be restricted by law.

The kinds of restrictions which the Williams Committee thought appropriate are detailed in Chap. 9 of the *Report.* Paragraph 9(15), for example, proposes the following:

> We think it should be unlawful to sell or display this material other than in separate premises, or at least a part of premises having a separate access from the street, to which no person under the age of eighteen should be admitted … To protect the unwary member of the public, we think it right that any

shop wishing to sell restricted publications should exhibit a warning notice at its entrance in such a way that an unsuspecting customer could not see any of the goods offered for sale until he had seen the sign (Williams 1979, p. 117).

Some of these recommendations were quickly incorporated into British law in the *Indecent Displays Act 1981*.

Wolff, as we saw, also doubts the practical usefulness of Peter Singer's work on animal welfare and animal liberation. But Singer's work—like that of Williams and Mill—has been much more influential, and focused, than Wolff allows (Bandler 1999). Leaving aside altogether the influence of Singer on this whole area of debate, and the fact that in 2005, he was named one of the hundred most influential people in the world by *Time* magazine (Caplan 2005); his campaign for animal rights has been sharply focussed from the 1990s onwards. In an article for *The Guardian*, in May 2006, he provided his readers with the following update:

> I founded the Great Ape Project together with Paola Cavalieri, an Italian philosopher and animal advocate, in 1993. Our aim was to grant some basic rights to the non-human great apes: life, liberty and the prohibition of torture (Singer 2006).

Singer concedes that their project had proven controversial: 'Some opponents argue that, in extending rights beyond our own species, it goes too far, while others claim that, in limiting rights to the great apes, it does not go far enough' (Singer 2006). Singer rejected both of these claims; but what I wish to stress for present purposes is the highly targeted nature of the Singer–Cavalieri proposal, and the further telling fact that in recent years, several jurisdictions—such as New Zealand, the Netherlands, and the UK—have placed a ban on experimentation with great apes, though not with macaques (see, for instance, Project R&R 2015; Taylor 2001).

8   Conclusion

On the basis of the foregoing history of ideas, I have no hesitation in concluding that philosophers are more than capable of having an impact on matters of public importance. The work of Williams and Warnock shaped and informed public debate on the issues of the law and pornography and the new reproductive technologies—and many of their recommendations made it into law. Singer (1990 [1975]) and Regan (2001) provided the intellectual foundation for the animal liberation movement, as well as being active campaigners themselves for that movement. Marcuse (1964), Cohen (1978), Wood (1981; see also Chap. 11), and Elster (1985) have made Marxism intellectually respectable. Beauvoir provided the intellectual foundation for feminism, as well as being actively involved in the women's liberation movement. Camus, in my opinion, wrote better about the death penalty than anyone else, then or since. Chomsky remains the most outspoken critic of American foreign policy, having been ably supported by Hampshire in the 1960s. Peter Singer's (2004) *The President of Good and Evil* and A.C. Grayling's (2007) *Among the Dead Cities* continue their work. J.J. Thomson (1971) convulsed the moral debate about abortion. Mill wrote powerfully about public policy and recreational stimulants, as well as the status of women. As a Member of Parliament, he also campaigned vigorously for women's suffrage. Engels—also an ardent feminist—provided a detailed roadmap for democratic socialism. These are my heroes.

I shall conclude with two recommendations.

1. Professional philosophers should devote more time to questions of public policy ('What should the law do about it?') than they have done, for the past four decades, to discussing moral issues. Courses in public policy, and in related areas of law, should be given more prominence in philosophy curricula. 'Assisted Suicide: The Philosophers' Brief', the *amicus curiae* submission to the US Supreme Court from the formidable team of Dworkin, Nagel, Nozick, Rawls, and Thomson (1997), gives a good idea of the kind of research and writing I have in mind.

2. Philosophers should give more attention to popular culture. This is mainly because popular culture has (probably) supplanted religion as the main source of moral insight and moral education in today's world. To give just three recent examples: Stieg Larsson's *The Girl with the Dragon Tattoo* maintains that people may be lied to and deceived, for the right reasons (Mahon 2012); the television drama series *Breaking Bad* would have us believe that it is possible to recover lost moral ground; and Clint Eastwood's *American Sniper* appears to assert that it is morally acceptable—even if it remains morally shocking—to shoot dead a child carrying an explosive,

which he will otherwise use to blow to pieces a dozen or so of your men. The Blackwell 'Philosophy and Pop Culture' series shows how fertile an area this can be for philosophical exploration, not to mention how useful it could be in attracting students to the subject!

NOTES

1. In the latter parenthesis, I am, of course, referring to a paper of Hare's (1967) published in *Mind*.
2. See Lukes (1985). There is, of course, a vast literature on the subject of Marxism and ethics. But for present purposes, I should like to draw attention to the following further contributions to that debate: Burke et al. (1981), Cohen (1995, 1997), Fromm (1961), Mahon (1990), Quinton (1979), Soper (1987), and Wood (1993). For material on 'ethical socialism', see Solzhenitsyn (1971).
3. Both neglect to mention Engels, who furnished detailed specifications for 'democratic socialism'—the first, transitional communist phase—in his publications of the late 1840s (see Mahon 1982, 2011).
4. Stuart Hampshire also published a highly appreciative review of *The Williams Report* in *The London Review of Books*, 24 January 1980, under the title 'Common Decency'.
5. In Ireland, the Commission on Assisted Human Reproduction, set up by the Minister for Health in March 2002, did not include one professional philosopher among its 19 members. However, one of the Commission's members— Dr. Aonghus Nolan, chief embryologist at the Galway Fertility Unit—had studied philosophy. Moreover, the ethics subcommittee contained some members who had also studied philosophy, including the sociologist Dr. Evelyn Mahon. Dr. E. Mahon also led the Trinity College Dublin research team that produced the hugely influential, government-commissioned report on *Women and Crisis Pregnancy* (Mahon et al. 1998), the first and only comprehensive piece of research on Irish women and abortion.
6. Its full, official, title is *Report of the Commission on Obscenity and Film Censorship*. For direct references to Mill, see, in particular, pp. 53–60.

REFERENCES

Anonymous. (1973, July 6). The clever men of Oxford. *New Statesman*, pp. 8–11.
Bandler, T. (1999, July 27). Furor follows Princeton philosopher. *The Boston Globe*, pp. 59–62.
Beauchamp, T. L., & Perlin, S. (Eds.). (1978). *Ethical issues on death and dying*. NJ: Prentice-Hall.

Burke, J. P., Crocker, L., & Legters, L. H. (Eds.). (1981). *Marxism and the good society*. Cambridge: Cambridge University Press.

Camus, A. (1995 [1957]). Reflections on the guillotine. In A. Camus (Ed.), *Resistance, rebellion, and death* (pp. 175–234). New York: Vintage.

Camus, A. (2006). In J. Levi-Valensi (Ed.), *Camus at combat*. Princeton: Princeton University Press.

Caplan, A. (2005, April 18). The 2005 time 100: Peter Singer. *Time*. Retrieved July 20, 2015, from http://content.time.com/time/specials/packages/article/0,28804,1972656_1972712_1974257,00.html.

Chomsky, N. (1972 [1968]). Philosophers and public policy. In V. Held, K. Nielsen, & C. Parsons (Eds.), *Philosophy and political action* (pp. 201–216). Oxford: Oxford University Press.

Cohen, G. A. (1978). *Karl Marx's theory of history: A defence*. Oxford: Clarendon Press.

Cohen, G. A. (1995). Equality for real. *Red Pepper*, 19(December), 16–17.

Cohen, G. A. (1997). The moral case for Marxism. *The Philosophers' Magazine*, 1(1), 38–42.

de Beauvoir, S. (1948). *L'Existentialisme et la sagesse des nations*. Paris: Agel.

De George, R. T. (Ed.). (1968). *Ethics and society*. London: Macmillan.

Duncan, E. A. (1980). Random thoughts on detachment and professionalism in moral philosophy. *Ethics*, 90(2), 264–270.

Dworkin, R., Nagel, T., Nozick, R., Rawls, J., & Thomson, J. J. (1997, March 27). Assisted suicide: The philosophers' brief. *The New York Review of Books*. Retrieved July 20, 2015, from http://www.nybooks.com/articles/archives/1997/mar/27/assisted-suicide-the-philosophers-brief/.

Editor. (1979, November 29). Reasonable men in a Soho street. *The Guardian*, p. 16.

Edwards, P., & Pap, A. (Eds.). (1973). *A modern introduction to philosophy* (3rd ed.). New York: The Free Press.

Elster, J. (1985). *Making sense of Marx*. Cambridge: Cambridge University Press.

Fromm, E. (1961). *Marx's concept of man*. New York: Frederick Ungar.

Grayling, A. C. (2007). *Among the dead cities: Is the targeting of civilians in war ever justified?* London: Bloomsbury.

Grove, V. (1989, November 26). Mary, past master of life's little mysteries. *The Sunday Times*.

Hampshire, S. (1967, September 7). Philosophy and madness. *The Listener*, pp. 289–292.

Hampshire, S. (1972). Russell, radicalism, and reason. In V. Held, K. Nielsen, & C. Parsons (Eds.), *Philosophy and political action* (pp. 258–274). Oxford: Oxford University Press.

Hampshire, S. (1976). Does a political cause ever give us the right to kill? *The New Review*, 2(24), 3–10.

Hampshire, S. (1980, January 24). Common decency. *The London Review of Books*, 2(1), 3–4.

Hampshire, S., Kolakowski, L., & Taylor, C. (1972, May 4). Is Marxism alive and well?. *The Listener*, pp. 583–585.

Hare, R. M. (1952). *The language of morals*. Oxford: The Clarendon Press.

Hare, R. M. (1967). Some alleged differences between imperatives and indicatives. *Mind*, 76(303), 309–326.

Held, V., Nielsen, K., & Parsons, C. (Eds.). (1972). *Philosophy and political action*. Oxford: Oxford University Press.

Hobsbawm, E. (2011). *How to change the world: Tales of Marx and Marxism*. London: Little, Brown.

Hudson, W. D. (1970). *Modern moral philosophy*. London: Macmillan.

Kautsky, K. (1906). *Ethics and the materialistic conception of history*. Chicago: C.H. Kerr and Company.

Knox, M. (1977, September 26). A meeting with Marcuse. *Time*, p. 12.

Kuykendall, E. (Ed.). (1970). *Philosophy in the age of crisis*. New York: Harper and Row.

Lukes, S. (1985). *Marxism and morality*. Oxford: Oxford University Press.

MacIntyre, A. (1964). Existentialism. In D. J. O'Connor (Ed.), *A critical history of western philosophy* (pp. 509–529). New York: The Free Press.

MacIntyre, A. (1971a, February 25). Conversations with philosophers—Alasdair MacIntyre talks to Bryan Magee about political philosophy and its emergence from the doldrums. *The Listener*, pp. 235–238.

MacIntyre, A. (1971b, July 29). Mr. Wilson's pragmatism. *The Listener*, pp. 150–151.

MacIntyre, A. (2013). On having survived the academic moral philosophy of the twentieth century. In F. O'Rourke (Ed.), *What happened in and to moral philosophy in the twentieth century?* (pp. 17–34). Indiana: University of Notre Dame Press.

Mahon, J. (1982). Engels and the question about cities. *History of European Ideas*, 3(1), 43–77.

Mahon, J. (1984). *An introduction to practical ethics*. Dublin: Turoe Press.

Mahon, J. (1990). Marx as a social historian. *History of European Ideas*, 12(6), 749–766.

Mahon, J. (2002). *Simone de Beauvoir and her Catholicism*. Galway: Arlen House.

Mahon, J. (2011). Social democracy "A Long Way from Marx". *Politico*. Retrieved July 20, 2015, from http://politico.ie/society/social-democracy-long-way-marx.

Mahon, J. E. (2012). To catch a thief: The ethics of deceiving bad people. In E. Bronson (Ed.), *The girl with the Dragon Tattoo and philosophy* (pp. 198–210). NJ: John Wiley and Sons.

Mahon, E., Conlon, C., & Dillon, L. (1998). *Women and crisis pregnancy*. Dublin: The Stationary Office.

Malcolm, N. (1967). *Ludwig Wittgenstein: A memoir*. Oxford: Oxford University Press.

Marcuse, H. (1964). *One dimensional man*. London: Routledge and Kegan Paul.

Marcuse, H. (1968). Ethics and revolution. In R. T. De George (Ed.), *Ethics and society* (pp. 133–147). London: Macmillan.

Mill, J. S. (1977 [1859]). In G. Himmelfarb (Ed.), *On liberty*. Harmondsworth: Pelican Books.

O'Grady, J. (2004, June 16). Obituary: Sir Stuart Hampshire. *The Guardian*, pp. 2–9. Retrieved July 20, 2015, from http://www.theguardian.com/news/2004/jun/16/guardianobituaries.obituaries.

Phillips, M. (1994, January 9). Moral torpor spawns designer babies. *The Observer*, p. 23.

Project R&R. (2015). International bans: Countries banning or limiting chimpanzee research. *Project R&R: Release and restitution for chimpanzees in US laboratories*. Retrieved July 20, 2015, from http://www.releasechimps.org/laws/international-bans.

Quinton, A. (1979, August 5). Pied piper of protest. *The Observer*.

Rachels, J. (Ed.). (1979). *Moral problems* (3rd ed.). New York: Harper and Row.

Rée, J. (1989, March 10). Clarity through ancient cobwebs: English philosophy in the 1950s. *Times Higher Education Supplement*.

Regan, T. (Ed.). (1980). *Matters of life and death*. New York: Random House.

Regan, T. (2001). *Defending animal rights*. Chicago: University of Illinois Press.

Singer, P. (1990 [1975]). *Animal liberation*. London: Jonathan Cape.

Singer, P. (2004). *The president of good and evil: Taking George W. Bush seriously*. London: Granta.

Singer, P. (2006, May 27). Great apes deserve life, liberty and the prohibition of torture. *The Guardian*. Retrieved July 20, 2015, from http://www.theguardian.com/commentisfree/2006/may/27/comment.animalwelfare.

Solzhenitsyn, A. (1971). *Cancer ward*. Harmondsworth: Penguin.

Soper, K. (1987). Marxism and morality. *New Left Review*, 163, 101–113.

Stevenson, C. L. (1944). *Ethics and language*. New Haven: Yale University Press.

Taylor, R. (2001). A step at a time: New Zealand's progress towards hominid rights. *Animal Law Review*, 7, 35–43.

Thomson, J. J. (1971). A defense of abortion. *Philosophy & Public Affairs*, 1(1), 47–66.

Warnock, M. (Chair). (1984). *Report of the committee of inquiry into human fertilisation and embryology*. London: Her Majesty's Stationary Office.

Weir, R. F. (Ed.). (1977). *Ethical issues in death and dying*. New York: Columbia University Press.

Williams, B. (Chair). (1979). *Report of the committee on obscenity and film censorship*. London: Her Majesty's Stationary Office.

Wilson, H. (1971). *The labour government 1966–70: A personal record.* London: Weidenfeld and Joseph.

Wolff, J. (2011). *Ethics and public policy.* London: Routledge.

Wood, A. W. (1981). *Karl Marx.* London: Routledge and Kegan Paul.

Wood, A. W. (1993). Marx against morality. In P. Singer (Ed.), *A companion to ethics* (pp. 511–524). Oxford: Blackwell.

Zohar, D. (1981, June 21). Is real life worth thinking about? *The Sunday Times.*

CHAPTER 4

Abortion and the Right to Not Be Pregnant

James Edwin Mahon

In his 1979 article 'The Ethics of Abortion', and in the two chapters 'Abortion' and 'Defences of Abortion' from his 1984 book, *An Introduction to Practical Ethics*, Joseph Mahon mounts an argument against abortion and criticizes several defences of abortion, including that of Judith Jarvis Thomson.[1] In this essay I am concerned with Mahon's argument against abortion, Thomson's defence of abortion, and Mahon's criticisms of her defence. I reject his argument, and I defend Thomson from his criticisms.[2] Although I highlight two problems with her argument, I conclude by offering remedies for these problems.

1 PRACTICAL ETHICS AND 'A DEFENSE OF ABORTION'

Judith Jarvis Thomson's 'A Defense of Abortion' was published in the very first issue of the journal *Philosophy & Public Affairs*, in 1971. The article that immediately followed it was 'Understanding the Abortion Argument', by Roger Wertheimer (1971). The third issue of the journal contained a response to Thomson by Baruch Brody (1972), 'Thomson on Abortion'. The fifth issue of the journal contained the article 'Abortion

J.E. Mahon
Department of Philosophy, CUNY-Lehman College, Bronx, NY, USA

© The Editor(s) (if applicable) and The Author(s) 2016
A. Fives, K. Breen (eds.), *Philosophy and Political Engagement*,
DOI 10.1057/978-1-137-44587-2_4

and Infanticide', by Michael Tooley (1972). The sixth issue of the journal contained another response to Thomson by John Finnis (1973), 'The Rights and Wrongs of Abortion: A Reply to Judith Thomson', as well as a response to Finnis from Thomson (1973), 'Rights and Deaths'.

It is not an exaggeration to say that the journal put the topic of abortion on the philosophical map and that Thomson's article did more than any other article, before it or since, to energize philosophical debate about abortion.[3] As Mahon says in introducing Thomson's argument, 'This paper has occasioned a large volume of discussion among professional philosophers, and is regarded as one of the best things yet written on this subject' (1984, p. 107). When James Rachels published the first edition of his important anthology of practical or applied ethics, *Moral Problems*, in 1975, he included Thomson's article. That book went on to sell 100,000 copies, in over three editions. Thomson's article remains one of the most reprinted philosophy articles of all time (Parent 1986).

Philosophy & Public Affairs was the official journal of the Society for Philosophy and Public Affairs. In his 1975 article 'Philosophy and Public Matters', Mahon points out that 'some North Americans engaged professionally in philosophy saw the need for a Society for Philosophy and Public Affairs (originally the Society for Philosophy and Public Policy), founded in May 1969 by Sidney Morgenbesser, Thomas Nagel, and others' (Mahon 1975, p. 7). Mahon returns to the subject of this society and their statement of purpose in 'The Emergence of Practical Ethics', the first chapter of *An Introduction to Practical Ethics*, where he says that 'The third area of ethics, and that which forms the subject area of this book, is that which, following the example of the young Australian philosopher, Peter Singer, I have called "practical ethics"', and which 'is a relatively recent phenomenon, and again one that is notably American in origin and practice' (Mahon 1984, pp. 12–13). The emergence of practical ethics in the late 1960s and early 1970s, Mahon says, had three causes. First, it was a reaction to the moral philosophy that had preceded it, which was dominated by metaethics and which was 'highly theoretical and abstract, rarely if ever concerning itself with real social and moral issues' (Mahon 1984, p. 16). Second, it was a reaction to the USA's involvement in the Vietnam War, which led to people questioning other 'issues of a practical and moral nature'. And, finally, it 'was a response, and the only decent response, to a widespread call for "involvement"' in the 1960s (Mahon 1984, p. 17).

What Mahon says here is correct and is repeated by Thomson (2013) herself in her autobiographical account of that time, 'How It Was'. But there is more to the story of the emergence of the topic of abortion, in particular, at this time. The original 'mission statement' of the Society for Philosophy and Public Affairs did not even mention the topic of abortion:

> The subject is not political philosophy or ethics in the abstract but rather concrete contemporary problems like conscription, police power, methods and occasions of warfare, treatment of individuals charged with crimes, population control, compensation for social disadvantages, eugenics, and so forth (quoted in Thomson 2013, pp. 49–50).

While Mahon is right in saying, in the chapter 'Abortion', that 'when philosophy, and especially ethics, became "practical" in the late 60s, one of the first issues to be scrutinized was abortion' (Mahon 1984, p. 88), it is at least arguable that this was in part due to the then current debate in the USA over the legalization of abortion. The case of *Roe v. Wade* first reached the US Supreme Court in 1970, although it was not decided until 1973, after the court had met a second time. At the time of her writing, in 1971, abortion was still prohibited in most states in the USA. As Thomson says:

> in most states in this country women are compelled by law to be not merely Minimally Decent Samaritans, but Good Samaritans to unborn persons inside them ... it does show that there is a gross injustice in the existing state of the law (Thomson 1971, p. 63).

When Ronald Dworkin anthologized Thomson's article in his collection, *The Philosophy of Law*, it was introduced as one of the essays that discussed 'issues of political philosophy that the United States Supreme Court has recently had to consider' (Dworkin 1977, p. 13). Thomson's own gloss on this is as follows

> Philosophers interested in ethics began publishing papers on topics that the standard philosophy journals had never published papers on before – we wrote on topics such as abortion, just war, the right to privacy, self-defense, and affirmative action and preferential hiring and the rights of women and minorities more generally. It was remarkable! Much of that material was first published in *Philosophy and Public Affairs*, which was founded by Marshall Cohen in 1971: it invited lawyers and political theorists to join moral philosophers in dealing with concrete moral issues and was an immediate success (Thomson 2013, p. 55).

Thomson's article was not merely groundbreaking because it addressed, with great philosophical sophistication, the topic of abortion—a topic that, more than 40 years later, continues to overshadow many important US Supreme Court cases.[4] It was also groundbreaking in terms of what it did for women. As N. Ann Davis has pointed out, the article was more instrumental than even John Rawls's *A Theory of Justice*, also published in 1971, in drawing more women into the growing philosophy and public affairs movement:

> The philosophy and public affairs movement did not begin with the publication of ADA ['A Defense of Abortion']. It already had roots, sources, and sustainers. But the publication of ADA helped expand its base. The reception of Thomson's article was no doubt affected by the recent publication of John Rawls's *A Theory of Justice*, which gave philosophers with interests in social and moral issues both the incentive to undertake serious work in moral and political theory, and an inspiring model of how work in that portion of philosophy could be both theoretically powerful and normatively rich. Nevertheless, it was the publication of ADA that provided the true catalyst in many cases: the spark that fused students' passionate interest in philosophy with the belief that the discipline might have a place for them, and the conviction that they might have something important to contribute to it. This was especially true, I think, for students of philosophy who were women. Thomson's work helped sustain both their self-esteem and their commitment through even the most difficult phases of graduate study (Davis 2001, pp. 85–86).

As Davis adds in a footnote: 'Within two weeks of the article's arrival in the library, every one of the female graduate students in philosophy had read it' (Davis 2001, p. 95, n. 5).

Thomson's article did more than draw women into the growing philosophy and public affairs movement. As Davis (2001, p. 85) says, 'Its style, too, was revolutionary'. It was not merely that Thomson argued for conclusions on the basis of moral intuitions about striking examples. All of these examples were also presented to readers in the form of a second-personal address:

> By casting her central example – the notorious, unconscious violinist – in the second person, Thomson showed philosophers that there was a viable alternative to the disengaged stance of the philosophical analyst, one that helped strengthen individual philosophers' convictions that they could – and should – be involved in social issues as committed participants, not merely as neutral observers or analysts (Davis 2001, p. 85).

Indeed, Thomson is responsible for what is surely one of the most famous sentences in all of moral philosophy: 'You wake up in the morning and find yourself back to back in bed with an unconscious violinist' (Thomson 1971, p. 113).

This revolution in style was extremely important because 'the topic of abortion' was one that 'had been tainted by people's (generally unvoiced) moralistic assumptions about sex and sexuality, and by their dismissive characterization of it as a "woman's problem"' (Davis 2001, pp. 88–89). By putting the example in the second person, Thomson made the male reader adopt the perspective of a pregnant woman:

> prior to the publication of ADA, women made only infrequent appearances in philosophers' examples. ... Thomson's creation of an example that both sought to model the intense physicality and overwhelmingness of pregnancy... and involved men as players – I am assuming that most professional philosophers in the early 1970s were male, and that Thomson knew that was the case – was, I think, brilliant (Davis 2001, p. 96).

Her article was thus revolutionary in being a *feminist* work. Indeed, the Good Samaritan Argument, in addition to being known as the 'Argument from Bodily Autonomy' (Feinberg 1980, p. 209), is also referred to as the 'Feminist Argument' (Singer 2011 [1979], p. 132). When Thomson returned to the subject of abortion in 1995, she explicitly cast the abortion debate in terms of its importance to women's equality:

> So this is an issue of great importance to women. Denial of the abortion right severely constrains their liberty, and among the consequences of that constraint are impediments to their achievement of equality (Thomson 1995, p. 20).

Even if those who formed the Society for Philosophy and Public Affairs in 1969 did not intend it, 'when philosophy, and especially ethics, became "practical" in the late 60s' it also became feminist.

2   THOMSON'S DEFENCE OF ABORTION

Thomson's defence of abortion is as follows. Everyone possesses the right to his or her own body. This is the right to bodily autonomy: 'My own view is that if a human being has any just, prior claim to anything at all, he has a just, prior claim to his own body' (Thomson 1971, p. 54). What this right amounts to is the right to refuse to allow another person to use my body. No one has the right to use my body without my permission.

In the case of pregnancy as a result of rape, the fetus has no right to use the woman's body, because the woman has not given the fetus permission to use the woman's body. As she says: 'I suppose we may take it as a datum that in a case of pregnancy due to rape the mother has not given the unborn person a right to the use of her body for food and shelter' (Thomson 1971, p. 57). Since the fetus has no right to use the woman's body, the woman may refuse to allow the fetus to use her body. If she refuses to allow the fetus to use her body, she is not violating any right of the fetus. However, the *only way* for a woman to refuse to allow a (non-viable) fetus to use her body is for her to have an abortion. This is simply a fact about human biology. Hence, in the case of a pregnancy as a result of rape, at least when the fetus is not viable, abortion violates no right of the fetus (Mahon 2014, p. 1431). In such a case at least, abortion is not a violation of the right to life of the fetus, because the right to life is the right not to be killed unjustly, and such a killing is not an unjust killing. Thus, we are led to

> the conclusion that unborn persons whose existence is due to rape have no right to the use of their mothers' bodies, and thus that aborting them is not depriving them of anything they have a right to and hence is not unjust killing (Thomson 1971, p. 58).

Of course, the woman may choose to allow the fetus to use her body. She may choose not to have an abortion. But since the fetus has no right to use her body, it follows that, if she does allow the fetus to use her body, and does not have an abortion, this is a *supererogatory* act on her part. If she allows the fetus to use her body, then she is being a 'Good Samaritan' to the fetus.

Thomson provides an example to support her argument. Imagine that you are kidnapped by a group of musical enthusiasts and wake up to find yourself in bed, hooked up to a violinist who is unconscious. The violinist has also been kidnapped by the same group of musical enthusiasts. The violinist has failing kidneys and requires the use of your kidneys for nine months in order to repair his kidneys. At the end of the nine months, he will be woken up from his unconscious state, healthy again, and you will be free to return to whatever you were doing before you were kidnapped. If you remain hooked up to the violinist, he will live.

But if you disconnect yourself from the violinist, he will die. According to Thomson:

> If anything in the world is true, it is that you do not commit murder, you do not do what is impermissible, if you reach around to your back and unplug yourself from that violinist to save your life (Thomson 1971, p. 52).

Since the unconscious violinist has no right to use your body, you do not violate any right of his by unhooking yourself from him and killing him. You do not violate his right to life, since his right to life does not extend to a right to use your body.

3   MAHON'S ARGUMENT AGAINST ABORTION

Mahon's argument against abortion is formulated provisionally as follows:

Killing an innocent and defenceless human being is wrong.
Killing a fetus is killing an innocent and defenceless human being.
Therefore, killing a fetus is wrong.
Therefore, abortion is wrong (Mahon 1984, p. 92).

In defence of the second premise, Mahon argues, 'the word "human" signifies, or denotes, a being at *some stage* of its development'. The life of this being, it is said, 'does not begin at birth but, on average, 38 weeks prior to its birth' (Mahon 1984, p. 93). The 'unborn or premature human being... is, as a rule, called the "foetus"'. Mahon distinguishes between being a 'human being' and being a 'person'. A 'person', he claims, is a

> biologically mature specimen of its kind, exhibiting in unequivocal measure those powers and proclivities, such as ratiocinative, moral, political, and productive powers and proclivities, that typify entities of that mature kind (Mahon 1984, p. 93).

By contrast, 'a human life, as distinct from the life of a person, begins at conception (or fertilization) and ends at death' (Mahon 1984, p. 95). To say that a fetus is a human being is simply to say that a fetus is member of the species *Homo sapiens*. Even if it were argued against Mahon that there are, or can be, persons who are not human beings (chimpanzees, dolphins, Martians, angels, God, et cetera), Mahon would still be correct in saying that (human) fetuses are human beings. Further, even if it were argued against Mahon that fetuses are persons, Mahon would still be correct in saying that they are human beings.

In defence of the second premise, Mahon also argues that the fetus 'is incapable of harbouring malevolent intentions' and that the fetus 'is defenceless or completely vulnerable to attack' (Mahon 1984, p. 94). These twin claims are not controversial. Mahon does consider an objection to the second premise made by G.A. Cohen.[5] The objection is that 'the concept of a human being is too wide' in this second premise, since, according to it, 'a *zygote*, i.e., what exists from conception to implantation about a week later, would qualify as a human being', and it is 'absurd' to claim that to kill a zygote is to 'kill an innocent and defenceless human being' (Mahon 1984, pp. 94–95). While admitting that the objection 'appears to be a very strong one', Mahon in the end rejects the charge that it is absurd to claim that to kill a zygote is to kill an innocent and defenceless human being. Its apparent absurdity stems from 'the tendency to date membership of the human race from the point of birth' and from 'the tendency to automatically think of human beings in terms of persons' (Mahon 1984, pp. 95–96). Both tendencies are misleading, since it is false that something is not a human being until it is born, and it is false that all human beings are persons.

In defence of the first premise, Mahon considers the objection that 'it forbids killing when there is, demonstrably, a right to kill. To be more precise, we do, conceivably, sometimes have the right to take innocent and defenceless human life' (Mahon 1984, p. 94). The strongest version of this objection, Mahon considers, is to be found in Thomson's defence of abortion.

Mahon summarizes Thomson's defence of abortion as follows: 'certain persons do not have the right to life', and 'the fetus is such a person' (Mahon 1984, p. 108). That is, the fetus lacks a right to life. Note that Thomson would reject this characterization of her argument. She holds that the fetus does have a right to life (or rather, she grants this for the sake of the argument; her own position is that a fetus in the early stages of pregnancy lacks a right to life).[6] This is the right not to be killed unjustly (i.e., the right not to be murdered). As she says: 'the right to life consists not in the right not to be killed, but rather in the right not to be killed unjustly' (Thomson 1971, p. 57). She simply rejects the argument that because a fetus, like everyone else who is innocent, has a right not to be killed unjustly, it follows that a fetus has a right not to be killed. Her argument is that, even if a fetus has a right to life, it is still morally permissible to kill a (non-viable) fetus, if this is the only way to stop the fetus from using your body. Human biology being the way it is, however, this *is* the only way.

The first of Mahon's criticisms of Thomson's argument that will be considered here is the criticism that the example involving the unconscious violinist fails to be analogous to pregnancy as a result of rape, because 'The woman is the *mother* of the fetus; no such relation exists, or at least no such relation has been postulated, between the kidney-captive and the violinist' (Mahon 1984, p. 110, emphasis in original).[7] Importantly, other philosophers have rejected the use of the term 'mother' to refer to the woman who is pregnant as a result of rape, although Thomson herself uses the term in her article. 'Mother', they argue, implies or connotes something more than the biological fact of being pregnant, in the form of a special relationship towards the fetus or a special responsibility for the fetus. In the case of unwanted pregnancy in general, and in the case of pregnancy as a result of rape in particular, however, there is nothing more than the biological fact of being pregnant. They would object to Mahon's characterization of the woman who is pregnant as a result of rape as a 'mother'.[8]

Mahon may be said to have considered Thomson to have responded in this vein to his disanalogy criticism. He says that 'She first points out that it is commonly believed that to say X is the mother of Y is to say that X has a *special responsibility* for Y' (Mahon 1984, p. 112), and he then quotes Thomson as saying: 'Surely we do not have any such "special responsibility" for a person unless we have assumed it, explicitly or implicitly' (Thomson, quoted in Mahon 1984, p. 113). The point is that 'mother' either does not imply any responsibility for caring for the fetus, or it implies having a responsibility for caring for a child that has been assumed, either explicitly or implicitly. Hence, someone who is pregnant as a result of rape is either a 'mother' who has not (or not yet) assumed responsibility for caring for a child or is not (or not yet) a 'mother'. As he says, 'Thomson attaches little fundamental importance to the hereditary relation between the mother and her unborn offspring', a hereditary relation which he characterizes as based on the fact that 'the make-up of the foetus is due, in part, to genes transmitted from the woman whose womb it occupies' (Mahon 1984, p. 113). What he says about the lack of importance of such a hereditary relationship for Thomson is quite correct, since such a relation exists in the case of a pregnancy that is the result of rape, and Thomson states explicitly that such a relationship does not imply any responsibility for caring for the fetus. The responsibility must be assumed. As Mahon summarizes Thomson's position, 'What matters basically is whether she wanted the child. If she did, then it has rights against her, and she has obligations toward it. If she didn't, then it has no rights against her' (Mahon 1984, p. 113).

This is basically right, although the final sentence here is somewhat misleading, since it is not true that the fetus has no rights against the pregnant woman. Thomson does hold that a fetus has rights against a pregnant woman. Most importantly, the fetus has the right not to be killed unjustly. It is just that a fetus does not have the right against the pregnant woman to use her body, and this right is the relevant right here. Thomson is quite clear that, if it were possible for the fetus to survive without using the pregnant woman's body (to be removed from her body), then it would be a violation of the fetus's rights—indeed, it would be murder—for the pregnant woman to kill the fetus: 'I agree that the desire for the child's death is not one which anybody may gratify, should it turn out to be possible to detach the child alive' (Thomson 1971, p. 66). As N. Ann Davis has correctly stated, the right that Thomson is defending in her article is the right to not be *pregnant*: 'her view of abortion [is] as essentially a form of pregnancy termination that involves fetal detachment, rather than as the deliberate termination of the life of the fetus' (Davis 2001, p. 93).

Mahon's belief that Thompson has already responded to his disanalogy criticism leads him to make his main criticism. Characterizing her argument as the argument that 'one cannot be responsible for someone unless one has promised to, or assumed responsibility for that person at some stage', Mahon argues that this is false:

> I can be responsible for the victims of a car crash, for instance (i.e., have moral duties towards them), even if I have never seen the victims before in my life, without ever having given an undertaking to help them, and without my having chosen to be the person on whom they now depend for help. How far this obligation goes is, of course, another thing. I certainly do not think it goes so far as to give one's life. If I am right about this, then there is at least one circumstance in which an abortion is morally justified, namely, where a woman has been raped, where she is pregnant as a result of being raped, and where her life is in imminent danger as a result of that pregnancy. In such a case, she is not morally obliged to sacrifice her life (Mahon 1984, pp. 113–114).

In order for this criticism to apply to Thomson's argument, it must be the case that someone who is the victim of a car crash has a right to be helped by a mere bystander, because the bystander is 'morally obliged' to help the victim. Similarly, a fetus has a right to use the pregnant woman's body, even in the case of pregnancy as a result of rape (at least when this does not involve the loss of the pregnant woman's life), because the pregnant woman is 'morally obliged' to bring the pregnancy to term.

It is important to see why Thomson would reject this criticism. According to Thomson, it is false that the car crash victim has a right to be helped by the bystander. The most that can be said is that the bystander ought to help the car crash victim. However, it does not follow from this that the car crash victim has a right to the bystander's help. From the fact that A *ought* to help B, it does not follow that B has a *right* to be helped by A. As she says:

> [S]uppose pregnancy lasted only an hour, and constituted no threat to life or health. And suppose that a woman becomes pregnant as a result of rape. Admittedly she did not voluntarily do anything to bring about the existence of the child. Admittedly she did nothing at all which would give the unborn person a right to the use of her body. All the same it might well be said ... that she *ought* to allow it to remain for that hour ... Now some people are inclined to use the term 'right' in such a way that it follows from the fact that you ought to allow a person to use your body for the hour he needs, that he has a right to use your body for the hour he needs, even though he has not been given that right by any person or act. They may even say that it follows also that if you refuse, you act unjustly toward him. This use of the term is perhaps so common that it cannot be called wrong; nevertheless it seems to me to be an unfortunate loosening of what we would do better to keep a tight rein on (Thomson 1971, p. 60).

It must be said that it remains ambiguous in Thomson's article as to what 'A has a moral obligation to B to ∅' means. It may mean the stronger 'B has a right to ∅ from A'. If it does, then 'A has a moral obligation to B to ∅' is not equivalent to, and cannot be derived from, 'A ought to ∅ (to B)'. Or, it may mean the weaker 'A ought to ∅ (to B)'. If it does, then 'B has a right to ∅ from A' is not equivalent to, and cannot be derived from, 'A has a moral obligation to B to ∅'. Because of this ambiguity in her article, it remains uncertain as to whether Thomson would argue that a bystander has no moral obligation to help a car crash victim, or whether she would argue that a bystander has a moral obligation to help a car crash victim, but that the car crash victim has no right to be helped by the bystander.

Nevertheless, Thomson does hold that the stronger 'B has a right to ∅ from A' is not equivalent to, and may not be derived from, the weaker 'A ought to ∅ (to B)'. As she says about moral requirements—which would appear to be equivalent to moral obligations—in discussing a variation on the violinist example in which the violinist only needs to use your kidneys for 1 hour in order to live:

> If anyone does wish to deduce "he has a right" from "you ought", then all the same he must surely grant that there are cases in which it is not morally required of you that you allow that violinist to use your kidneys, and in which he does not have a right to them, and in which you do not do him an injustice if you refuse (1971, p. 61).

Thomson would therefore reject Mahon's claim that a car crash victim has a right to be helped by a bystander, and that it would be unjust of the bystander not to help the victim.

Mahon could reply by adapting an argument from Peter Singer (1972). Imagine that you come across a child drowning in a shallow pond. Even if you have not assumed any responsibility whatsoever to take care of drowning persons, such as becoming a life guard, and even if the child is a complete stranger, it still seems that the child has a right to be rescued by you, when all it would take to save the child is to wade into the shallow pond and pull the child out of the water. In the case of pregnancy as a result of rape, it could be argued, the fetus is in a similar position to the child in the shallow pond. Without the use of the pregnant woman's body, the fetus will die. Even if the pregnant woman has not given the fetus permission to use her body, it still seems that the fetus has a right to use her body, when all it would take is 9 months of her time (or at least until the fetus is viable). Indeed, Thomson says that her argument holds even if 'pregnancy lasted only an hour, and constituted no threat to life or health'. Surely, the fetus has a right to use her body for 1 hour.

It is important to understand that Thomson would reject this argument. In her article, she provides the following counterargument, using a pair of examples:

> [T]o deprive someone of what he has a right to is to treat him unjustly. Suppose a boy and his small brother are jointly given a box of chocolates for Christmas. If the older boy takes the box and refuses to give his brother any of the chocolates, he is unjust to him, for the brother has a right to half of them. ...

Suppose that box of chocolates I mentioned earlier had not been given to both boys jointly, but was given only to the older boy. There he sits, stolidly eating his way through the box, his small brother watching enviously. Here we are likely to say, "You ought not to be so mean. You ought to give your brother some of those chocolates." My own view is that it just does not follow from the truth of this that the brother has any right to any of the chocolates. If the boy refuses to give his brother any, he is greedy, stingy, callous – but not unjust. ...
  So my own view is that even though you ought to let the violinist use your kidneys for the one hour he needs, we should not conclude that he has a right to do so – we should say that if you refuse, you are, like the boy who owns all the chocolates and will give none away, self-centered and callous, indecent in fact, but not unjust. And similarly, that even supposing a case in which a woman pregnant due to rape ought to allow the unborn person to use her body for the hour he needs, we should not conclude that he has a right to do so; we should conclude that she is self-centered, callous, indecent, but not unjust, if she refuses (1971, pp. 56, 60–61).

According to Thomson, if you do not allow the violinist to use your kidneys for just 1 hour, then you are callous, self-centred, et cetera, but you are not unjust. This is because he has no right to use your kidneys. Similarly, if the woman who is pregnant as a result of rape does not allow the fetus to use her body for just 1 hour, she is callous, self-centred, et cetera. But she is not unjust. This is because the fetus has no right to use the pregnant woman's body. Likewise, if you do not help the child drowning in the shallow pond, by wading in and saving him, you are callous, self-centred, et cetera. But you are not unjust. This is because the child has no right to be rescued by you. As it has been said:

> If I choose to refrain from saving the toddler drowning in the mud puddle, I would not be violating the moral right of the toddler, but I would still be acting as a "moral monster" (Liberto 2012, p. 397).

Finally, if the woman who is pregnant as a result of rape does not allow the fetus to use her body for 9 months, then she is not callous or self-centred, et cetera. She is merely not being a Good Samaritan.
  It is now possible to return to the first premise of Mahon's argument. It does seem that there is a right to kill an innocent and defenceless human being. When an innocent and defenceless human being is using your body without your permission, and the only way to refuse to allow this innocent

and defenceless human being to use your body is to kill this innocent and defenceless human being, then you have a right to kill this innocent and defenceless human being. This is because the innocent and defenceless human being lacks a right to use your body, and you have a right to your own body. Mahon's argument against abortion must be rejected.

4   THOMSON AND INDECENCY

Although I have defended Thomson's argument above, there are at least two problems with it. The first is a problem with her terminology. This requires some explaining. Thomson concludes the article with the following:

> First, while I do argue that abortion is not impermissible, I do not argue that it is always permissible. There may well be cases in which carrying the child to term requires only Minimally Decent Samaritanism of the mother, and this is a standard that we must not fall below. I am inclined to think it a merit of my account precisely that it does *not* give a general yes or a general no. It allows for and supports our general sense that, for example, a sick and desperately frightened fourteen-year-old schoolgirl, pregnant due to rape, may *of course* choose abortion, and that any law which rules this out is an insane law. And it also allows for and supports our sense that in other cases resort to abortion is even positively indecent. It would be indecent in the woman to request an abortion, and indecent in a doctor to perform it, if she is in her seventh month, and wants the abortion to avoid the nuisance of postponing a trip abroad (Thomson 1971, pp. 65–66).

Here, Thomson distinguishes between an abortion where the woman is not 'indecent' (the 14-year-old pregnant rape victim), and an abortion where the woman is 'indecent' (the 7-month pregnant woman who wishes to go on holiday). In saying that the woman in the second example is 'indecent', Thomson would appear to be saying that she is callous, self-centred, et cetera, although her action is not unjust. Her behaviour falls below the standard of being a 'Minimally Decent Samaritan', which is 'a standard that we must not'—that is, ought not—'fall below'. Nevertheless, this woman does not violate a right of the fetus.

A term that captures this type of behavior is *suberogatory*.[9] As Julia Driver explains: 'Suberogatory acts are acts that we ought not to do, but which are not forbidden ... The suberogatory is "mere badness"' (Driver 1992, p. 291). Thomson, it would seem, holds that 'a frivolous abortion... is bad' and that 'bad abortions' are 'suberogatory' (Driver 1992, p. 292).

If a pregnant woman who has an abortion in the seventh month of pregnancy to go on holiday is (merely) 'indecent', however, and the abortion is (merely) suberogatory, then this must be because, even in the seventh month of her pregnancy, the fetus has no right to use the pregnant woman's body. This means, first, that the fetus in this example must not be viable, because Thomson insists that 'should it turn out to be possible to detach the child alive' an abortion at 7 months would be a violation of the fetus's right not to be killed unjustly. Second, since there is no indication that the pregnancy was the result of rape, it means that whether or not the pregnancy is the result of rape is ultimately irrelevant to the question of whether or not the fetus has a right to use the woman's body. The only thing that is relevant is whether or not the woman wishes to allow the fetus to use her body.

If this is correct, then Thomson *does* give 'a general yes' to the question of the permissibility of (voluntary) abortion, at least when the fetus is not viable: (voluntary) abortion is *always* permissible.[10] Abortion *never* violates the right to life of a fetus. Thomson does indeed embrace the '"extreme" liberal position' that has been attributed to her by Driver: 'a liberal should view all (early) abortions as permissible even when the mother is quite healthy and could take care of the baby without difficulty' (Driver 1992, p. 289).[11]

The problem with this conclusion is that Thomson claims that she does *not* 'give a general yes or a general no' to the question of the permissibility of abortion, and that she does *not* 'argue that it is always permissible' to have an abortion when the fetus is not viable.

She could avoid the contradiction by arguing that her use of 'permissible' and 'impermissible' is equivalent to her use of 'decent' and 'indecent'. She could say that when she talks about 'a standard that we must not fall below' in our behaviour towards other people—the standard of being a Minimally Decent Samaritan, that is, the standard of being decent—she is talking about the standard of what is 'permissible' behaviour towards other people. The woman who has an abortion in the seventh month of her pregnancy would therefore be acting *impermissibly*. Meanwhile, the 14-year-old rape victim who has an abortion would be acting *permissibly*.

If Thomson defended herself in this way, however, she would have to admit that her use of 'permissible' and 'impermissible' is different from that of most moral philosophers and common usage.[12] Normally, when you say that someone is acting callously, or self-centredly, et cetera, but is not violating anyone's rights, you are saying that she is *not* acting impermissibly. Indeed, suberogatory actions are precisely actions 'that are permissible, though bad' (Driver 1992, p. 291). If Thomson identified acting impermissibly with acting indecently but not violating anyone's rights, then she would be saying that someone can be acting both impermissibly and justly, which is a highly unusual claim. It would also mean that indecent abortions are not suberogatory actions after all, since suberogatory actions are those actions that 'are deserving of negative evaluation, without being actually wrong, where wrong just means "impermissible"' (Driver 1992, p. 286, n. 2).[13]

This first terminological problem with her argument can be remedied in one of two ways, in order to avoid a contradiction. Thomson can state explicitly that by 'impermissible' she merely means acting in a way that is 'indecent' (callously, self-centredly, et cetera), and that by 'permissible' she merely means acting in way that is 'decent' (not acting callously, self-centredly, et cetera). Or she can alter the claims in her conclusion. She can say that 'I do ... argue that it is always permissible [although not always decent, to have an abortion when the fetus is not viable]', and 'I am inclined to think it a merit of my account precisely that it does *not* give a general yes or a general no [as to whether or not an abortion is decent, although it does give a general yes or a general no as to whether or not an abortion is permissible, namely, a general yes]'.

The second problem with her argument is a more serious problem, because it is a problem with the argument itself. *Why* is having an abortion (of a non-viable fetus) in the seventh month of pregnancy, in order to go on a holiday, (merely) 'indecent'? It seems clear that the pregnancy was desired, and that the woman originally expected to bring the pregnancy to term. More importantly, since the woman is in her seventh month of pregnancy, it might be thought that the fetus has acquired the right to use the woman's body by now. Has the fetus not acquired such a right? If so, what is her argument?

At one point in the article Thomson says: 'Suppose a woman voluntarily indulges in intercourse, knowing of the chance that it will issue in pregnancy, and then she does become pregnant' (Thomson 1971, p. 57). About this hypothetical situation, she comments:

> It seems to me that the argument we are looking at can establish at most that there are *some* cases in which the unborn person has a right to the use of

its mother's body, and therefore *some* cases in which abortion is unjust killing. There is room for much discussion and argument as to precisely which,
if any (Thomson 1971, p. 59).

The 'if any' here is very telling. Thomson provides no example of a case
in which a non-viable fetus has acquired a right to use the woman's body.
She provides no example of an abortion that is an unjust killing.

The closest that Thomson comes to providing an example of an unjust
killing is the following:

> If a set of parents do not try to prevent pregnancy, do not obtain an abor-
> tion, and then at the time of birth of the child do not put it out for adoption,
> but rather take it home with them, then they have assumed responsibility for
> it, they have given it rights, and they cannot *now* withdraw support for it at
> the cost of its life because they now find it difficult to go on providing for it
> (Thomson 1971, p. 65).

Importantly, this is not a case of an abortion. It is a case of parents with-
drawing 'food and shelter' from the child they have taken home with
them, resulting in the child's death (since no one else is apparently available to take care of the child). The example is not analogous to pregnancy,
because having a claim to food and shelter from other people is different
from having a claim to use another person's *body* for food and shelter.

I take Thomson to hold that there is *no* case in which a (non-viable)
fetus acquires a right to use the pregnant woman's body, and that *no*
abortion (of a non-viable fetus) is unjust. The problem is that she has
provided no argument for this conclusion.

This second problem, too, can be remedied.[14] In addition to its being
true that no one has the right to use my body without my permission;
it is also true that I may revoke this permission at any time. I am always
free to refuse to allow another person to use my body, and I am always
free to refuse to allow another person to *continue* to use my body, even
if I have allowed the person to use my body up until now. My freedom
to decide if someone may or may not use my body is *inalienable*. Since I
may refuse to allow another person to use my body, even if this results in
the person's death, I may refuse to allow another person to continue to
use my body, even if this results in the person's death, despite the fact that
I have allowed the person to use my body up until now. This argument
is implied by her claim that 'if a human being has any just, prior claim to

anything at all, he has a just, prior claim to his own body', and, perhaps, by comments such as the following: 'Women have said again and again, "This is *my* body!" and they have reason to feel angry, reason to feel that it has been like shouting into the wind' (Thomson 1971, p. 53).[15]

NOTES

1. The two other defences of abortion he criticizes are Kamm (1976) and Dooley-Clarke (1981). On a different point, I should apologize in advance for any confusion that results in my writing about someone who shares my name—namely, my father.
2. My defence of Thomson is very much in the spirit of Boonin (2002).
3. An equally historically important article on abortion is that by Philippa Foot (1967). It should not be lost on us that Philippa Foot was another prominent woman philosopher at a time when there were much fewer women in philosophy. Foot and Thomson, between them, may be said to have created the 'Trolley Problem', perhaps the most famous 'problem' of modern moral philosophy.
4. To give just one example, the recent 2014 US Supreme Court decision, *Burwell v. Holly Lobby*, essentially concerns the question of whether for-profit corporations are exempt from the mandate of the Affordable Care Act to pay for Plan B, *ella*, et cetera, for their employees, because those running the corporations consider these to be abortifacients rather than contraceptives. For the background to this debate, see Hrobak and Wilson (2014).
5. Sadly, G.A. (Jerry) Cohen, a friend of my father's from my father's sabbatical year at University College London in 1979–1980, died in 2009 and could not be a contributor to this volume.
6. As Thomson says, 'we have only been pretending throughout that the fetus is a human being from the moment of conception. A very early abortion is surely not the killing of a person' (Thomson 1971, p. 66).
7. Space constraints prohibit discussion of every one of Mahon's objections to Thomson's argument. I have selected the two most important criticisms.
8. For an argument against using the term 'mother' to refer to a woman who is an 'abortion candidate', see Nancy Davis (1984).
9. An older term for this kind of action was 'offence'. See Chisholm (1963). See also Mellema (1987) and Mahon (2006).
10. The assumption throughout this essay is that the abortion under discussion is a voluntary abortion, and not one that is coerced or performed without the consent of the pregnant woman.
11. Footnote 9 on the same page attributes this position to Thomson. Note that Driver says about this position that 'no consideration is given to the fetus in

determining the permissibility of the abortion' (1992, p. 289, n. 9). I would prefer to say that moral consideration is given to the fetus—Thomson assumes for the sake of the argument that a fetus is a person—but that the fetus, despite its moral status, is judged to fail to have a right to use the pregnant woman's body, which is the only right that would make the abortion impermissible.

12. My thanks to Melina Bell for discussion of the normal moral philosophical usage of these terms.

13. For this reason, Liberto (2012, p. 399) is incorrect when she says that Thomson 'suggests that it is probably morally impermissible for the older brother to refuse to share the chocolates' with the younger brother. The older brother is being callous, self-centred, et cetera, but he is not doing anything impermissible.

14. There remains a third problem. *Why* is having an abortion (of a non-viable fetus) in the seventh month of pregnancy, in order to go on a holiday, 'indecent' at all? What is the argument for this claim? Lack of space prohibits discussion of this third problem.

15. The argument of the penultimate section of this essay was first presented in a talk at 'Roe at 40—The Controversy Continues', a symposium at Washington and Lee University School of Law, on 8 November 2013. For discussions about the argument contained in that talk (a version of which was later published [Mahon 2014]), I would like to thank Melina Bell. For an exchange about what Thomson says in her article about permissibility, impermissibility, and indecency, I would also like to thank Jessica Gordon-Roth. For clarification of Thomson's argument, I would like to thank David Boonin. For a discussion about the suberogatory and Thomson's argument, I would like to thank Julia Driver. Over the years, I have benefitted from discussing Thomson's article with many different undergraduates and law students at Washington and Lee University, and I would like to take this opportunity to thank them for these discussions. I first discussed the topic of abortion with my parents, Joseph Mahon and Evelyn Mahon, as a teenager in the context of the passing of the Eighth Amendment to the Constitution of Ireland in 1983, which attempted to copperfasten a ban on abortion in Ireland. Years later, I helped proofread my mother's report to the Irish government, *Women and Crisis Pregnancy* (Mahon et al. 1998). I am happy that the occasion of my father's retirement from teaching philosophy has afforded me the opportunity to write on this topic, even if I disagree with the position he defended in his early writings (he has since moved on). Finally, I would like to thank the University of International Business and Economics in Beijing, China, for affording me the opportunity to complete work on this essay in the summer of 2015.

REFERENCES

Boonin, D. (2002). *A defense of abortion.* Cambridge: Cambridge University Press.

Brody, B. (1972). Thomson on abortion. *Philosophy & Public Affairs,* 2(3), 335–340.

Chisholm, R. M. (1963). Supererogation and offence: A conceptual scheme for ethics. *Ratio,* 5, 1–14.

Davis, N. (1984). Abortion and self-defense. *Philosophy & Public Affairs,* 13(3), 175–207.

Davis, N. A. (2001). Fiddling second: Reflections on "A Defense of Abortion". In A. Byrne, R. C. Stalnaker, & R. Wedgwood (Eds.), *Fact and value: Essays on ethics and metaphysics for Judith Jarvis Thomson* (pp. 81–96). Cambridge, MA: MIT Press.

Dooley-Clarke, D. (1981, September 11). Just exceptions to moral principles. *The Irish Times.*

Driver, J. (1992). The suberogatory. *Australasian Journal of Philosophy,* 70(3), 286–295.

Dworkin, R. (Ed.). (1977). *The philosophy of law.* Oxford: Oxford University Press.

Feinberg, J. (1980). Abortion. In T. Regan (Ed.), *Matters of life and death.* Philadelphia, PA: Temple University Press.

Finnis, J. (1973). The rights and wrongs of abortion: A reply to Judith Thomson. *Philosophy & Public Affairs,* 2(2), 117–145.

Foot, P. (1967). The problem of abortion and the doctrine of double effect. *Oxford Review,* 5, 5–15.

Hrobak, R. M., & Wilson, R. F. (2014). Emergency contraceptives or abortion-inducing drugs? Empowering women to make informed decisions. *Washington and Lee Law Review,* 71(2), 1385–1428.

Kamm, F. M. (1976). Review of Marvin Kohl, The morality of killing: Sanctity of life, abortion, and euthanasia. *Philosophical Review,* 85, 124–126.

Liberto, H. R. (2012). Denying the suberogatory. *Philosophia,* 40(2), 395–402.

Mahon, E., Conlon, C., & Dillon, L. (1998). *Women and crisis pregnancy: A report presented to the Department of Health and Children.* Dublin: The Stationary Office.

Mahon, J. (1975). Philosophy and public matters. *Understanding,* pp. 5, 5–11.

Mahon, J. (1979, November 10). The ethics of abortion. *Irish Medical Times.*

Mahon, J. (1984). *An introduction to practical ethics.* Dublin: Turoe Press.

Mahon, J. E. (2006). The good, the bad, and the obligatory. *Journal of Value Inquiry,* 40(1), 59–71.

Mahon, J. E. (2014). Innocent burdens. *Washington and Lee Law Review,* 71(2), 1429–1472.

Mellema, G. (1987). Quasi-supererogation. *Philosophical Studies,* 52(1), 141–150.

Parent, W. (1986). 'Preface' to J.J. Thomson, *Rights, restitution, and risk: Essays in moral theory* (pp. vii–x). Cambridge, MA: Harvard University Press.

Rachels, J. (Ed.). (1975). *Moral problems*. New York: Harper & Row.

Rawls, J. (1971). *A theory of justice*. Cambridge, MA: Harvard University Press.

Singer, P. (1972). Famine, affluence, and morality. *Philosophy & Public Affairs*, 1(3), 229–243.

Singer, P. (2011 [1979]). *Practical ethics* (3rd ed.). Cambridge: Cambridge University Press.

Thomson, J. J. (1971). A defense of abortion. *Philosophy & Public Affairs*, 1(1), 47–66.

Thomson, J. J. (1973). Rights and deaths. *Philosophy & Public Affairs*, 2(2), 146–159.

Thomson, J. J. (1995). Abortion. *Boston Review*, 20(3), 11–15.

Thomson, J. J. (2013). How it was. In S. M. Cahn (Ed.), *Portraits of American philosophy* (pp. 47–61). Lanham, MD: Rowman & Littlefield.

Tooley, M. (1972). Abortion and infanticide. *Philosophy & Public Affairs*, 2(1), 37–65.

Wertheimer, R. (1971). Understanding the abortion argument. *Philosophy & Public Affairs*, 1(1), 67–95.

CHAPTER 5

Acts, Omissions, and Assisted Death: Some Reflections on the Marie Fleming Case

Richard Hull and Annie McKeown O'Donovan

This essay looks at one recent case that has triggered widespread public debate. Marie Fleming, confined to a wheelchair and in the final stages of multiple sclerosis (MS), recently asked the High Court in the Republic of Ireland to rule as to whether she had the constitutional right to be assisted in taking her own life. The Court ruled that she did not have that right and, throughout the deliberations, a strong moral distinction was drawn between letting nature take its course via palliative care or withdrawal of treatment and physician assistance to bring about death. The position of the Court was that physician assistance is impermissible, while corresponding omissions that let nature take its course are generally permissible.

That position will be questioned and criticized here. It can be seen to rely heavily on the distinction between harmful acts and omissions and, through analysis of this case, it will become clear that a strong moral emphasis on the distinction between acts and omissions can do a lot of work in our assessment of critical situations. The reasoning behind such an emphasis will be explored. It will be argued that the most compelling philosophical basis for a moral emphasis on the distinction between acts and omissions lies in the structural difference entailed, where acts interfere

R. Hull (✉) • A.McKeown O'Donovan
National University of Ireland, Galway, Republic of Ireland

© The Editor(s) (if applicable) and The Author(s) 2016
A. Fives, K. Breen (eds.), *Philosophy and Political Engagement*,
DOI 10.1057/978-1-137-44587-2_5

with a victim in a way that omissions do not. That is, in the absence of harmful acts as opposed to omissions, the victim would usually have and be able to maintain the good that s/he has. As such, that basis does not apply to the same extent in the Marie Fleming type of case, since she was imminently unable to maintain the good that she had, in this case her life.

In the light of this analysis, it will be suggested that assisted suicide can be morally justified in the advanced stages of terminal illness, both from within our traditional moral outlook and in a limited way that can resist any inevitable descent down a slippery slope. That said, it will also be argued that we should continue to question our traditional moral landscape and encourage more action in the light of our humanitarian convictions. This implies, in turn, a clear need for more critical philosophical discourse and persuasive analysis in the public sphere. A public and more accessible role for philosophical analysis could assist in clarifying conceptual confusions, more deeply question the legitimacy of different approaches to pressing issues, work towards sensible and progressive social development, and, at the very least, perform the critical function of discriminating good from less good arguments.

1   Overview of the Case

Marie Fleming was diagnosed with MS in 1989, aged 35 years. In her memoir, we witness an open, honest, and rational account of an individual's reasoning behind the desire to end her own life. Fleming begins by describing a typical day in her life in the summer of 2013, before her death in December of that year. She lists the different coloured pills she had to take daily, the elements of daily life which brought her joy, such as being able to listen to the radio, and the elements which brought her great sorrow and pain, such as thirst and difficulties swallowing due to atrophied throat muscles (Fleming and Leonard 2014, p. 5). She tells us stories from her life, culminating in the final chapters documenting the experience of deciding that she did not want to die of MS, but at her own hand at a time of her choosing, when the symptoms of her MS were severe enough to comprise a life she no longer felt was worth living.

Once Fleming had made the decision to end her life, she was shocked to find that, given she would need assistance in dying, this act would constitute a crime in accordance with the *Criminal Law (Suicide) Act* (1993).[1] She and her family had taken it for granted up to that point that, should they ask for assistance, it would be provided. This led to a period of fear and insecurity before Fleming decided, with the support of her partner, Tom Curran, that she would try to achieve the death she wanted.

Article 40 of the Constitution of Ireland concerns fundamental human rights. Included here is the statement that 'All citizens shall, as human persons, be held equal before the law. This shall not mean that the State shall not in its enactments have due regard to differences of capacity, physical and moral, and of social function' (Bunreacht na h'Éireann/Constitution of Ireland, Article 40.1). In 1993, the Irish law regarding suicide changed, making suicide legal and recognized as a right—that is, that one has the right to take one's own life. Since Fleming required assistance in all aspects of daily living, it logically entailed that she would also need assistance with the action to end her life. 'Yet if someone has a disability, that means they are unable to take their own life. So it seemed ... that those rights were in conflict', says Fleming (2014, p. 233) in her memoir.

This conflict of rights inspired Fleming and Curran to take their Case to the High Court. Ultimately, they were challenging the constitutionality of the ban on assisted suicide contained in the *Criminal Law (Suicide) Act* of 1993, saying that it was incompatible with the *European Convention on Human Rights Act 2003*.

The Court ruled against Fleming, but this case brought widespread attention to the difficulties surrounding the issue of assisted dying. The ruling recognized a series of serious philosophical dilemmas, and here the focus will in particular be on the distinction between acts and omissions. This ethical issue is recognized and referred to repeatedly throughout the Court judgement, yet that is all there is: repeated reference. There is no substantial analysis or justification for the assumption, advocated in the ruling, that assisting an individual in circumstances such as Fleming's is morally wrong. It will be argued here that although a distinction between action and omission certainly does exist, the moral weight it is granted does not hold as much strength in a case such as Marie Fleming's, when the weight is seen to lie in the fact that, in the absence of the act in question, one would otherwise be alive.

2   Exposition of the Case

The case that Marie Fleming brought before the Court transpired as follows. 'In the proceedings, the plaintiff's claim' is stated as for:

1. An order declaring that section 2, subsection (2) of the Criminal Law (Suicide) Act of 1993 is invalid having regard to the provisions of the Constitution of Ireland.

2. An order declaring that section 2, subsection (2) of the Criminal Law (Suicide) Act 1993 is incompatible with the rights of the plaintiff pursuant to the European Convention on Human Rights and Fundamental Freedoms.
3. In the alternative, an order directing the third named defendant, within such time as to this Court shall seem just and appropriate, to promulgate guidelines stating the factors that will be taken into account in deciding, pursuant to section 2, subsection (4) of the Criminal Law (Suicide) Act 1993, whether to prosecute or to consent to the prosecution of any particular person in circumstances such as those that will affect a person who assists the plaintiff in ending her life.[2]

The judgement ruling describes MS in clinical terms before going on to highlight Fleming's case. At the time of the ruling, the Court stated that Fleming was 'almost totally physically helpless and [required] assistance with all aspects of her daily living' (Kearns 2013, section 12). It may be of interest to note that, at this early stage of the ruling, it is recognized that Fleming needed '*assistance* with all aspects of daily *living*' (Kearns 2013, section 12, emphasis added). However, that this assertion might logically entail assistance with *dying* is not recognized in any meaningful way.

In a quantitative measure of her level of disability, Marie Fleming's consultant neurologist, Professor Niall Tubridy, assessed her as 8.5 on the Expanded Disability Status Scale (EDSS), but at the time of the ruling believed she had deteriorated and said she was 9 at best, most likely 9.5, with the next step on the EDSS being 10, representing death from the disease.[3] Fleming was, at this point, experiencing a rapid deterioration of her condition, along with intense pain, and she was consuming the maximum doses of analgesia possible without becoming comatose. From this assessment, it is immediately clear that a salient difference between harmful acts and omissions, that one would otherwise be alive in the case of harmful acts as opposed to omissions, does not apply with much force in this case. That is to say, Marie Fleming was sadly about to die, whether by act or omission, and she did indeed die less than a year after the ruling was heard. This argument will be explored in more detail, utilizing Kagan's analysis, later in the chapter.

Fleming counted herself lucky that her MS did not impair her cognitive functions (Fleming and Leonard 2014, p. 224). On the other hand, this meant that she was completely aware at all times of her other impairments;

and she stated that she lived 'with little or no dignity' (Kearns 2013, section 20). Her enduring cognitive functions were discussed in the judgement in the reports of Fleming's advisors—Professor Niall Tubridy, consultant neurologist, Dr. Paul Scully, consultant psychiatrist, Dr. Niall Pender, clinical neuropsychologist, and Dr. Ann-Marie O'Farrell, general practitioner—who all advised against palliative care on the grounds that it would exacerbate the worst parts of Fleming's condition and require more medication. The reports stated that 'the plaintiff's mind and its forceful clarity "is all that Marie has left" … the plaintiff's strong wish is to pre-serve this mental clarity as it constitutes her one remaining faculty' and, by implication, to die before it is lost (Kearns 2013, section 21). Ultimately, '[h]er wish and her request to the Court was for assistance in having a peaceful dignified death in the arms of her partner and with her children in attendance' (Kearns 2013, section 22).

Professor Margaret Battin, whose views were sought during the case, is an advocate of assisted dying. The discussion with Professor Battin dur-ing the case does not tackle the acts and omissions distinction (Kearns 2013, section 25–33). This is worthy of note given that in the discourse involving Dr. Tony O'Brien and Professor Robert George, two opponents of assisted dying, the subject *is* raised.

Dr. Tony O'Brien, a consultant physician in palliative care, describes palliative care as a medical intervention which is concerned with quality of life, involving pain and symptom management, and psychological, social, emotional, and spiritual support (Kearns 2013, section 35). A related and interesting question is that of who decides that a person's quality of life is acceptable? The presumption here seems to have been that pain and symptom management, along with psychological, social, emotional, and spiritual support, will occur in the context of palliative care, irrespective of quality of life. However, in a case where an individual who has half a step on the EDSS scale to go before death, and who is judged to be of sound mind on a number of levels, decides that death, now, is a more attractive option than prolonging her current quality of life, which, on all accounts, will only deteriorate, it would appear that palliative care has little or noth-ing to offer. In such circumstances, the unquestioned belief in maintain-ing and preserving life, albeit in the most supportive manner possible, does fall into doubt and it should at least be considered that death, along with action to bring about death, can actually constitute a moral good in these circumstances. Philippa Foot writes, for example, that 'we are talking about death understood as a good or happy event for the one who dies' and only cases where we are 'opting for death for the sake of the one who dies' (Foot 1977, p. 86). Frances Kamm puts it slightly differently, that we are considering cases where 'death is a lesser evil and not going on living is the greater good' (Kamm 2013, p. 59).

Dr. O'Brien is quoted in the case as saying that patients 'are going to die with or without palliative sedation; they are dying as a direct, unavoidable and inevitable consequence of their underlying disease process' (Kearns 2013, section 37). From this view, the cessation of treatment with the foreseen consequence of death is interpreted as 'letting nature take its course' rather than hastening death, which is directly contrasted with actively taking steps to bring about death.

In relation to an inability to communicate at the end of life, Dr. O'Brien said that 'where patients lose the ability to speak ... there are other ways in which they can communicate their needs very efficiently and effectively' (Kearns 2013, section 41). Again, it is pertinent to highlight this assertion, which may, of course, be of great comfort and solace to some, because it begs the question as to who is the judge of efficient and effective communication? The question is also raised as to whether *all* communicated needs would be acknowledged or indeed acted upon. There is an obvious danger here of both power and autonomy being lost; and that loss being obscured by an explanation of the very processes in question. That explanation can also, in some cases, support a conclusion in which one already believes, hence the need for further analysis. The conclusion being questioned here is that active physician assistance in patient death is impermissible, while corresponding omissions that let nature take its course are generally not.

As the case progressed, it was said that:

> In line with the sentiments expressed ... the Court would observe that there are profound and difficult moral, ethical, philosophical and religious views on the question of end-of-life decisions such as the issue in controversy here. These are questions which are best left to public discourse and political debate and do not in and of themselves directly impinge on our analysis. If, accordingly, the plaintiff's constitutional rights extend as far as the matter claimed, then the fact that she is exercising those rights in a manner and for a purpose which some might consider contrary to their own ethical, moral or religious beliefs – or even the prevailing mores of the majority – is irrelevant (Kearns 2013, section 51).

This section suggests that Fleming's circumstances were going to be considered narrowly and strictly from the point of view of the law.

However, this was repeatedly shown not to be true, since a number of ethical, political, and moral questions *were* considered and *did* influence the ruling. These include assumptions about the morality of intention (sections 38, 47, and 93), the public interest (section 83), and the inevitability of descending down a slippery slope (sections 76, 81, 87, and 122), which will be discussed later. Most obvious, and most important for the analysis here, is the unquestioned assumption of a moral difference between actions and omissions. For example, in section 53, the Court stated that there is 'a real and defining difference' between the decision of a competent adult who declines treatment, allowing the course of the disease to cause death, and the taking of *active steps* by *another* to bring about the end of life of another. The ruling states that the latter is 'a totally different matter' (Kearns 2013, section 53). We will argue that, indeed, there is a conceptual difference between actions and omissions. However, as already mentioned, we will also argue that the transition from a conceptual difference to a moral difference is by no means straightforward, especially in this kind of case. This claim will shortly be explored more fully.

Section 55 addresses the practical difference between action and omission. It states that:

> the taking of active steps by a third party to bring about death is an entirely different matter [in comparison to the withdrawal of treatment], even if this is desired and wished for by an otherwise competent adult who sincerely and conscientiously desires this outcome and even if again ... the difference in some particular cases between the two types of decisions may sometimes be nuanced and blurred (Kearns 2013, section 55).

There is no justification offered for this stance, which could be said to be rather an oversight, especially in light of the recognition of the 'nuanced and blurred' nature of such cases. The judgement is clearly against the aiding and abetting of a suicide by another party, yet it did not seem to be able to articulate *why* this distinction is so very important in a case which purportedly was to consider the individual facts and not allow ethical or moral beliefs to influence the ruling. Indeed, the judgement goes on to say that, if it were possible for the Court to make an exception for Ms. Fleming without any wider consequences, there would be a good deal to be said in favour of this. However, circumstances were not such that this was a possibility: 'the Court is mindful that any legislative solution would have to be of *general* application and that this is true *a fortiori* of any judicial decision that the Court might be called upon to make' (Kearns 2013, section 55).

The discourse goes on to examine the perceived threats posed by the legalization of physician-assisted suicide, namely, variations of the slippery-slope argument. Difficulties ensuring safeguards, the fear of coercion, and threats to vulnerable groups are all mentioned to that effect. Section 69, however, includes an alternative view. It is recognized here that physician-assisted suicide could be presented 'as a humanitarian measure designed to assist the gravely ill via a form of agency to achieve that which they could (and, in many cases, perhaps would) freely do if they were able bodied', but that this cannot be realized in Ireland due to the fear of the 'objective moral dimensions' which would affect the physician and lead to complacency in the maintenance of statutory safeguards (Kearns 2013, section 69). This alternative view reinforces the suggestion that the distinction between action and omission in cases such as Marie Fleming's is complicated, and that it cannot be pinned down in these cases with as much force and assurance as in other situations, such as the classic example put forward by James Rachels.[4]

Section 72 grants that 'it is true that under our proportionality analysis a complete statutory ban which overrides or significantly interferes with a constitutional right requires compelling justification' (Kearns 2013, section 72). This point leaves the door open for a change in the future and the Court recognized that this is an issue which will continue to rear its head. In addition, Battin (2005, p. 18) notes that 'in the developed world, with its sophisticated health-care systems, the majority of the population of these countries dies at comparatively advanced ages of degenerative diseases with characteristically long down-hill courses, marked by a terminal phase of dying', again highlighting the likely endurance of this issue in the future.

Sections 75 and 76 can be taken to imply that the Court ruled against Fleming out of fear, and not because of a lack of compassion or understanding of the nuances or differences amongst individuals who wanted an assisted death:

> The Court appreciates ... Ms. Fleming's perspective [that] it seems unfair that she is condemned by the law and society to endure that which, for the rest of the able-bodied population, we could not endure and would not personally tolerate ... Yet the fact remains that if this Court were to unravel a thread of this law by even the most limited constitutional adjudication in her favour, it would – or, at least, might – open a Pandora's Box which thereafter would be impossible to close (Kearns 2013, sections, 75, 76).

In Section 106, the judgement refers to the Diane Pretty case (*Pretty v. Director of Public Prosecutions* 2001) in the UK, where 'the applicant suffered from a debilitating motor neurone disease and was terminally ill. She sought the assistance of her husband to help her end her own life, but only if there could be an assurance that he would not be prosecuted for helping her to do so'. Lord Bingham, the Senior Law Lord in the Pretty case, 'stressed the difference between the cessation of medical treatment on the one hand and active assistance to end life on the other' (Kearns 2013, section 106). This case has strong similarities to that of Marie Fleming and, again, the distinction between omission and action was highlighted. However, the distinction is not addressed in any substantial way in the Fleming case further to the reference here. Again, its gravity is mentioned, but without further analysis of what that entails or what the actual implications are of the distinction in this particular circumstance.

In Section 122, the alleged violation of the equality guarantee is dismissed. The judgement acknowledges that when the *Criminal Law (Suicide) Act* (1993) was passed, it made no exception for those in circumstances such as Fleming's, but it is claimed that the differential treatment is amply justified because of the 'profound difference between the law permitting an adult to take their own life on the one hand and sanctioning another to assist to that end on the other' (Kearns 2013, section 122). Again, the distinction between omission and action is alluded to in the context of assistance, but there is no elaboration with respect to the assumption of the profound moral difference in this context. If we take the moral difference as being constituted by the idea that when omitting to act, the individual would die as a matter of nature taking its course, as opposed to death directly resulting from an action where, in the absence of that action, the victim would otherwise be alive, then the distinction seems to decline in relevance. This is because, in the case of late-stage terminal illness, the individual will very soon die whether via act or omission. So, in this type of case, it is more difficult to unquestioningly accept adherence to the acts/omissions distinction. That distinction will now be more fully explored.

3   ACTS AND OMISSIONS

The Court's comment that 'the taking of active steps by a third party to bring about death is an entirely different matter [in comparison to the withdrawal of treatment]' can be seen to be a clear endorsement of the commonly held view that our actions are more morally significant than our omissions.[5] The idea here is that taking active steps to bring about death is both different to and more morally significant than 'allowing the course of the disease to cause death' via, for example, cessation of treatment. More generally, a strong moral emphasis on the distinction between acts and omissions can do a lot of work in our assessment of critical situations, as evidenced by other high profile cases and a wide range of current public debates (with corresponding debates about agents' responsibility).[6] It reflects the intuitively appealing view that we are more morally responsible for what we actually *do*, rather than what we allow to happen in a given situation. This view, in turn, is a strong candidate for justifying the current status quo reflected by the Court judgement in the Marie Fleming case: that it is morally acceptable to 'let nature take its course' (because we are not *doing* anything harmful), but morally unacceptable to take active steps to hasten death in accordance with the plaintiff's wishes (because we *are* doing something). However, whether this view is defensible across the board—and in this case in particular—is highly questionable.

While the acts/omissions distinction is deeply entrenched in our common sense morality, it is difficult to know what we can coherently say about it, other than simply stating the position and assuming it to be true. This is especially the case in situations where the result of either act or omission will be similarly severe, or the result of omission will be more severe than an alternative act. There are a variety of approaches to the distinction that are worthy of consideration and we will consider three of them here. One view is that there is no real difference between acts and omissions in this context, that actions are not different to, nor more morally significant than, omissions. What matters, on this account, is the desired outcome, along with the most humane way to bring it about. James Rachels points out in the context of terminal illness, for example, that letting nature take its course can be slow and painful, whereas taking active steps to bring about death can be relatively quick and painless. Given that can be the case, Rachels argues that, once the initial decision not to prolong life has been made, active assistance is actually preferable to letting nature take its course. To say otherwise, he argues, 'is to endorse the option that leads to more suffering rather than less, and is contrary to the humanitarian impulse that prompts the decision not to prolong life in the first place' (Rachels 1999, p. 228).

Rachels's argument about our humanitarian impulse with respect to suffering is highly pertinent to the Marie Fleming case, as the Court at least tacitly acknowledged. However, Rachels wants to collapse the moral emphasis on the acts/omissions distinction and, indeed, the distinction itself, which many consider to be too radical a move.[7] It could be said, then, that Rachels's position is both conceptually problematic and unlikely to be persuasive in the public sphere, given a deeply entrenched belief in *some* distinction between acts and omissions. Another option is to retain the moral emphasis on the distinction, but to adjust the definition of actions and omissions. This is the strategy of Warren Quinn (1989).

Quinn might well have been entirely sympathetic to Marie Fleming's case and might have agreed with Rachels's point about minimizing suffering in the case of an inevitable (and identical) outcome. However, he also wants to defend the idea that actions are more morally serious than omissions. To do this in a way that copes with problematic cases like his 'Rescue' examples and the Trolley Problem, he redefines intentional omission as action or, as he puts it, 'positive agency'.[8]

Quinn starts by defining harmful positive agency as 'harm occurring because of what the agent does (because of the existence of one of his actions)', as opposed to harmful negative agency, which is where harm occurs 'because of what the agent did not do but might have done (because of the noninstantiation of some kind of action that he might have performed)' (Quinn 1989, p. 294). He then tackles the Trolley Problem, which challenges any reliance on the acts/omissions distinction as the sole basis for moral judgement. The scene is set with a runaway trolley (or train) threatening five people trapped on the track on which it is moving. They will all die if the driver does nothing, but be saved if s/he switches to a side-track on which only one person is trapped. There seems to be good reason here for the driver to switch the tracks and save the five, yet making the switch seems to count as the more reprehensible positive agency, as opposed to the 'entirely different' and conventionally less reprehensible alternative of doing nothing. A moral emphasis against doing harm suggests that switching tracks would be wrong in this case, which is wildly counterintuitive to many. With that in mind, Quinn argues that not switching tracks in this case is really a form of positive agency. He contends that if the driver fails to switch tracks with the aim of preventing the death of the person on the side-track, 'it is because he intends that the train continue in a way that will save the man. But then he intends that the train continue forward past the switch, and this leads to the death of the five'. So, argues Quinn, 'his choice is really between two different positive options—one passive and one active. And that is why he may pick the alternative that does less harm' (Quinn 1989, p. 305).

Thus, on Quinn's account, where omission is 'strategic and deliberate', it should count as positive agency. 'To the idea of positive agency', he maintains, 'we must therefore add positive agency by this special kind of inaction'.[9] If we apply this analysis to the Marie Fleming case, then the 'real and defining difference' between the decision to withdraw treatment (or to let nature take its course) and 'the taking of active steps by a third party to bring about death' seems to somewhat dissolve because, on Quinn's account, both are instances of positive agency, the latter obviously so and the former also so in being 'strategic and deliberate'. Moreover, given Rachels's observations about suffering and, indeed, Marie Fleming's observations about her own suffering, the arguments in favour of picking 'the alternative that does less harm' and assisting the plaintiff with her own death are more than a little compelling.

Having said that, Quinn's analysis, while coping well with problematic counter-examples, arguably fails to strike the right chord with respect to our common sense notion of acts and omissions, of what 'doing' is, as opposed to 'not doing' or 'allowing'. As such, it may also fail to be persuasive in the public sphere, even if it is more conceptually refined than Rachels's view. There is also a danger, as Jonathan Glover notes, of 'fitting our beliefs to our conduct rather than our conduct to our beliefs' (Glover 1977, p. 110). As we have seen, Rachels suggests that acts are not different to, nor more morally significant than, omissions. Alternatively, Quinn attempts to retain the moral emphasis on the acts/omissions distinction, but he redefines what should count as action (or positive agency) in order to do so. A third alternative is to retain the conventional distinction between actions and omissions, but to challenge the moral significance of that distinction in particular cases. That will be the approach taken henceforth.

If we do not want to argue for an equivalence between acts and omissions, or redefine omissions in problematic cases so that they count as acts, we have to look elsewhere to find a 'real and defining difference' between acts and omissions. Leaving aside for now the issue of attaching moral significance to the distinction, a compelling and defensible philosophical basis for a distinction between acts and omissions has been developed by Shelly Kagan. While Kagan does not defend the moral relevance of the distinction between acts and omissions (or doing and allowing), he does articulate an important 'structural difference' between the two (Kagan 1989, p. 118).

That is, in the case of doing harm, the good that the victim has prior to the agent's act—for example, his life—'is one that he has and can maintain independently of the agent', whereas, in the case of allowing harm, 'the very fact that aid from the agent is required by the victim brings out the fact that the good in question is not one that is independent of the agent' (Kagan 1989, pp. 117–8). To put it more crudely, when we kill a victim, they would not have otherwise died, but when we fail to save a victim, they would have died anyway (had we not been there, for example). Kagan suggests that this structural difference may provide the key, for some, to the offensiveness of doing harm. It certainly denotes a difference that can usually be found between acts and omissions on our common sense understanding. It can also explain why, in a revised version of the Trolley Problem, where one person is trapped on the track and one is on a side-track to which we can switch the train, we tend not to want to intervene. However, the interesting thing about the difference articulated by Kagan for the analysis here is that, while it is convincing as to the source of our objection to harmful acts, that difference does not forcefully apply in the Marie Fleming case.

Using Kagan, we can acknowledge that there *is* a defensible difference between acts and omissions, contra Rachels and without a Quinn-like redefinition. It implies that, in the exact same circumstances and where the outcome will be the same, omission is preferable to action given that, for example, the subject of lethal harmful action would otherwise be alive. This, in turn, points towards the importance of the circumstances of each particular case where intervention is requested and it is crucial to note here that, in the case of late-stage terminal illness, the subject of action would *not* otherwise be alive, at least not for very long.[10] That is to say, the good that the victim has cannot be durably and independently maintained, so the structural difference that is the source of the resistance to act falls away. Thus, even on a very defensible reading of the acts/omissions distinction, there is very little structural difference between the taking of active steps by a third party and the withdrawal of treatment in the Marie Fleming case. As such, it is hard to see that there is much of a moral difference either. This is especially the case, given that the plaintiff both desired the taking of active steps and considered it to be preferable to the withdrawal of treatment. Indeed, given that she was between 9 and 9.5 on the Expanded Disability Status Scale, it can be argued that, altogether, action was more morally justifiable than omission in this case. By implication, it was morally permissible to assist Marie Fleming with her own death and the above considerations should be taken seriously in future if similar cases come before the Irish High Court and other courts.

A further implication of this argument, which could be useful in the public domain, is that it need not open a 'Pandora's Box', as the Court feared at the time. That is to say, while the analysis suggests that active assistance is justified in cases of terminal illness in their final stages, this in no way implies a wider justification of physician assistance or any inevitable descent down a slippery slope. On this analysis, we can legitimately restrict assistance to cases of late-stage terminal illness and defensibly resist the sanctioning of assistance in cases where the patient would otherwise be alive, cases that for many are a lot more unsettling.[11] It is, then, an argumentative framework that enables us to act on our humanitarian impulse, an impulse that the Court clearly shared, without becoming vulnerable to slippery-slope arguments and the more sensationalist claims that tend to attach to them.

Of course, there are many other arguments, like arguments about personal autonomy, which might encourage a much wider justification of active assistance to end life on request. They will not be considered here. What we have merely tried to show is that the pervasive resistance to act in the Marie Fleming case (and cases like it) is without foundation. And while many might want to go much further, an argument has been presented that shows how the issue could defensibly progress in a limited and least controversial way, avoiding the opening of a Pandora's Box and working within, rather than being opposed to, the currently prevailing moral landscape.

While working within the currently prevailing moral landscape may have tactical or strategic advantage in the public domain, it is worth noting that the prevailing moral landscape is certainly not beyond reproach. Indeed, perhaps the most obvious example where continued adherence to the acts and omissions distinction is morally unsettling is with regard to world poverty. Just as the resistance to act can be criticized in the Marie Fleming case, Jonathan Glover has recently argued that 'the relative weakness of our moral concern about the human devastation caused by poverty is an excellent candidate for some sharply sceptical interrogation'. He writes about our 'moral paralysis' with respect to this issue:

> The paralysis is real. According to one recent estimate, starvation and preventable diseases kill 30,000 children every day. They cause a child's death roughly every three seconds, round the clock every day of the year. Suppose these deaths were not mainly far away, located in many different places.

Suppose they all happened in one place and we were there. We would be overwhelmed by the horror and sadness of it all, and overwhelmed by the moral urgency of putting a stop to it. But, not having had that experience, we are not overwhelmed. What in our psychology protects us from the urgency? What are the sources of our moral paralysis? (Glover 2010, p. 272).

While there are obviously a multitude of issues bound up with such a vast problem, continuing to subscribe to the belief that our omissions are much less morally significant than our actions is unlikely to help to solve it. Indeed, as Glover puts it in an earlier work, 'it may well be because of tacit acceptance of the acts and omissions doctrine that we acquiesce in the worst evils in the world' (Glover 1977, p. 112). As we have argued, rethinking the distinction, even in the limited sense proposed here, might benefit people unfortunate enough to find themselves in a position similar to that of Marie Fleming. In time, rethinking the distinction and working towards more of a match between our conduct and our humanitarian sympathies might also have much wider moral benefits.

4   Conclusion

It has been argued here that adherence to the moral emphasis on the distinction between acts and omissions tends not to be very sophisticated, as evidenced by the deliberations of the Court in the Marie Fleming case. Analysis of that distinction suggests that assisted suicide in cases like that of Marie Fleming is permissible. On its most defensible reading, the acts and omissions distinction does not apply to these sorts of cases in the way that it is commonly held to apply, since the requested act does not interfere with the independent maintenance of life in the way that it normally would. While the analysis suggests that assisted suicide is therefore justified in cases of terminal illness in their final stages, this in no way implies a wider justification of assisted suicide or any inevitable descent down a slippery slope.

Moreover, with respect to other issues where the acts and omissions distinction is commonly invoked, taking poverty as an example, a singular emphasis on that distinction clearly does not provide us with a complete moral picture or a convincing moral justification of continued inaction. Students of philosophy, in our experience, get very passionate about precisely these sorts of debates and distinctions. Academics can make a valuable contribution to their community if they promote more nuanced analyses of such debates and distinctions in the public sphere. This is especially the case where conventional views both rest on shaky foundations and stand in the way of sensible and progressive social change.

NOTES

1. Section 2(2) of the law states that: 'A person who aids, abets, counsels or procures the suicide of another, or an attempt by another to commit suicide, shall be guilty of an offence and shall be liable on conviction on indictment to imprisonment for a term not exceeding fourteen years'.
2. Kearns (2013, section 3). The case was judged by a three-judge High Court, comprising the President of the High Court, Mr. Justice Nicholas Kearns, and Mr. Justice Paul Carney, and Mr. Justice Gerard Hogan.
3. Kearns (2013, section 19). The Expanded Disability Status Scale (EDSS) is a method of quantifying disability in MS and monitoring changes in the disability over time. The scale was developed by a neurologist named John Kurtzke in 1983 and is widely used in clinical trials and in the assessment of people with MS. The EDSS ranges from 0 to 10 in 0.5 increments that represent higher levels of disability, and scoring is based on examination by a neurologist (see Kurtzke 1983).
4. Rachels (1975, pp. 78–80) puts forward the analogy of Smith and Jones, two individuals who both have inheritance to gain in the event of the death of their 6-year-old cousin. Both individuals want the child dead. In the first instance, Smith acts and drowns the child in the bath. In the second instance, Jones sets out to kill the child, but happens upon the 6-year-old drowning in the bath of his own accord and stands by and watches—an omission of action with the same direct consequence as the action taken by Smith. While designed to make us worry a lot about some omissions, this example illustrates the structural difference explored by Kagan (1989) that we discuss later in the chapter.
5. Kearns (2013, section 55). While other distinctions can combine with and contribute to the view expressed in the Court's comment, like the distinction between intention and foresight and the distinction between passive and active treatment options, our sole focus here will be on the distinction between acts and omissions.
6. See, for example, the case of Savita Halappanavar, where the point has been made that action in the form of a termination was seen as less morally defensible than omitting to act and waiting for the foetal heartbeat to stop—an event which was inevitable (Holland 2012). The reluctance to perform a termination was reported to have contributed to the death of Savita Halappanavar.
7. For example, Rachels (1999, p. 230) contends that '[l]etting someone die … is a kind of action'.

8. Quinn's 'Rescue III' example, for instance, is a variation of the Trolley Problem, where we have the choice to stop a train or to let it continue on automatic control when one person is trapped ahead on the track. If we stop the train and free the trapped person, the rescue mission to save five others will be aborted (Quinn 1989, p. 298).
9. Quinn (1989, p. 301). For further discussion of this position, see Hull (2007, pp. 53–8).
10. Development of this position in a practical sense would require agreement as to how close to the end of one's life one might reasonably be expected to be.
11. See, for example, the case of Daniel James (Booth 2008). As recorded in a 2014 *Guardian* article, there are other high profile cases, notably in Belgium, that would not be sanctioned by the reasoning here. These include a 44-year-old transsexual woman, 'whose botched sex-change operation left her with physical deformities that she felt made her look like a "monster"; and 45-year-old identical twins who were deaf and going blind and believed they had nothing left to live for' (Guardian Staff 2014). Of further interest to the analysis here, is that the article also notes that more recent legislation in Belgium legalizing euthanasia for children stipulates that minors must be terminally ill, close to death, and suffering beyond any medical help. Views about euthanasia and euthanasia for children aside, these legislative stipulations do reflect the arguments of the position developed here.

REFERENCES

Battin, M. P. (2005). *Ending life: Ethics and the way we die.* Oxford: Oxford University Press.

Booth, R. (2008, October 18). "He wasn't prepared for a second-class life": Why injured rugby star went to Switzerland to die. *The Guardian.* Retrieved July 20, 2015, from http://www.theguardian.com/uk/2008/oct/18/11.

Bunreacht na h'Éireann—Constitution of Ireland. (1937/2013). Retrieved July 20, 2015, from http://www.irishstatutebook.ie/en/constitution/.

Criminal Law (Suicide) Act, 1993. (1993). Retrieved accessed July 20, 2015, from http://www.irishstatutebook.ie/eli/1993/act/11/enacted/en/print.

Fleming, M., & Leonard, S. (2014). *An act of love: One woman's remarkable life story and her fight for the right to die with dignity.* Dublin: Hachette Books Ireland.

Foot, P. (1977). Euthanasia. *Philosophy & Public Affairs, 6*(2), 85–112.

Guardian Staff. (2014, October 17). Euthanasia and assisted-suicide laws around the world. *The Guardian.* Retrieved July 20, 2015, from http://www.theguardian.com/society/2014/jul/17/euthanasia-assisted-suicide-laws-world.

Glover, J. (1977). *Causing death and saving lives.* Harmondsworth: Penguin Books.

Glover, J. (2010). Responses: A summing up. In A. N. Davis, R. Keshen, & J. McMahan (Eds.), *Ethics and humanity: Themes from the philosophy of Jonathan Glover* (pp. 237–282). Oxford: Oxford University Press.

Holland, K. (2012, November 14). Woman "denied a termination" dies in hospital. *The Irish Times.* Retrieved July 20, 2015, from http://www.irishtimes.com/news/woman-denied-a-termination-dies-in-hospital-1.551412.

Hull, R. (2007). *Deprivation and freedom.* New York: Routledge.

Kagan, S. (1989). *The limits of morality.* Oxford: Clarendon Press.

Kamm, F. M. (2013). *Bioethical prescriptions: To create, end, choose, and improve lives.* Oxford: Oxford University Press.

Kearns, N. (2013). [2013] IEHC 2 *Fleming-v-Ireland & Ors.* Dublin: High Court. Retrieved July 20, 2015, from http://www.courts.ie/Judgments.nsf/0/911C B02A6531C7A380257AEF0037C379.

Kurtzke, J. F. (1983). Rating neurological impairment in multiple sclerosis: An Expanded Disability Status Scale (EDSS). *Neurology,* 33(11), 1444–1452.

Pretty v. Director of Public Prosecutions. (2001). UKHL 61, [2002] 1 A.C. 800.

Quinn, W. S. (1989). Actions, intentions and consequences: The doctrine of doing and allowing. *The Philosophical Review,* 98(3), 287–312.

Rachels, J. (1975). Active and passive euthanasia. *New England Journal of Medicine,* 292(2), 78–80.

Rachels, J. (1999). Active and passive euthanasia. In P. Singer & H. Kuhse (Eds.), *Bioethics: An anthology* (pp. 227–230). Oxford: Blackwell Publishing.

PART II

Ethical Commitment and Political Engagement

CHAPTER 6

Writing as Social Disclosure: A Hundred Years Ago and Now

Alasdair MacIntyre

1

It is a familiar truth that from the late eighteenth century onwards, one striking feature of social history is the extent to which voices that had hitherto gone unheard begin to be heard. In protests and riots, in early forms of trade union organization, in movements for the suffrage and for Catholic emancipation, in churches and in cooperative societies, even through participation in revolution, the deprived are heard and speak in a multiplicity of voices. The poor and the excluded are also, to a quite new extent, spoken about and written about by those concerned about the implications of their deprivation for the larger society and about what responses should be made to them and to what they are saying. So it was in Ireland, Scotland, England, and the USA, in Germany, France, and elsewhere. Each national culture has its own story, but here I shall be concerned only with the English-speaking story and indeed only with some few episodes in it. What I want to remark on is a notable contrast between the early twentieth century and the early twenty-first century in the way in which poverty and deprivation are attended to and written about.

A. MacIntyre
University of Notre Dame, Indiana 46556, IN, USA

© The Editor(s) (if applicable) and The Author(s) 2016
A. Fives, K. Breen (eds.), *Philosophy and Political Engagement*,
DOI 10.1057/978-1-137-44587-2_6

99

Begin with the present. We now think about poverty, hunger, and homelessness in a number of ways: as reduced and reducible globally by economic growth, as one index among several of the success or failure of government policies, as providing occasion for philanthropy both on a large and a small scale. What we do not think about very much is how poverty and deprivation are recurrently generated and regenerated within and by advanced economies, how our economic system is such that those least able to afford to do so, including the children of the poor, are made to pay a significant part of the costs that are the counterpart of the benefits that the more privileged receive, and how the gross inequalities of our economic system are a practical denial of our common humanity. The use of these last words may seem to many nowadays rhetorical overkill, if only because expressions such as 'common humanity' are for the most part no longer used in our culture with a shared determinate meaning, but only, if at all, for their emotive effect.

When I say 'we', to whom do I refer? Ours is a culture of elites— political, financial, media, academic—each drawing happily on resources provided by the others. It is the leading members of those elites who determine which topics provide the focus for our national conversations, whose opinions are treated seriously and whose with dismissive contempt or not at all, and which are the alternative courses of action between which governments choose. It is elites that supply what is taken to be the expertise to which the nonexpert should defer. When I say 'we', I am therefore inescapably, if unhappily, speaking as myself, like you, my reader, a member, even if an outlier, of those elites, someone often trying to edge into their conversations. But, if I have difficulty in making my voice heard, this is nothing compared to the obstacles now encountered by the most deprived and excluded. Their voices are indeed heard from time to time in this or that local situation, often as a result of the admirable work of community and trade union organizers, but for the most part it is not just that their voices go unheard, but that they themselves have never had an opportunity to learn how to articulate effectively what it is most urgent for them to say. This is unsurprising, if one considers the facts of gross educational inequality in our metropolitan cultures.

Those who most need an education in our society, if they are to understand their own condition and act effectively to remedy it, are those least likely to receive it. Deprivation in respect of money, housing, and access to health care is generally accompanied by educational deprivation, while those who do receive an excellent education are taught to think in certain

received ways, so that, when the facts of poverty are brought to their attention, they think about them as raising issues to be debated along with other
issues in the arenas of politics, as matters for expert enquiry, as occasion for
philanthropy, but not as an affront to our moral being, not as disquieting,
not as putting in question the established social and cultural order. Nor
is this surprising. Those authors whom they read in books, magazines,
and newspapers and those to whom they listen or whom they watch on
television or film or the internet, generally give them little reason to make
thought about poverty central to their lives, let alone to be affronted or
disquieted by it. Writing no longer functions as a form of social disclosure.

2

Contrast matters in England one hundred years ago. There was, unlike
now, a steadily increasing proportion of the population devoted to reading. There were, just as now, numerous writers competing for their attention. Begin with some background facts. Charles Booth had published the
first volume of his investigations into poverty in London in 1889. The 17
volumes of the third edition of *Life and Labour of the People in London*
appeared in 1902–1903 (Booth 1902–1903). Booth had initially gone to
work with his team of investigators, among them his cousin, Beatrice Potter,
later Beatrice Webb, expecting to refute the claim by H.M. Hyndman that
25 % of Londoners lived in abject poverty. What his investigations disclosed
was that the true figure was 35 %. 1889 was also the year of the great Dock
Strike in London's East End. The voices of the leaders of the dockwork-
ers and of their supporters were clearly and widely heard. Notable among
those supporters was Cardinal Manning, who anticipated the teaching of
Leo XIII's encyclical of 1891, *Rerum Novarum*, that the labouring poor
needed trade unions. 'We have been under the despotism of capital', he
wrote to Archbishop Walsh. 'The union of labourers is their only shelter'
('Manning to Walsh', 1 March 1890, quoted in Leslie 1921, p. 376).

This new consciousness of poverty as an evil found political expression. Charles Booth was a Liberal. Hyndman was a Marxist who had led
the first British socialist party, the Social Democratic Federation. Beatrice
Webb joined the Fabian Society. Working class Catholics found a political home in the newly formed Labour Party. One political effect was the
Old Age Pensions Act of 1908. It provided noncontributory pensions for
those 70 years old and over of five shillings for single individuals and seven
shillings and sixpence for married couples, but restricted them to those

whose annual income was no more than 31 pounds and ten shillings, who had lived in the UK for at least 20 years, and who passed tests of good moral character. The pension was intentionally low, so that workers would be motivated to save for their old age. The ideal worker presupposed by the Act was British, sober, anxious to work even for low wages, thrifty, law abiding, and deferential. The Act was undeniably an important step forward, but it expressed the standpoint of those concerned not with poverty as such, but only with the poverty of the deserving poor. It was that standpoint which was put in question by some early twentieth-century debates, debates that had three characteristics. First, poverty was presented as a, perhaps the, great evil of the age, one that it was urgently necessary to abolish. Second, the framework of argument in terms of which the critique of poverty was carried through was philosophical, although not academic. And, third, the audience intended by the debaters was as great a part of the reading and the theatre-going public as they could persuade to attend to them by the exercise of their literary and dramatic skills. The particular extended debate on which I want to focus attention is that in which the major protagonists were George Bernard Shaw and G.K. Chesterton.

Begin with Shaw. From his contributions to *Fabian Essays* in 1889, through such plays and essays as *Man and Superman* and *The Revolutionist's Handbook* (whose purported author is a central character in *Man and Superman*, John Tanner) in 1902–1903, to *The Intelligent Woman's Guide to Socialism and Capitalism* in 1928, Shaw's writings give expression to two fundamental convictions, his statements of which are remarkably consistent through time. The first has to do with poverty. Poverty is a matter not only of deprivation, but of degradation. In *Fabian Essays*, Shaw (1889, p. 21) had said of the working class that 'their poverty breeds filth, ugliness, dishonesty, disease, obscenity, drunkenness, and murder'. Later in *The Intelligent Woman's Guide* he was to argue that 'Such poverty as we have today in all our great cities degrades the poor, and infects with its degradation the whole neighborhood in which they live. And whatever can degrade a neighborhood can degrade a country and a continent and finally the whole civilized world, which is only a large neighborhood' (Shaw 1928, p. 42). The rich, too, are degraded both by their own way of life and by the effects of poverty.

Shaw found the way of life of the poor personally offensive. 'Socialism abhors poverty', he was to write in *The Intelligent Woman's Guide*, and he commended a 'hearty dislike and disapproval of poor people. ... Under Socialism people would be prosecuted for being poor as they are now for being naked' (Shaw 1928, p. 95). What should replace the relationships of rich and poor? Shaw's answer to this question reveals a second fundamental conviction. The only tolerable and the only desirable society is one in which equality of income has been achieved. Only equality of income will rescue us from the corruptions of rich and poor. Those who exercise political authority and those who supply professional services will, like the hitherto rich and the hitherto poor, act well, as they have it in them to act, only when provided with equal incomes which they can increase only by increasing to an equal extent the income of everyone else.

We may be surprised to discover that Shaw numbers among the enemies of egalitarian socialism thus conceived trade unionists, whose systematic defence of their own particular interests too often subverts the honour and kindliness of individual trade unionists. We will be less surprised once we have taken note of another of Shaw's fundamental convictions. Consider the character of John Tanner, the male protagonist in *Man and Superman*. Tanner's socialism is Shaw's socialism, and those critics who have claimed that in portraying Tanner Shaw was portraying himself are not to be refuted by pointing to Tanner's ineffectiveness. For in Shaw's plays, generally those characters who stand for the right and the good are less effective than those who have intelligently come to terms with the realities of money and power. It is the Inquisitors, and not St. Joan, who finally prevail. But what then is to be done? The political gradualism of *Fabian Essays* is no longer a source of hope. The institutions of the present—government agencies, political parties, and trade unions—are all obstacles to, rather than agents of, change. What we have to hope for and can hope for is the emergence of a new kind of human being, something that we will not recognize so long as we see the Ann Whitefield of *Man and Superman* as no more than an engaging and designing woman, manipulating John Tanner into marriage, rather than as an emblem of and an agent of the Life Force that will produce the Supermen of the future.

It is in Tanner's dream in Act III of that play that we are introduced to the concept of the Life Force by Don Juan Tenorio, Tanner's reimagined self. Don Juan has had to learn from Woman, and could only have learned from Woman, 'to say "I am; therefore I think". And also "I would think more; therefore I must be more"'. What being more and thinking more has enabled Don Juan—Tanner transformed in imagination—to become is a philosopher, someone dedicated to discovering the inner will of the world, someone through whose actions that will fulfils itself. Shaw as philosopher, composing the speeches to be uttered by Don Juan, took himself to have grasped the central message of nineteenth-century philosophy.

His introduction to that philosophy had been his study of Wagner and the authors to whom that study had sent him were most of all Schopenhauer see his remarks in *The Perfect Wagnerite* of 1898—and, to some extent, Nietzsche. His conceptions of a will to life, of the relationship of the individual will to that of the species, and of the part played by erotic love in furthering the designs of the Life Force he took from Schopenhauer, especially from Schopenhauer's (1936 [1819]) 'Metaphysics of the Love of the Sexes'. The concept of the Superman in whose emergence those designs are achieved is Shaw's transformation of Nietzsche's *Übermensch* (Nietzsche 2006 [1892]).

To critics justly complaining that Shaw misread and misrepresented Schopenhauer and that he travestied Nietzsche, that he distorted their ideas for his own purposes, Shaw's reply would have been that this was indeed so, but that nonetheless they should have been grateful. For he had shown a larger public what their ideas amounted to when translated into dramatic terms. Only when philosophical ideas are translated into those terms can such a public understand their significance. Theatre is one of the testing grounds of philosophy, one of the places where lay audiences can become engaged in and by philosophical debate. This is not of course anything like an adequate answer to the charge of misrepresentation, but it does propose a different and enlarged conception of philosophical enquiry and debate from that either of Schopenhauer and Nietzsche themselves or of their twentieth-century academic exponents at work in departments of philosophy. Yet at this point someone may interrupt to ask 'But what has this intervention in philosophy to do with Shaw's concern for the abolition of poverty and the establishment of equality of income?'

The answer would have been that it is only in the perspective afforded by a philosophical account of human being and becoming that we can understand ourselves adequately and that, only if we understand ourselves adequately, will we recognize the deprivations and deformations of ourselves and our relationships that are the outcome of that system of private property which results in gross inequality of income and gross poverty. To fail to recognize the part that poverty plays in human life, to regard it with any degree of complacency, is to fail as a human being, as one through whom the Life Force is at work. We need economic expertise to understand the causes of poverty, but it is to philosophy that we must look if we are to evaluate our responses to it and the damage that both it itself and inadequate responses to it do to human beings. So Shaw. In advancing these views, he was of course, and knew himself to be, contributing to a wide ranging debate with protagonists of rival standpoints: among them H.G. Wells and Rebecca West, Robert Blatchford and a variety of Socialists, including the author of *The Ragged-Trousered Philanthropists* (Tressell 1914), the Cambridge precursors of Bloomsbury, Bertrand Russell, and D.H. Lawrence. If from among these I choose to focus on G.K. Chesterton, it is because Chesterton's abhorrence of poverty and its effects matched Shaw's, even if they gave significantly different accounts of the condition of the poor and of how that condition is to be remedied.

3

Chesterton's polemics against Shaw focused on what he rightly took to be the absurdity of Shaw's conception of and faith in the Superman. As early as 1905 his essays in *Heretics* included one on Shaw, and in his weekly column in the *Illustrated London News* Shaw was a frequent target. It was there that he argued that what he had called Shaw's religion of the Superman was deeply at odds with his socialist convictions: 'for a Socialist to talk about the Superman is incomprehensible as well as contemptible' (Chesterton 1987, p. 236, 19 December 1908). Why so? Chesterton was a radical egalitarian of a kind very different from Shaw and he took it that socialists, if they were consistent, should be similarly egalitarian, something quite incompatible with belief in the coming of a Superman. He expressed his strongest condemnation of his contemporaries by saying of them that 'Men feel that cruelty to the poor is a kind of cruelty to animals. They never feel that it is an injustice to equals; nay it is a treachery to comrades' (Chesterton 1906, p. 277). His own standpoint he was to define trenchantly: 'To say that I do not like the present state of wealth and poverty is merely to say that I am not the devil in human form' ('Why I Am Not a Socialist', *The New Age*, 4 January 1908, reprinted in Chesterton 1981, p. 189).

In his *Autobiography,* he would describe his starting point: 'I saw our industrial civilization as rooted in injustice ... It was my instinct to defend the rights of man as including the rights of property, especially the property of the poor' (Chesterton 1936, p. 354). What began as instinct Chesterton developed into reasoned argument, an argument about what we owe to each other as human beings and an argument about the rights and wrongs of property. What justice requires is not only equal treatment of each other in important respects, but equal responsibility for each other. To violate justice is to deny our shared humanity, to treat others as less than human, and so to act as less than human. By and large, so Chesterton argued, poor people act well in these respects. By and large, the rich do not. About property he took an interestingly different view from Shaw. '"Property"', he wrote in his column, 'means (as to its original meaning) the fact that something is *proper* to somebody. Property is propriety. Now it is obvious that in modern England and America property is gross impropriety. In fact it is shocking indecency' (Chesterton 1987, p. 215, 14 November 1908). The rights of poor people to have property have been infringed and ignored by the system of property rights. So there must be a redistribution of property, but not as the Socialists, whether Fabian like Shaw, or Bolshevik like Lenin, propose. For they believe 'that the means of production ought all to belong to the State' (Chesterton 1987, p. 50, 22 February 1908). But this would involve an unprecedented concentration of power in the hands of a dominant few, one that would be as dangerous and harmful as the concentration of wealth in the hands of the few. Power and property both need to be widely and democratically distributed. Yet socialists are to be praised, even if socialism is to be rejected. So Chesterton joined with the Irish Nationalist member of parliament, Tom Kettle, in praising Socialism for 'its sincerity, its thirst for abstract fairness, its pity, its Christian anger' (Chesterton 1987, p. 50, 22 February 1908).

Chesterton, unlike Shaw, was a radical democrat. But, unlike many exponents of democracy, he took tradition with great seriousness. In *Orthodoxy* in 1908, he wrote that 'tradition is only democracy extended through time. It is trusting to a consensus of common human voices. ... Tradition means giving votes to the most obscure of all classes, our ancestors. It is the democracy of the dead' (Chesterton 1908, pp. 84–85). That consensus of common human voices over time speaks very differently from the manufactured consensus of this or that moment in modern party politics. It speaks consonantly with Christian faith. It speaks to and of both material and moral needs that are often unrecognized as well as unmet. So Chesterton as a radical critic of the established order found himself at odds with such other critics of that order as Shaw. But about the overriding political and human importance of the present misdistribution of wealth under capitalism they were in agreement. Why then did their disagreements matter so much to them?

Both took it that the problem of poverty would never be adequately addressed, if treated in isolation or as a problem only or primarily for experts. How we think about poverty depends in their view upon how we think about human beings and their social relationships, and how we think about human beings and their relationships is a matter for philosophical enquiry and debate. Without such enquiry and debate things will go very wrong. But on what philosophical resources are we to call? It is in answering this question that Shaw and Chesterton disagree most deeply. For Shaw, as we have seen, we need to learn from Schopenhauer and Nietzsche, even if the lessons to be learned from them, as presented by Shaw, would have surprised Schopenhauer and both surprised and horrified Nietzsche. To learn those lessons we will have to transcend the limitations of any traditional religious view of things. For Chesterton, by contrast, it is only through the recovery of the tradition of Catholic Christianity that we and other plain people will once again understand ourselves and others as we are and as we, all of us, know ourselves to be, when we are sufficiently truthful. A central task of philosophy is to vindicate this knowledge of moral and other truths that plain people commonly possess, by exposing the false philosophical claims of those who attempt to discredit this common sense of humankind, a common sense commonly shared by the poor, but rarely acknowledged by the rich. For Chesterton, the philosopher who provides what is most needed is Thomas Aquinas, although it took him a long time to recognize this (Chesterton 1933).

A first reaction by contemporary readers is going to be one of incredulity. Can Shaw and Chesterton really be asking us to believe that in order to think rightly and searchingly about poverty we have to reckon with the philosophical issues over which Aquinas, on the one hand, and Schopenhauer and Nietzsche, on the other, are in conflict? What Shaw and Chesterton would reply is that those who doubt the relevance of philosophy in their everyday thinking and acting, even if they do not recognize it, presuppose the truth of philosophical theses quite as contentious as any advanced by Aquinas, Schopenhauer, or Nietzsche, and that, more specifically, how they think about poverty is determined by their allegiance to those philosophical theses. We are all of us, on their view, philosophers, even if only some of us are aware of it. If we remain unaware of it, we become the victims of our unacknowledged philosophical allegiances. To this there will be a second response, that Shaw and Chesterton are philosophically unqualified, that Shaw's Schopenhauer is not Schopenhauer and his Nietzsche is not Nietzsche and that Chesterton's Aquinas is a grossly simplified and unsubtle version of Aquinas. To this, Shaw and Chesterton would have replied somewhat differently.

For Shaw, the charge that his expressions of Schopenhauer's and Nietzsche's ideas are misleading caricatures would have left him unimpressed. What he had taken from them and put into presentable form were, on his view, those of their theses that were both rationally justifiable and relevant to the twentieth-century condition, theses concerning the primacy of the will, the nature of practical intelligence, the past from which we have emerged and the future towards which we can be directed, the illusions from which we need to be rescued. If Schopenhauer and Nietzsche thought otherwise, so much the worse for Schopenhauer and Nietzsche. For Chesterton, the reply would have been that Aquinas and other philosophers may indeed have had much more to say than his selective use of their thoughts suggested, but that his simplified presentation of those thoughts was accurate and to the point. Chesterton took Aquinas to be someone from whom he himself was still learning at the same time as he attempted to communicate Thomistic thoughts to others. Both Shaw and Chesterton would have emphasized the importance of the genres in which they wrote. Philosophical theses, no matter how cogently they are argued, will never be recognized as socially and politically important so long as that argument takes place only in academic settings. It is only when philosophy is presented as theatre or in the novel or in journalistic commentary that it will find that audience or those readers who most need it.

What audience was that? What readers were these? They were, as I noticed earlier, members of a general educated public, who in significant numbers went to the same plays or read reviews of those plays, read the same books or reviews of those books, subscribed to the same newspapers and periodicals, knew the same music hall songs. They expected Chesterton in his column to comment on Shaw's plays and Shaw to respond to Chesterton. They knew both Shaw and Chesterton as contributors to debates with a variety of others. The vast majority of them had not had a university education. They were largely, although not exclusively, middle class, and to influence them was to influence public opinion more generally. How they thought about poverty was therefore of great importance. Radical change could, of course, result only from political debate in and out of parliament between the protagonists of the major parties and their critics on poverty, on unemployment, pensions, and other welfare benefits, on redistributive taxation, and on political action. But how those issues are thought about and the terms of such debate depend in key part on the general culture of the educated public, and it was to transforming that culture that Shaw, Chesterton, and their fellow debaters had dedicated themselves.

What that public needed to learn, so Shaw and Chesterton agreed, was that how one responds morally and politically to gross human poverty that is close at hand is a measure of one's success or failure as a human being. And to understand that this is how one needs to understand oneself is to have begun to think philosophically. Much then depends on how well or badly one thinks philosophically. Nothing less is the message of Shaw and Chesterton.

4

One hundred years later, some of Shaw's plays are still regularly produced and Chesterton's books still find significant numbers of readers. But those who provide Shaw with a continuing audience are rarely those who now read Chesterton. H.G. Wells is read by almost no one, Rebecca West mostly by those interested in the history of feminism, while Lytton Strachey and D.H. Lawrence each have their own small and often academic set of readers. Russell as philosopher and logician is as notable as he ever was. Russell as social critic and moralist is left to his biographers. What has been almost entirely lost, one hundred years later, is any sense of these and other such writers as having been participants in a set of complex cultural and philosophical debates of potential political significance. And with it, there has been lost any sense of what the absence of such debate in our own culture might signify.

To this it will be objected that we still have writers who present themselves to their audiences as Shaw and Chesterton did, as protagonists in key moral debates, most notably perhaps Tom Stoppard, whose philosophical preoccupations have provided matter for his dramatic art from *Jumpers* to *Darkside,* and whose ethical concerns are evident throughout his work. But Stoppard's plays do not provide a counter example to my thesis. His allusions to philosophy never suggest to his audience that they too are or might become philosophers. And his moral concerns are very different from those of Shaw and Chesterton.

What then is it that we are missing? It is twofold. First, there is no one culturally influential, as Shaw and Chesterton were influential, who now contends in the public realm that it is our attitudes to poverty and destitution that are the measure of our humanity and that, in order to understand human nature and human relationships rightly, one must understand peculiarly modern poverty as the evil that it is. Second, there is no one culturally influential, as Shaw and Chesterton were influential, who now contends in the public realm that to understand poverty in this way is above all a philosophical task. What has changed and why?

There is of course nowadays much genuine concern with poverty among economists, in the politics of welfare, and in public and private philanthropy. Global economic growth has rescued many, many millions from the very worst extremes of poverty, one of the few things for which the protagonists of free market economies have reason to congratulate themselves. The effects of welfare legislation are recurrently debated in the legislatures of advanced countries. And there are numerous, entirely admirable, philanthropic enterprises concerned with alleviating poverty and its consequent ills in this or that part of the world. What is too often missing in our most advanced societies, as I remarked earlier, is any sense that ours is a social and economic order that in its cities continually regenerates and perpetuates poverty, that in making a few very rich indeed makes a much larger number very poor, that provides no work for many and no effective welfare for many needy children. Such poor, for those of us who inhabit cities, are our near neighbours. Generous philanthropy directed towards the urban poor is indeed admirable, but the philanthropic are rarely, if ever, invited to reflect that it is their own support for and complacency with the established social and economic order, the order from which they derived the riches that they now generously distribute, that results in so much of the poverty that they rightly deplore.

Given these absences and omissions, it is unsurprising that we find few voices arguing that the moral measure of a human being is her or his attitude to the very needy, especially the very needy who are close at hand. But this is also unsurprising for quite another reason. For, if there were such voices, where would they find expression? And who would be there to listen to them? In many advanced countries, a much larger proportion of the population has received some form of higher education than was the case a hundred years ago, something at which both Shaw and Chesterton would have rejoiced. But the effect has not been to bring into being a larger educated public, actual or potential participants in large-scale fundamental debate on fundamental issues. What we have instead are a multiplicity of educated publics, each with its own providers of whatever particular aspects of the culture—literary, dramatic, operatic, historical, political, military, information theoretic, scientific, technological, philosophical, theological, antitheological—are their peculiar concern and each with its own consumers of those particular aspects. It is not that within each of these particular areas there are not disagreements and debates, but that there is no general cultural debate in which our most widely shared assumptions can be put in question. This situation has been a long time in the making.

Consider first the political failures of both Shaw and Chesterton and the political defeat of Marxism. That Shaw's faith in the emergence of a Great Man was as absurd as Chesterton had claimed became widely evident when Shaw was taken in, first, by Mussolini's bombastic charades and then by Stalin's tyrannical power. Chesterton's distributism, although it provided an intellectually and morally powerful critique of the capitalist order, was never translatable into a realistic political programme for local, let alone central, government. Those failures left Marxism in its different versions as the only apparent systematic cultural and political critique of the capitalist world order. But Marxism, whatever the degree to which it has remained undefeated in this or that respect as history and as theory, has for a long time now been incapable of advancing a politics capable of challenging the capitalist world order. So politically the only choices have been between different varieties of capitalism, free market capitalism, social democratic capitalism, Chinese or Cuban state capitalism. It is not that nothing significant turns on these choices, but that, when they are the only choices, it becomes all too easy to take for granted as ineliminable the condition of the urban poor in advanced societies. The poor tend not to vote and, as the conservative political columnist Christopher Caldwell has pointed out, the political parties are devoted to maximizing their electoral advantage. Thus, 'the poor wind up an afterthought' (Caldwell 2013). In California, by the best measure that we have, 22 % of the population and over one quarter of the children, many of them immigrants, live in poverty. Yet the Governor of California (Jerry Brown) is able to speak of this as 'the flip side of California's incredible attractiveness' (Siders 2013).

The occasion for Caldwell's remarks was the publication in 2013 of Pope Francis's Apostolic Exhortation, *Evangelii Gaudium*, where Francis reiterated the Catholic Church's call for solidarity with the poor and condemned free market capitalism. Yet even sympathetic reporters of Francis understand what he says as a matter of a Catholic talking to Catholics, interesting for those who happen to be interested in such things, but not something of general import for an educated public, since we now live in a secularized culture. Again, how different this is from Shaw and Chesterton! Shaw believed that what he took to be the content of Christianity now had to be translated into secular terms—in this he was among the successors of Hegel and Feuerbach—and that one of his tasks as a dramatist was to effect this translation. For the conventional secular morality of the nineteenth century he had only contempt. Its notion of 'Duty' was a special object of mockery. But he was, of course, an atheist. Christian dogma, so he urged, should be abandoned, but the specifically Christian concern for the poor was not just to be preserved, but transformed into a twentieth-century politics.

Chesterton, as a Catholic, argued that no such translation of Christianity into secular terms was possible or needed and that it is only from within a theological understanding of human nature that the concern of the gospels for the poor can be adequately understood and politically embodied. Both agreed that without general assent to the teaching of the gospels - that human beings define themselves in key part by their attitudes to the poor - any culture will be itself impoverished. The continuing secularization of the past hundred years, whether it issues, as in the UK and Europe, in an exodus from the churches or, as in the USA, in a largely secularized practice of religion, has deprived the Christian message concerning the poor of any large impact, except as a call to philanthropy.

It is not just that there has been a decline in religious belief and practice. Ours is now a culture in which the large questions about human existence to which the great religions have advanced answers, the questions that provide philosophical enquiry with its starting point, are seldom asked. There is indeed a deep resistance to opening up those questions and so making us aware of those shared presuppositions that we have been taking for granted. Philosophy has become an activity for the class room, for the college student, for the 18- to 22-year old. It is not matter for serious adult thought, unless one happens to be one of those adults who teach it to college students. Such teachers are generally taken to be, and generally take themselves to be, practitioners of a specialized discipline, indeed nowadays of a series of specialized subdisciplines, and, as with the practitioners of other such disciplines, they have had to learn how to write in the idiom of their fellow specialists, so making themselves increasingly inaccessible to the general reader. So the question of how we should evaluate ourselves as human beings, and with it the question of what significance our attitudes to the urban poverty of our nearby neighbourhoods have for that evaluation, goes unasked by the lay public and unanswered by the professional philosopher.

It is not that academic philosophers have nothing significant to say about poverty. Peter Unger (1996) and Peter Singer (1972) among others have argued forcefully and admirably that many of us have an obligation to contribute a far higher proportion of our income and our time to fighting poverty than in fact we do. John Rawls (1971) and others have elaborated principles of justice that require distributions of power, wealth, and income to be justified by their effects in improving the condition of the least well off. But, given the place that philosophical writing has in our culture, those contentions have minimal impact in those debates from which public policy emerges. Tell almost any member of the present day general public, whatever their social class or education, that it is to philosophy that she or he needs to go, if they are to understand what they most need to understand about themselves and why a concern for the condition of the poor should be important to them, and they will take you to babble. Yet this is not only because they have learned to identify philosophy with academic philosophy as currently practiced. What more is involved?

5

It is a distinctive feature of the cultures of advanced societies that we lead increasingly compartmentalized lives. On any given day, someone may find herself moving again and again from one type of activity to another, as a parent giving her children breakfast and taking them to school, as an office manager arranging files and ordering supplies, as a friend meeting a friend for lunch, as a motorist filing an insurance claim through her agent, as a parent once more, giving her children their evening meal, as a member of a neighbourhood association attending an evening meeting. In each of these roles she meets with a different set of people. Each area of her activity has its own norms, including distinctive conversational norms, so that what is appropriate behaviour in one context may be quite inappropriate in another.

Those who have learned to structure their lives in this way may from time to time find themselves having to ask 'How am I doing as a parent, as a colleague in the workplace, as a neighbour, or as a friend?', but there will be nowhere in their lives where they have occasion to ask 'How am I doing as a human being?' Or rather, when they do ask a question that takes that form, it will almost certainly be because they have become conscious of not functioning well as parent or spouse or in the workplace and are looking for therapeutic help. For them to do well or badly as a human being just is to function well as parent and as spouse and in the workplace and elsewhere. The self has become invisible, except in its role playing and role management.[1] But, when it does become thus invisible, there is no longer occasion for the kind of philosophical self-questioning that Shaw and Chesterton hoped to elicit. And it is not only the self that becomes invisible.

Plain people learn to think, sometimes in highly sophisticated ways, about their situations and their problems as parents, as at work in this or that workplace or as out of work, as members of this or that organization, and the like. What in a highly compartmentalized culture they do not learn to think about is compartmentalization itself, about the workings of the social and cultural order which they inhabit, and about the ways in which they may be shaped by that order. So those workings and that order become something taken for granted rather than something to be put in question. This means that they are, even when highly educated, very different from the audiences and the readers addressed by Shaw and Chesterton. Anyone who now wishes to communicate what Shaw, Chesterton, and many of their contemporaries wished to communicate must first ask where and how she or he will find others to address.

Both Shaw and Chesterton understood themselves as having a vocation. Their task was to find those genres in which, by focusing attention on this or that particular situation or problem, they could disclose to others truths about themselves and their social relationships of which their readers and audiences would otherwise be unaware. Both understood, as well as anyone ever has, how to write so as to achieve this effect. It is important that this is something that we no longer know how to do.

NOTES

1. For other treatments of compartmentalization, see 'Moral Philosophy and Contemporary Social Practice: What Holds them Apart?' and 'Social Structures and their Threats to Moral Agency' in, respectively, volumes one and two of my *Selected Essays* (2006a, 2006b).

REFERENCES

Booth, C. (1902–1903). *Life and labour of the people in London* (3rd ed.). London: Macmillan.

Caldwell, C. (2013, November 29). The new world pope shifts church politics south. *Financial Times*. Retrieved July 20, 2015, from http://www.ft.com/cms/s/0/219f84be-5797-11e3-86d1-00144feabdc0.html#axzz3jlLsWLHu.

Chesterton, G. K. (1905). *Heretics*. London: John Lane and Company.

Chesterton, G. K. (1906). *Charles Dickens: A critical study*. London: Methuen.

Chesterton, G. K. (1908). *Orthodoxy*. London: John Lane and Company.

Chesterton, G. K. (1933). *St. Thomas Aquinas*. London: Sheed & Ward.

Chesterton, G. K. (1936). *Autobiography*. London: Sheed & Ward.

Chesterton, G. K. (1981 [1908]). Why I am not a socialist. *The Chesterton Review*, 7(3), 189–195.

Chesterton, G. K. (1987). In L. J. Clipper & G. J. Marlin (Eds.), *Collected works, Vol. XXVII: Illustrated London news, 1908–10*. San Francisco: Ignatius Press.

Leslie, S. (1921). *Henry Edward Manning: His life and labours.* London: Burns, Oates, and Washbourne.

MacIntyre, A. (2006a). *The tasks of philosophy: Selected essays* (Vol. 1). Cambridge: Cambridge University Press.

MacIntyre, A. (2006b). *Ethics and politics: Selected essays* (Vol. 2). Cambridge: Cambridge University Press.

Nietzsche, F. (2006 [1892]). *Thus Spoke Zarathustra* (A. Del Caro, Trans.). Cambridge: Cambridge University Press.

Pope Francis. (2013). *Evangelii Gaudium.* Retrieved July 20, 2015, from http://w2.vatican.va/content/francesco/en/apost_exhortations/documents/papa-francesco_esortazione-ap_20131124_evangelii-gaudium.html.

Pope Leo XIII. (1891). *Rerum Novarum.* Retrieved July 20, 2015, from http://w2.vatican.va/content/leo-xiii/en/encyclicals/documents/hf_l-xiii_enc_15051891_rerum-novarum.html.

Rawls, J. (1971). *A theory of justice.* Oxford: Oxford University Press.

Schopenhauer, A. (1936 [1819]). The metaphysics of the love of the sexes. In *The world as will and representation. Vol. II: Supplements to Part IV, Chapter XLIV* (E. J. Payne, Trans., pp. 531–567). New York: Dover.

Shaw, G. B. (1889). The basis of socialism: Economic. In G. B. Shaw (Ed.), *Fabian essays in socialism* (pp. 3–29). London: W. Scott.

Shaw, G. B. (1898). *The perfect Wagnerite.* London: Grant Richards.

Shaw, G. B. (1903). *Man and superman: A comedy and a philosophy.* Westminster: Archibald Constable & Co.

Shaw, G. B. (1928). *The intelligent woman's guide to socialism and capitalism.* London: Constable and Company.

Siders, D. (2013, November 7). Jerry Brown says poverty, joblessness due to California being "A Magnet". *The Sacramento Bee.* Retrieved July 20, 2015, from http://blogs.sacbee.com/capitolalertlatest/2013/11/jerry-brown-calls-poverty-flip-side-of-californias-incredible-attractivenes.html.

Singer, P. (1972). Famine, affluence, and morality. *Philosophy & Public Affairs,* 1(3), 229–243.

Tressell, R. (1914). *The ragged-trousered philanthropists.* London: Grant Richards.

Unger, P. (1996). *Living high and letting die: Our illusion of innocence.* Oxford: Oxford University Press.

CHAPTER 7

Ethics, Markets, and Cultural Goods

Russell Keat

1 INTRODUCTION

This chapter considers some possible justifications for cultural institutions being supported by the state, rather than the provision of cultural goods being left to the market. In doing so, it also addresses more general issues about the legitimate aims of state action, including especially the proper grounds for political choices between different economic arrangements.

Without defining what count as 'cultural activities', I will take these to include the various arts, broadcasting, and academic research. 'Support by the state' may range from tax breaks, grants, and other measures that protect these from the full impact of the market, to securing their provision as a public service, as in the case of broadcasting. I shall also take it that state support does not imply state *control*.[1]

Broadly speaking, arguments for the non-market provision of goods and services may appeal either to considerations of distributive justice or to concerns about the character and quality of the items concerned. Justifications for public healthcare provision, for example, appeal primarily to the former: what is at issue is ensuring that access to this service is based on

R. Keat
University of Edinburgh, Edinburgh, UK

© The Editor(s) (if applicable) and The Author(s) 2016
A. Fives, K. Breen (eds.), *Philosophy and Political Engagement*,
DOI 10.1057/978-1-137-44587-2_7

need and not income or wealth, something that the market cannot achieve. By contrast, justifications for public service broadcasting or for the support of other non-market cultural institutions appeal primarily to the latter: it is the supposedly negative implications of exclusively commercial provision for the nature of the cultural goods made available that is at issue.[2]

Thus, the case for cultural institutions being supported by the state depends on judgements being made about the *value* of what is thereby provided and its superiority to what would be achieved by markets alone. Critics, consequently, may say: such judgements are not only highly problematic, but should anyway be ruled out as grounds for state action. To allow them any such role is at odds with a principle widely endorsed in liberal political theory: that the powers of the state should not be employed to aid or hinder the realization of particular 'conceptions of the good' (see, for example, Arneson 1987; Dworkin 1985; Rawls 1971). Instead, the state should restrict itself to securing a just framework within which individuals may freely pursue their own understanding of what the good life consists in.

According to this principle of state *neutrality*, then, judgements about 'the good', or what will here be called *ethical* judgements, should play no part in political decisions and debates.[3] One might call this 'the exclusion of ethics from politics', which implies also its exclusion from any contribution from philosophy to political debate (see Raz 1986, pp. 134–63). I shall be arguing against such exclusion later on in this chapter. But I shall also be questioning a further (and crucial) assumption made by those who invoke the principle of neutrality in opposing state support for cultural activities, namely that 'leaving such activities to the market' *is* consistent with that principle, whereas using the powers of the state to secure their non-market provision is *not*.

The market, on this view, is the ideal economic institution for a neutralist state to support. In market economies, there is no role for collective ethical judgements about what is to be produced. The only authoritative judgements of value are those made by individuals, and in particular by consumers in deciding what they think is worth purchasing (Hayek 1976, pp. 107–32; for an analysis of this view, see O'Neill 1998, pp. 64–72). The market's distributive consequences may, of course, be regarded as unjust and redistributive measures taken to remedy this. But this is a matter of improving people's chances of achieving what they themselves value, as distinct from making collective judgements about what is valuable.

On this view, then, the support provided by the state for market institutions is consistent with the principle of neutrality, whereas state support for non-market cultural institutions is not. I shall argue against this view, suggesting instead that both arguments for the non-market provision of cultural goods *and* for the market itself may quite properly appeal to collective judgements about the human good. Allowing a place for ethics in politics need present no threat to liberal principles, but deepens the basis upon which political choices between market and non-market institutions can be made. And I shall also suggest that, if the place of ethics in politics is accepted, this provides an important reason for supporting non-market cultural institutions.

However, these issues about ethics, politics, and neutrality are not addressed until later sections of this chapter. Before reaching that point, I will say something about how I first became interested in the proper relationship between cultural institutions and the market, and about how the problems that emerged for the approach that I initially took led me to consider some broader issues about the nature of market institutions and their possible justifications. I hope readers will not find this mode of presentation unduly self-indulgent; it is intended as a convenient way both of explicating the relevant conceptual linkages and of indicating how 'philosophical' engagements with public matters sometimes proceed.

2   CHANGES TO BRITISH CULTURAL INSTITUTIONS IN THE 1980s

My interest in cultural institutions and the market began while working in a university that, like others in Britain during the mid-1980s, was coming under increasing pressure to adopt the organizational forms and outlook of commercial enterprise. Unlike the public utilities and nationalized industries, universities were not being privatized, but they were being encouraged or required to operate in a far more 'business-like' manner: students were to be seen as consumers, prospectuses refashioned as promotional literature, peer judgements replaced by performance indicators, the costs of space usage attributed to departments, and so on. Similar changes were taking place in other cultural institutions. Public subsidies for the arts were not removed, but the Arts Council made business plans and marketing strategies a condition of its financial support. The BBC remained a public service broadcasting institution, but through a series of organizational changes became more difficult to distinguish from its commercial counterparts.[4]

Like many others, I felt there was something seriously wrong with all this: that it would damage the integrity of cultural institutions and their potential value for society. But I found it difficult to construct a theoretical justification for this intuitive response. In particular, two bodies of literature with which I was reasonably familiar proved not to be helpful. First, there were the continuing debates about social justice stimulated by Rawls's (1971) work in political philosophy. However, what was problematic about these changes did not seem to be a matter of distributive injustice. With relatively minor exceptions (such as the introduction of entry charges for museums and galleries), the costs of access to cultural institutions were not being increased: tuition at universities remained free and the price of a TV license stayed roughly the same.[5] What worried critics of BBC reforms was not that access to TV would be denied to those with less money, but that there would be fewer programmes worth watching. Second, there were the critiques of the market (and commodification) in the Marxist tradition. From this perspective one would object to any *extension* of the market because one objected to the market *as such*. But in the absence of any preferable alternative to the market (as the primary means of coordination in a modern economy), these critiques seemed unpersuasive; all the more so given that the only 'actual' alternative, state socialism, was not only economically inferior but—unlike the market—apparently incompatible with basic elements of liberal democracy. Further, the proponents of market socialism had shown, in my view, that much of what is objectionable about *capitalist* market economies can be removed in a system of workers' cooperatives that preserves the market and is hence compatible with civil and political liberties (Miller 1990; Nove 1983; Selucky 1979). But there would still be a need to decide on the proper relationship between cultural institutions and the market in this socialist market economy.

So to justify the protection of cultural institutions from the market, it seemed that one could draw neither on arguments against injustice nor on arguments against the market *tout court*. Instead, the case would have to be made in terms of the market's proper scope or boundaries: of which kinds of activities are, and are not, appropriately governed on this basis. The book that encouraged me to think about the problem in this way was Michael Walzer's *Spheres of Justice*, published in 1983, in which he urged political philosophers to take proper account of the highly differentiated nature of modern societies, comprising a number of spheres (family, polity, economy, and so on) that differ in their institutional character and the kinds of social goods that are created, distributed, and enjoyed within them.[6]

It is a central responsibility of (modern) politics, Walzer argued, to maintain the boundaries between these spheres, so as to prevent any one of them coming to dominate the others. This applies especially to the *market*, the sphere of money and commodities. Walzer has no objection to the market as such, provided it is kept in its proper place. He accepts this is difficult to achieve because of its inherently expansive tendency. But he suggests that this can be (and to a significant extent actually is) dealt with through a series of what he calls 'blocked exchanges', that is, prohibitions on the sale or purchase of various items.[7]

However, despite the attractiveness of Walzer's overall framework, this focus on blocked exchanges did not seem helpful in addressing the issues about cultural institutions and the market with which I was concerned. For whereas, for example, the sale or purchase of political office would rightly be seen as corruption, and that of friendship services as undermining the character of this valued relationship, the same could hardly be argued in the case of theatre tickets or lectures on political philosophy. Further, the defence of non-market cultural institutions, such as public service broadcasting, does not imply or require that their commercial counterparts should be prohibited.[8]

What these disanalogies suggested was that instead of focusing on issues about the *exchange* of cultural goods, it might be more fruitful to consider the effects of the market on how cultural goods were *produced* (see Keat 2012). That is, the problem was not whether the proper nature of cultural goods would be undermined by possessing the status of commodities, but whether the pressures imposed on cultural institutions by operating as commercial enterprises in the market might damage or reduce their ability to produce cultural goods of sufficient value. But to show that this was so would require some account of how cultural institutions and activities were best organized and conducted, and of why it was that the market posed a threat to this.

In thinking about how to do this, it was Alasdair MacIntyre's *After Virtue*, first published in 1981, that seemed to provide some possible answers. What was especially attractive was its account of what he called a *practice*: a form of social activity in which the primary aim is to do or achieve what is good, valuable, or admirable, judged in terms of the criteria shared by those who engage in it. This account of practices seemed to capture a great deal of the distinctive nature and value of the cultural activities with which I was concerned. In the next two sections, I shall first outline the way in which I tried to use MacIntyre's account, and then consider some problems this encountered.

3   MacIntyre, Practices, and Cultural Institutions

A practice, MacIntyre says, is any complex form of cooperative activity in which goods that are *internal* to this are realized in trying to achieve the *standards of excellence* appropriate to, and partly definitive of, the activity concerned (MacIntyre 1985, p. 187). A wide range of social activities can potentially be practices, including the various arts and sciences, sports and games, the conduct of politics and households, and 'productive' activities such as farming, fishing, and the making of objects that satisfy human needs.

The standards of a practice, says MacIntyre, define what count as good or bad—genuine or spurious, exemplary or worthless, et cetera—instances of the activity. It is by reference to these standards that the success of people's performance of the activity and the value of their contributions to the practice are judged. Without being willing to accept the authority of these judgements, individuals will be unable to appreciate and enjoy the internal goods of the practice, which can be understood only in terms of its specific character: for example (mine, not MacIntyre's), the elegance of a scientific theory or the truthfulness of a theatrical performance.

Internal goods differ radically from what he terms *external* goods, such as money, power, and status (MacIntyre 1985, pp. 188–91). When people are motivated primarily by the pursuit of external goods, what counts as success in terms of a practice's own standards is valued only instrumentally, as a way of achieving something that could equally well be achieved by other means, and not intrinsically, as is the case with internal goods. MacIntyre argues, however, that external goods are necessary for practices, since these cannot survive or flourish without the support of *institutions*, which are 'involved in acquiring money and other material goods ... are structured in terms of power and status, and ... distribute money, power and status as rewards'(MacIntyre 1985, p. 194).

Ideally, the institutional use of external goods should enhance the practice's ability to pursue and develop its particular goals, to operate in accordance with its standards, and to generate for its participants the shared appreciation and enjoyment of its internal goods. But this positive role for institutions is difficult to ensure, since external goods always have the potential to undermine the integrity of practices. It is partly for this reason that MacIntyre (1985, p. 191) also emphasizes the role of the moral virtues, especially courage, honesty, and justice, which may enable practitioners to resist the pressures generated by external goods.

By insisting on the need for institutions, MacIntyre's account steers one away from regarding external goods as inherently antithetical to practices, and instead directs attention to identifying those institutional forms that are conducive to their integrity and those that are not. Amongst the latter, he believes, are the capitalist market and the modern business corporation. But in *After Virtue* he says rather little about just why this is so. So in drawing on his work to justify opposition to the commercially modelled reshaping of cultural institutions, I tried to spell out why this would be damaging for the practices they had previously supported (Keat 1991, 1994).

The basic idea was that, in a market economy, firms are subject to various pressures that require them to act in ways they might otherwise not wish to, on pain of going out of business. In particular, the pressures of competition from other firms often have this effect (and this would be just as much so for cooperatives in a market socialist economy). The market does not compel firms to aim only at maximizing their profits, but it does require them to remain profitable and it will not protect them from the effects of their competitors' decisions. And what this means is that any firm in which production is, at a certain time, being conducted in a practice-like manner may perfectly well find itself, at a later time, unable to continue to do so.

There are many specific reasons for which this may occur. The one that I focused on was the potentially problematic relationship between consumer preferences and a practice's standards (Keat 1991, 2000, pp. 19–32). In a market economy, firms have to be able to satisfy consumer preferences (as indicated by their willingness to pay) in a profitable manner. But there is no guarantee that these preferences, or the judgements on which they are based, will be consistent with a practice's standards or will remain so even if at one time they were. Correspondingly, there is no guarantee that firms that otherwise wish to act in accordance with a practice's standards will be able to afford to do so, especially when one or more competitors find ways of catering for those consumers' preferences that are at odds with the practice's standards. The previously practice-based firms will find themselves unable to act for practice-consistent reasons; to do so will be too costly, demanding material sacrifices that even their morally virtuous members cannot be expected to make.[9]

On further reflection, however, I began to have serious doubts about this argument. Although it was constructed with cultural practices in mind, it seemed to rely on claims that would apply equally well to practices of any kind. It thus implied that markets are antithetical to the conduct of any kind of activity as a practice, including that of economic production. But the more of the relevant economic literature I read, the less plausible this seemed to be (Keat 2000, pp. 111–32, 2008a). It looked, instead, as if there could be, and indeed were, many cases of practice-like production *within* market economies; or at least, as the work of some comparative political economists that I came across later on seemed to imply, within a certain *kind* of market economy.

In the next section, I shall consider some of this work and its bearings upon the relationship between cultural institutions and the market. But before that, I will draw attention to a different set of issues raised by this attempt to construct a MacIntyrean defence of non-market cultural institutions.

Even if it were true that the market is inimical to cultural activity as a practice, this would not by itself justify the provision of state support for cultural institutions. To do so, one would need also to show that they are sufficiently valuable to justify this (quite costly) allocation of societal resources; otherwise, there seems no reason why cultural practices should not simply be pursued in people's leisure time (as indeed they often are, to considerable effect). I shall say more about how this might be shown in Sect. 6, but some preliminary points can usefully be made here.

First, what makes these institutions valuable must be to do with the cultural goods they help create and not with their benefits for those who work in them. No doubt the life of a cultural practitioner is often enjoyable and fulfilling, but to support cultural activities because they are good for practitioners would unfairly privilege them over others who have to earn their living without such advantages. Second, it seems unlikely that the MacIntyrean account itself can provide any basis for judging the value of a practice and of what it generates, as distinct from judging what is done within any such practice. Both the internal goods of practices, and their standards of excellence, are specific to the practice concerned. These standards tell us what is good or valuable within a practice, but not what makes for a good or valuable practice.[10]

Finally—and returning now to the main theme of Sect. 1—to appeal to the value of these institutions as a reason for providing state support for them will most likely be at odds with the neutrality principle, with its exclusion from politics of judgements about the good. At the time when I was working on the ideas outlined in the present section, this was not a problem with which I was much concerned; it became so only some years later. By then, and quite fortuitously, it turned out that the political economy literature I had been working on for quite different reasons might also provide the basis for a response to the neutrality objection. At least, that is what I shall try to argue in the next two sections.

4   Two Kinds of Market Economy

In *Varieties of Capitalism* (2001), Peter Hall and David Soskice identify and explore the institutional differences between what they call 'liberal' and 'coordinated' market economies (LMEs and CMEs). Taking the UK and USA as exemplifying the former, and Germany the latter, they argue that the different institutional arrangements of LMEs and CMEs impact significantly on the organization and behaviour of firms. I shall argue that, because of these differences, one may reasonably expect CMEs to be conducive to the conduct of economic production as a practice, or at least a good deal less inimical to this than are LMEs.[11]

The institutional differences identified by Hall and Soskice (2001, pp. 8–21) include those concerned with ownership and finance, with the internal governance of firms, and with inter-firm relationships. The first difference, they argue, makes firms in CMEs less vulnerable than those in LMEs to the pressures of short-term profitability and to the subordination of production decisions to financial imperatives. The second reduces considerably the extent of intra-firm hierarchy and the exercise of 'managerial prerogative' in CMEs, by comparison with LMEs. The third enables various forms of cooperation between firms in CMEs, by contrast with the exclusively competitive relations that obtain in LMEs. This is due to the existence of industry-wide associations, to which all firms in a given industry belong and which play a major role in research and development, in technology transfer, and in systems of education and training.

Hall and Soskice argue that, because of these institutional differences, firms in CMEs are more likely than their LME counterparts to compete in terms of quality rather than price and to make more extensive use of workers who are equipped with high levels of technical skill, are subject to less intrusive monitoring, and have more opportunities for taking initiatives (Hall and Soskice 2001, p. 39). Such differences would be important for any ethical evaluation of the kinds of work provided by the two kinds of market economy, since they could be expected to affect significantly the opportunities for intrinsic satisfactions. However, MacIntyrean practices are not just a matter of the development and exercise of complex skills and judgement, and the intrinsic satisfactions generated by these, but also of engagement in a shared activity with its own standards of excellence and the possible enjoyment of internal goods dependent on this. It is here, I suggest, that the industry-wide associations of CMEs, and their role, *inter alia*, in education and training, are especially relevant.

As Hall and Soskice (2001, pp. 25–7) emphasize, the skills acquired through such training are applicable across all firms in a particular industry. There is also a strong emphasis on apprenticeship, along with other elements of a craft-oriented conception of training. Taken together with other features of CMEs, such training could be regarded, I suggest, as providing an appropriate form of induction into a shared activity that goes beyond the boundaries of individual firms, has its own standards of excellence that set the terms for competition between them, and potentially enables workers to participate in, contribute to, and experience the benefits of something quite close to the nature of a MacIntyrean practice. In LMEs, by contrast, such possibilities could be expected to be relatively slight, given the absence of industry-wide associations with comparable powers and functions, together with other institutional differences already noted.[12]

Without claiming that CMEs are entirely conducive to the conduct of production as a practice, the argument I have just sketched does, I think, cast serious doubt on markets being inherently incompatible with practices. So what are the implications of this for my earlier argument that cultural practices need to be institutionally protected from the market?

It might be thought that if CMEs are conducive to production as a practice, all that is needed to ensure the flourishing of cultural practices is to establish this kind of market economy, the assumption being that it is only LMEs from which they require protection. But this 'optimism' about cultural practices and CMEs would not be justified, for at least two reasons. First, it might be that CMEs are incompatible with specifically *cultural* production as a practice, even though they are compatible with production as a practice in other cases. If this were so, it would suggest that what was wrong with the earlier argument is that it did not engage with what is distinctive about cultural practices, relying only on generic considerations. I think there is something to be said for this view, but I shall not try to remove this defect here.

Second, even if specifically cultural practices *are* compatible with CMEs, an otherwise well-functioning CME might nonetheless be entirely devoid of cultural production (and cultural goods), since a fundamental feature of any kind of market economy is that there are no specific products whose provision can be guaranteed to be provided (this is why planning is always needed in wartime economies, for instance). So a case might still have to be made for the state to support cultural institutions, and, as noted at the end of the previous section, this will require not only defensible judgements about their ethical value, but a response to the neutralist objection to state action based on *any* such ethical grounds. However, as I shall now argue, what has just been said about different kinds of market economy points towards a possible way in which this neutralist objection can be effectively 'disarmed'.

5   Ethics and the Choice of Economic Institutions

Suppose that a political community were choosing between the two types of market economy described above, and hence deciding on which set of institutional arrangements the powers of the state will be used to support. If what I argued in the previous section is broadly correct, this political choice will have a significant and ethically relevant impact on the kinds of *work* available for the community's members. Working in firms engaged in practice-like production differs significantly in the kinds of goods (and ills) that may be experienced from working in firms that are not.[13] The two sorts of firm—and, likewise, the market economies underpinning them—thus differ in the relative ease or difficulty with which particular work-related 'conceptions of the good' can be realized within them. This is because the goods concerned are institutionally dependent: they are embedded in forms of social activity that require particular institutional arrangements, arrangements which themselves depend, in various ways, on state action. Moreover, for any society there will be limits on the range of possible goods available to people, since the choice to establish and support one institutional arrangement necessarily closes off access to goods made possible by alternative institutional arrangements (Keat 2011a, pp. 361–2). The question thus necessarily arises of *which* institutional arrangement—as well as its associated goods—is to be preferred.

In this situation, I suggest, it would be perfectly reasonable for the ethically relevant differences described above to be taken into account in choosing politically between the two types of market economy, and hence for the respective ethical merits (and defects) of work performed as a practice, and work that is not, to be debated. The decision on how the powers of the state should be used would thus be based (in part) on ethical considerations. But this, it seems, is ruled out by the principle of state neutrality. The principle thus requires citizens to ignore the ethically relevant and predictable consequences of their decisions; it absolves them, in effect, from taking collective responsibility for these consequences and from the need to debate their ethical character.

What the principle requires is not impossible; I am not trying to 'disprove' it here. But I do want to suggest there is no obvious reason why this limitation on political reasoning and responsibility should be accepted. In particular, although the neutrality principle has been widely endorsed by liberal political philosophers, it is hard to see what recognizably liberal principles or values would be threatened by permitting a political choice between these two types of market economy (in part) on these kinds of ethical grounds. Both in theory and in practice, both sets of economic institutions seem perfectly (or at least equally) compatible with the standard array of liberal rights, and with the exercise of individual autonomy (Keat 2011a, pp. 358–64).[14]

I will now take this argument one stage further, by considering another (hypothetical) political choice. This time it is between *any* kind of market economy and some kind of *non-market* economy—whether, for example, in the guise of state socialism, guild socialism, or a form of non-market, community-based local economy—so that one possible decision is to use the powers of the state to establish and maintain the institutional framework required by a market economy. Here too, I suggest, there will be ethically relevant differences between the market and non-market alternatives: differences in the set of goods that each of them makes possible, and in the kinds of life they make it relatively easy or difficult to lead.

Most obviously, this will be so with respect to *consumption*. The (apparently unique) dynamism of market economies with respect to both wealth generation and product innovation enables people in market economies to live in ways that are otherwise unlikely to be available. Issues such as the *ethical value* of this 'material well-being', and its possibly negative impact on other modes of well-being—such as enjoyment of the good of production or the bonds of solidarity definitive of tightly integrated communities—made available by alternative economic arrangements, should surely be seen as relevant, and legitimate, in making this political choice.

Less obviously, perhaps, market economies also differ radically from non-market alternatives in the ethical character of its central form of transaction, contractual *exchange*. Economists tend to think of this simply as a means by which individuals can achieve the goals they have, independently of this device. For many liberal political philosophers, by contrast, it is a concrete manifestation of individual liberty (see, for example, Booth 1993). But exchange can also be seen as a specific social relationship, constituted in part by a complex set of obligations and rights, that may itself be valued as a particular kind of social good (or judged to be a social ill) (see Durkheim 1984 [1893]; Keat 2013, pp. 175–81, 2015, pp. 197–8). The value of exchange, I suggest, is itself a matter for ethical debate that belongs quite properly to the political choice between market and non-market economic institutions.

As in the case of a choice between the two kinds of market economy, a political community could decide to exclude these ethical considerations if it so wished. But what has just been said should at least serve to undermine the view that *only* market economies are consistent with the principle of neutrality. Sometimes this view is held because it is thought that the market itself is neutral: that market institutions do not discriminate between conceptions of the good, but only between different individuals' ability to realize their own (Arneson 1987, p. 537). What is wrong with this view, I believe, emerges clearly from considering what might be involved—as revealed by reflection upon the goods of consumption and exchange—in a political choice between market and non-market economies.

What also emerges, I suggest, is the implausibility of invoking the principle of neutrality to oppose the provision of state support for non-market cultural institutions. As I noted in the opening section, it is widely believed that any justification for protecting cultural activities from the market in this way depends on ethical judgements about their value, and is thus incompatible with state neutrality, whereas this is not so for the justification of market institutions themselves. It is this supposed asymmetry that has now been challenged, since the justification of market institutions *also* hinges on ethical judgements.

The neutralist objection to state support for non-market cultural institutions is thus disarmed. There is no more reason to exclude ethics from political decisions about departures from the market than from political decisions to accept the market itself. More generally, one should regard all these decisions as part and parcel of the overall responsibility that citizens have to determine collectively their society's economic arrangements, a task that includes also the setting of boundaries between different institutional domains, and in which ethical reasons (along with liberal principles and considerations of justice) have a legitimate role throughout.

6   CULTURAL GOODS AND PUBLIC SERVICE
     BROADCASTING

In this penultimate section, I return to the question posed at the end of Sect. 3, of how one might show that cultural goods are sufficiently valuable for the state to support cultural institutions when it seems likely that the market might 'fail to deliver'. There are, I suggest, at least two ways of approaching this. The first points to the direct contribution of cultural goods to human well-being; the second to their role in what might be termed 'ethical reflection'. I shall focus mainly on the latter, not because it is more important than the former (with which it is also fully compatible), but because it is more closely related to other central themes in this chapter.

Adopting the first approach involves making the same kinds of judgement as those briefly noted in the previous section, in considering what might make one kind of economy ethically preferable to another (about the nature of work, the possibilities for consumption, et cetera). They are probably best made within a framework such as that proposed by Martha Nussbaum (1990, 2000), in which various human 'functionings' are identified, each of which is either essential for a minimally decent existence or central to a flourishing one. Political communities should provide their members with the possibility of achieving these, without requiring them actually to do so. Cultural goods might then be valued because, for example, they enable people to develop and exercise their imaginative capacities, to engage in various forms of aesthetic appreciation and enjoyment, and so forth.

By contrast, the second approach builds on an important feature of at least many cultural goods: that, in addition to what might be termed their 'first order' value (of the kinds just illustrated), they also have a 'second order' value in helping people to *reflect on* ethical questions, since they directly or indirectly explore the nature and possibilities of human well-being, the kinds of life that are worth living, the reasons for valuing different kinds of goods, and so on. This is most obviously so in the case of intellectual disciplines such as philosophy. But what is involved in such ethical reflection is not exclusively cognitive or theoretical in character; it is also affective and experiential, and hence aided as much, or indeed more, by imaginative engagement with the kinds of concrete depictions and explorations of people's lives to be found in novels, films, drama, and many other cultural goods (see Beiner 2014, p. xiii; Murdoch 1982).

The value of ethical reflection for individuals, and hence of the cultural goods that help them in deciding on what to aim at in their own lives, is widely recognized.[15] But if, as I have argued, ethical judgements are also required at the collective level, in making political decisions about institutional arrangements, then the value of cultural goods may also reside in their contribution to properly 'informed' public debate. I shall now develop this argument by considering its implications for the ways in which public service broadcasting (PSB) might be justified, taking the BBC as an example.

The BBC has for many years presented itself as having three main aims: to *inform*, to *educate*, and to *entertain*. These aims are generally seen as being pursued through different categories of programmes, respectively: news, current affairs, and documentaries; arts, history, and sciences; and soap operas, sitcoms, and popular drama series. I shall refer to these as 'News', 'Arts', and 'Soap'. Broadly speaking, in debates about the BBC and its continued funding (through the license fee), the first of these has been regarded as the easiest to justify, and the third as the hardest. But I shall question this, along with the assumed differences in the nature of their respective justifications.

The provision of News is typically supported on the grounds that it contributes significantly to the effective operation of democracy: citizens and political leaders need to be well-informed if decisions are to be made on a proper basis (Lukes 2005). For News to perform this function, one might argue, it needs to be both 'serious' in its selection of topics (for example, avoiding celebrity trivia) and 'impartial' or 'objective' in its treatment of these. In both respects, one might have reasonable doubts about the likely performance of commercially provided News (unless this is carefully regulated by statutory bodies, such as Ofcom).

This 'democratic' justification for PSB is generally regarded as applying only to News. By contrast, Arts provision is usually supported by appealing to (what I have called) the 'first order' value of cultural goods, especially those associated with 'high' as opposed to 'popular' culture. And defenders of PSB often find it difficult to justify the provision of Soap at all, except by arguing that a broadcaster such as the BBC would lose some of its audience for News and Arts if it did not also provide these 'entertaining' programmes that can equally well be provided commercially (Graham and Davies 1997).

However, if political choices and decisions depend partly on ethical considerations, and if (many) cultural goods also have a second-order value as resources for ethical reflection, the 'democratic' justification for PSB can be extended not only to Arts, but also, I would argue, to Soap, especially if the kind of case powerfully made by John Mepham (1990) is accepted. Mepham argues that (what he calls) 'TV fictions' can at their best perform similar, and similarly valuable, functions to those performed by their high-culture counterparts. In particular, he says of soap operas that:

> They can, at their best, produce a constant stream of puzzles relating to the morals and tactics of everyday affairs and offer to the viewer a range of possible solutions which can be mulled over, assessed, assimilated or rejected. They can expand the viewer's sense of what is possible, enhance his or her vocabularies and repertoires of words, gestures and initiatives. They are the great laboratory of modern everyday life. Of course, they can only achieve these things if they are of high quality (Mepham 1990, p. 67).

It might also be argued that there are analogues, for high-quality Soap, of the requirements for 'impartiality' and 'seriousness' in high-quality News: one might contrast, for example, the ethical reflection enabled by high-quality Soap with the distortion and obfuscation about human well-being in TV advertising (an extremely well-resourced cultural product). More generally, there is a similar need for integrity in both. That of Soap, and hence its ability to contribute to ethical reflection, is compromised when, for example, undue attention to viewing figures leads to the introduction of sensational events that require characters to act in an *out of character* manner, doing things that makes no sense, given who they are and how they have previously behaved. This is a serious failing in any (realist) drama: the sacrifice of character to plot.

However—as BBC Soap has amply demonstrated in recent years (witness the frequent sensationalism of *EastEnders*)—the provision of Soap as an element in PSB by no means ensures that it will be high-quality Soap. Much will depend on the specific organizational model that is adopted by (or imposed upon) PSB providers, and on the extent to which, for example, marketing and financial considerations are permitted to impact directly on the 'creative' processes of cultural production.[16] What is needed, I suggest, is an organizational design compatible with the conduct of cultural production as a practice.

Here I return to the concerns noted in Sect. 2, that cultural institutions such as the BBC might lose their integrity by being remodelled as commercial enterprises, despite not being privatized or fully marketized. What might now be added to this, as my discussion of varieties of capitalism in Sect. 4 indicated, is that it may also matter *which* model of commercial organization is thus imposed or adopted. In the UK, as one might expect, governments have since the 1980s chosen a model drawn from liberal, rather than coordinated, market economies. This, if my previous argument is correct, has damaged the prospects for cultural production as a practice within the UK, and hence the potential value of cultural goods for political choices and decisions properly informed by ethical considerations.

7   SOME FINAL THOUGHTS

These claims about cultural goods and the institutional choices and frameworks that facilitate or impede their realization clearly need a good deal of further development to be convincing. In particular, the remarks just made about the negative impact of certain organizational forms on the quality and value of the cultural goods that public service broadcasting can provide are supported here only by somewhat speculative theoretical claims about varieties of capitalism and MacIntyrean practices, and by impressionistic judgments about (changes in) the ethical value of TV programmes.

What is required, therefore, is both more detailed empirical investigation of cultural institutions such as the BBC, exploring the effects of organizational change on the decisions made within them, and more fully articulated reflection on the criteria to be employed in making ethical judgments about cultural goods. Both social science and philosophical ethics thus have crucial roles to play, and although these disciplines are distinct they they need to be practised in close relation to one another. The questions addressed by social scientists must be informed by an understanding of what makes institutions matter, in normative terms, and philosophers must recognise the socially embedded character and institutional dependence of the goods and ills with which they are concerned.

But whatever the specific results of these enquiries about cultural institutions turn out to be, there are at least two points of principle that remain, if what I have argued in this chapter is broadly correct. First, the ethical interest in cultural goods is a legitimate public interest and an appropriate basis for political and economic action, contra the principle of state neutrality. Second, cultural goods are an essential part of a good society and a democratic polity. Thus, if we fail to secure the conditions for their continued existence and flourishing, we will have failed in one of our key responsibilities as citizens.

And it is not just a matter of our responsibilities, but of our rights. All too often market institutions are presented by their advocates as sacrosanct, as if any kind of 'political interference' with them is inherently illegitimate. But these institutions are established and sustained by the state, and both their specific character and their proper scope are legitimate objects of political choice, guided *inter alia* by specifically ethical considerations.

NOTES

1. State support of the British Broadcasting Corporation (BBC), the key UK public service broadcasting organization, takes the form of a license fee levied on households possessing a TV, the state itself having no direct control over programming or the internal governance of the organization (Keat 2011b, pp. 61–2). Note, on a different point, that in addition to state support and market provision, many cultural goods are also provided through voluntary and unpaid cultural activities in the form of amateur orchestras, choirs, et cetera.

2. Justifications for the public provision of some other goods, such as education, may appeal both to distributive justice and to the character or nature of the good concerned.

3. By 'ethical judgements', I mean judgements as to what is 'good' or has 'value' for human beings, in contrast to 'moral judgements', which concern what is 'just' or 'right'. For fuller discussions of the distinction between these types of judgement, see Habermas (1993) and Keat (2008b).

4. For critical analyses of these organizational changes, see McGuigan (1996) and Leys (2001).

5. Of course, free university tuition in the UK came to an end later on, with the passage of *The Teaching and Higher Education Act* in 1998, which introduced a means-tested annual fee of £1000. Since then, the average annual tuition fee for students in England and Wales has increased to £9000.

6. A similarly differentiated understanding of modern society underpins Habermas's (1987) later social theory and his 'colonization thesis', the claim that serious social pathologies arise when market imperatives invade non-market spheres of life (see Keat 2008b).

7. Such 'blocked exchanges' include, for example, prohibitions on the purchase of people, of political office, of exemptions from general duties, and of friendship (Walzer 1983, pp. 100–3). Admittedly, Walzer's main concern was with questions of distributive justice, which I had decided were not relevant, but it seemed his framework could also be used (and was implicitly so used by Walzer) in thinking about how to protect the integrity and distinctive value of social goods.

8. Commercial broadcasters may well, however, be subject to statutory regulation. Within the UK, the body charged with this task is the Office of Communications (Ofcom), established by the *Communications Act 2003* (see Keat 2011b)

9. For an illustration of this point, see MacIntyre's (1994, pp. 284–6) discussion of the contrast between practice-based and non-practice-based fishing crews.

10. In relation to this issue, see also Miller's (1994, p. 250) distinction between 'self-contained' practices, such as games and sport, 'whose *raison d'être* consists entirely in the internal goods achieved by participants and the contemplation of those achievements by others', and 'purposive practices', such as architecture or farming, 'which exist to serve social ends beyond themselves'.

11. I should add here that I employ Hall and Soskice's analysis of the varieties of capitalism for theoretical purposes that are very different to theirs (see Keat 2008a, p. 88).

12. Where workers in CMEs generally acquire industry-specific skills, workers in LMEs are typically equipped with a combination of 'generic' skills applicable in any industry and 'firm-specific' skills acquired within a particular firm. On the significance of different skills-training regimes, see Estevez-Abe et al. (2001).

13. We should note here that while CMEs, as in the case of Germany, allow greater scope for production as a practice and are more egalitarian in terms of income distribution than most LMEs, they display much higher levels of gender inequality and of occupational segregation than those found in LMEs such as the UK and USA (Estevez-Abe et al. 2001, pp. 155–60; Keat 2008a, pp. 90–1). These less desirable features of CMEs as they currently exist would also have to figure in any choice between the two types of market economy.

14. With Raz (1986) and others (Sher 1997; Wall 1998; see also Chap. 8), I believe the core tenets of liberalism are in no way undermined by allowing perfectionist considerations as to the good a central place within political decision-making. For a defence of this 'liberal perfectionism', see Keat (2008b, 2009).

15. Both neutralist liberals, such as Dworkin (1985), and liberal perfectionists, such as Raz (1986), are largely in agreement on the connection between ethical reflection and the availability of valuable cultural options, on the one hand, and the capacity of individuals to realize autonomy, on the other.

16. On the growth of the 'managerial prerogative' within creative industries and the increasing subordination of artistic autonomy to financial and market imperatives, see Hesmondhalgh (2007), Hesmondhalgh and Baker (2011), and Keat (2011b).

References

Arneson, R. (1987). Meaningful work and market socialism. *Ethics*, 97(3), 517–545.

Beiner, R. (2014). *Political philosophy: What it is and why it matters.* Cambridge: Cambridge University Press.

Booth, W. J. (1993). *Households: On the moral architecture of the economy.* Ithaca, NY: Cornell University Press.

Durkheim, E. (1984 [1893]). *The division of labour in society* (W. D. Halls, Trans.). Basingstoke: Macmillan.

Dworkin, R. (1985). Liberalism. In R. Dworkin (Ed.), *A matter of principle* (pp. 181–204). Oxford: Oxford University Press.

Estevez-Abe, M., Iversen, T., & Soskice, D. (2001). Social protection and the formation of skills: A reinterpretation of the welfare state. In P. Hall & D. Soskice (Eds.), *Varieties of capitalism: The institutional foundations of comparative advantage* (pp. 145–183). Oxford: Oxford University Press.

Graham, A., & Davies, G. (1997). *Broadcasting, society and policy in the multimedia age.* Luton: University of Luton Press.

Habermas, J. (1987). *The theory of communicative action: Vol. II. System and lifeworld—A critique of functionalist reason.* Cambridge: Polity Press.

Habermas, J. (1993). On the pragmatic, the ethical, and the moral employments of practical reason. In J. Habermas (Ed.), *Justification and application: Remarks on discourse ethics* (pp. 1–18). Cambridge: Polity Press.

Hall, P., & Soskice, D. (2001). An introduction to varieties of capitalism. In P. Hall & D. Soskice (Eds.), *Varieties of capitalism: The institutional foundations of comparative advantage* (pp. 1–68). Oxford: Oxford University Press.

Hayek, F. A. (1976). *Law, legislation and liberty: Vol. II.* London: Routledge and Kegan Paul.

Hesmondhalgh, D. (2007). *The cultural industries* (2nd ed.). London: Sage.

Hesmondhalgh, D., & Baker, S. (2011). *Creative labour.* London: Macmillan.

Keat, R. (1991). Consumer sovereignty and the integrity of practices. In R. Keat & N. Abercrombie (Eds.), *Enterprise culture* (pp. 216–230). London: Routledge.

Keat, R. (1994). Scepticism, authority, and the market. In R. Keat, N. Whiteley, & N. Abercrombie (Eds.), *The authority of the consumer* (pp. 23–24). London: Routledge.

Keat, R. (2000). *Cultural goods and the limits of the market.* Basingstoke: Palgrave Macmillan.

Keat, R. (2008a). Practices, firms and varieties of capitalism. *Philosophy of Management, 7*(1), 77–91.

Keat, R. (2008b). Social criticism and the exclusion of ethics. *Analyse und Kritik, 30*(2), 291–315.

Keat, R. (2009). Anti-perfectionism, market economics and the right to meaningful work. *Analyse und Kritik, 31*(1), 121–138.

Keat, R. (2011a). Liberalism, neutrality and varieties of capitalism. In N. H. Smith & J.-P. Deranty (Eds.), *New philosophies of labour* (pp. 347–370). Leiden: Brill.

Keat, R. (2011b). Political philosophy and public service broadcasting. *Public Reason, 3*(2), 61–79.

Keat, R. (2012). Market limits and their limits. *Economics and Philosophy*, 28(2), 251–263.

Keat, R. (2013). The ethical character of market institutions. In M. Del Mar & C. Michelon (Eds.), *The anxiety of the jurist* (pp. 173–194). Farnham: Ashgate.

Keat, R. (2015). Towards a critical ethical economy. In A. Bielskis & K. Knight (Eds.), *Virtue and economy* (pp. 191–211). Farnham: Ashgate.

Leys, C. (2001). *Market-driven politics: Neoliberal democracy and the public interest*. London: Verso.

Lukes, S. (2005). Invasions of the market. In M. Miller (Ed.), *Worlds of capitalism* (pp. 298–314). New York: Routledge.

MacIntyre, A. (1985 [1981]). *After virtue: A study in moral theory* (2nd ed.). London: Duckworth.

MacIntyre, A. (1994). A partial response to my critics. In J. Horton & S. Mendus (Eds.), *After MacIntyre: Critical perspectives on the work of Alasdair MacIntyre* (pp. 283–304). Cambridge: Polity Press.

McGuigan, J. (1996). *Culture and the public sphere*. London: Routledge.

Mepham, J. (1990). The ethics of quality in television. In G. Mulgan (Ed.), *The question of quality* (pp. 56–72). London: British Film Institute.

Miller, D. (1990). *Market, state, and community*. Oxford: Oxford University Press.

Miller, D. (1994). Virtues, practices and justice. In J. Horton & S. Mendus (Eds.), *After MacIntyre: Critical perspectives on the work of Alasdair MacIntyre* (pp. 245–264). Cambridge: Polity.

Murdoch, I. (1982). Philosophy and literature: Dialogue with Iris Murdoch. In B. Magee (Ed.), *Men of ideas* (pp. 262–284). Oxford: Oxford University Press.

Nove, A. (1983). *The economics of feasible socialism*. London: George Allen & Unwin.

Nussbaum, M. (1990). Aristotelian social democracy. In R. B. Douglas, G. M. Mara, & H. S. Richardson (Eds.), *Liberalism and the good* (pp. 203–252). New York: Routledge.

Nussbaum, M. (2000). *Women and human development: The capabilities approach*. Cambridge: Cambridge University Press.

O'Neill, J. (1998). *The market: Ethics, knowledge and politics*. London: Routledge.

Rawls, J. (1971). *A theory of justice*. Oxford: Oxford University Press.

Raz, J. (1986). *The morality of freedom*. Oxford: Clarendon.

Selucky, R. (1979). *Marxism, socialism, freedom*. London: Macmillan.

Sher, G. (1997). *Beyond neutrality: Perfectionism and politics*. Cambridge: Cambridge University Press.

Wall, S. (1998). *Liberalism, perfectionism and restraint*. Cambridge: Cambridge University Press.

Walzer, M. (1983). *Spheres of justice*. New York: Basic Books.

CHAPTER 8

In Defence of Meaningful Work as a Public Policy Concern

Keith Breen

Now it is a good and desirable thing, truly, to make many pins in a day; but if we could only see with what crystal sand their points were polished – sand of the human soul, much to be magnified before it can be discerned for what it is – we should think that there might be some loss in it also (Ruskin 2007 [1853], p. 165).

In the above oft-quoted lines, John Ruskin raised as a question of public concern the wide-ranging impact of the work people do on their lives and characters. Like Adam Smith (1979 [1776], p. 782) before him, who in his ambivalent account of the modern division of labour condemned this division for rendering workers 'as stupid and ignorant as it is possible for a human creature to become', Ruskin deplored the damaging effects of meaningless, alienated work on the human personality, deeming it scandalous and unnecessary. To his mind, the possibility of enjoying meaningful work was both a defining mark of the good society and a reasonable expectation of all.

In this chapter, I wish to lend support to Ruskin's argument. I do so by challenging three distinct claims to the effect that the demand for meaningful work, grounded upon an ethical ideal of such work as partly constitutive

K. Breen
Queen's University, Belfast, Northern Ireland

© The Editor(s) (if applicable) and The Author(s) 2016
A. Fives, K. Breen (eds.), *Philosophy and Political Engagement*,
DOI 10.1057/978-1-137-44587-2_8

of a good human life, is either not a *significant*, not a *feasible*, or not an *acceptable* concern of public policy in liberal capitalist societies. These different claims against institutionalizing an ethic of meaningful work in capitalist market economies are underpinned, I suggest, by three variously influential organizing narratives relating to the role of ethical norms within economic relations or within public deliberation over these relations. The claim from insignificance operates in accordance with a narrative of *effacement*, which holds, as exemplified in Jürgen Habermas's social theory, that the modern economic realm is governed by market and organizational imperatives wherein ethical norms and values have little or no factual purchase. The claim from unfeasibility, differently, hinges upon a narrative of *impossibility*, namely, that the normative order of advanced capitalism, while defined by ethical values of a sort, is inimical to the realization of genuinely meaningful work. Key theorists advancing this view include Max Weber and, more importantly for my purposes, Alasdair MacIntyre. The third claim, that an ethical ideal of meaningful work is an unacceptable concern for public policy design, rests in contrast upon a narrative of *exclusion* advanced by some liberal theorists committed to state neutrality over conceptions of the good. As argued by Will Kymlicka and others, meaningful work is, under this perspective, a real good that many citizens properly aspire to, but a good that ought not to be privileged over other goods and which should therefore be excluded from public justifications of and arguments for economic policy.

In what follows, I argue that these three narratives are unconvincing, that meaningful work remains a significant, feasible, and acceptable public policy issue. I begin, however, by clarifying the concept of 'meaningful work' intended here and the specific goods associated with it.

1   What is 'Meaningful Work'?

It is necessary to be precise as regards the sense of meaningfulness entailed by the concept of 'meaningful work', since work can be experienced as meaningful along a number of discrete dimensions. For instance, we may experience our work as meaningful on account of the wider social ends it serves, such as advancing a worthy cause or fulfilling an essential social function, even when the work itself holds few other attractions. Alternatively, we may derive genuine meaning from our social relations at work, taking pleasure in the camaraderie, feeling of solidarity, and opportunities for play in an otherwise unappealing workplace. Or we may, quite differently, view our work as meaningful solely on account of the external goods that contingently accrue from it, the money, power, or status it grants us.[1]

All these dimensions are important. We typically, and rightly, view work that has no social purpose, that is characterized by negative social relations, or that does not give rise to sufficient external goods as bad work, to be avoided where possible. However, the dimension of meaningfulness of primary significance in the concept of 'meaningful work', as well as the value attaching to such meaningfulness, is different from these other dimensions in arising from the content and conduct of work, the *intrinsic* characteristics of work as experienced by workers. Following Richard Arneson, we can define 'meaningful work' along this intrinsic dimension as 'work that is interesting, that calls for intelligence and initiative, and that is attached to a job that gives the worker considerable freedom to decide how the work is to be done' (Arneson 1987, p. 522). Meaningful work, so defined, has sui generis value in facilitating the enjoyment of (at least) three goods internal to the work itself. First, in allowing for considerable discretion in the conduct of work, meaningful work grants workers significant decision-making powers and thus freedom understood in the Kantian sense of self-determination and autonomy. Second, in requiring the exercise of intelligence and initiative, meaningful work also involves the acquisition of significant levels of skill and the development of workers' capacities. It therefore allows for individual freedom understood in the Aristotelian sense of self-realization, that is, of workers having the opportunity to exercise and advance their potentialities and talents. The third internal good associated with meaningful work, gestured to by Arneson's inclusion of the word 'interesting' in his definition, is the experience of the unique value of a specific way of life—whether that of a carpenter, teacher, or scientist—and the gradual cultivation of a professional identity in which individuals can take pride.

Although people's understandings of a particular job will vary, it would be a mistake to conceive of meaningful work as a subjective category dependent upon individual preferences that are unamenable to intersubjective assessment (Hsieh 2008, p. 75). Against subjectivist perspectives, the intrinsic meaningfulness of work is objectively ascertainable in terms, for example, of the level of initiative permitted, the educational and skills base required, the authority relations in operation, and whether the work enables or impedes the development of a professional identity. We can see this if we compare meaningful work with work as experienced under the modern 'detailed division of labour', in which work processes are divided up into discrete tasks and workers assigned to a limited number of these tasks.[2] Jobs structured in accordance with the detailed division of labour— including line assembly and manufacture, numerous service occupations, much clerical work, and so forth—are guided by organizational principles that together represent the antithesis of meaningful work. As explained by Harry Braverman (1998, pp. 77–83), the first of these principles dictates the disconnection of work from the proficiencies and knowledge of workers, with the result that worker expertise ceases to be essential. A second principle entails the separation of 'conception', the design of work processes, from 'execution', the act of carrying these out, and a consequent division between managers and engineers, on the one hand, and the mass of workers, on the other. A further principle, following the second, stipulates precise managerial oversight of all phases of a standardized work process. Objectively viewed, the degrading effects of these principles on workers are clear: the loss of an understanding of and control over the conduct of work, the acquisition of, at best, minimal skills, and the reduction of work to the performance of routine tasks. And ethically viewed, such work can be condemned, as it was condemned by Ruskin, precisely because it denies workers the internal goods of autonomy, self-realization, and professional self-respect definitive of meaningful work.[3]

2   NARRATIVES OF EFFACEMENT

One way in which the demand for meaningful work as a reasonable expectation suffers suppression is through the acceptance of visions of the economic realm which accord that realm little ethical significance in and of itself. Despite being conceived as a critical analysis of modern society with emancipatory intent, Jürgen Habermas's (1987a) mature social theory espouses a vision of this sort. My argument here is that this theory and its organizing narrative should be rejected for mischaracterizing economic life as largely independent of ethical norms and for thereby veiling or effacing the normative landscape of existing economies.[4]

Making this argument, however, requires first ascertaining why Habermas characterizes economic life in the way he does. Underlying Habermas's conception of the economic realm is a critique of Marx. Although wishing to retain historical materialism in substantially revised form, he reproaches Marx's *praxis* philosophy for equating emancipatory human activity with 'social labour'. The effect of this mistaken equation, Habermas claims, is a reduction of social reality to economic endeavour and the technical forces of production underpinning the economic sphere. While not Marx's intention, his elevation of social labour 'could very quickly be misinterpreted in a mechanistic manner' in which the movement of history is conceived primarily in terms of material causal laws (Habermas 1973, p. 169). Confusing social emancipation with technological progress, this misinterpretation in turn lends plausibility to the belief in technological determinism and technocracy: if the movement of history is impelled by material causal laws, then those with knowledge of these mechanisms should alone rule. The threatened conclusion is a 'scientization' of politics, the identification of political activity with expert administration, and thus a denial of the moral-ethical content of socio-political life, the demand that citizens be positioned to freely deliberate over and determine their collective futures (Habermas 1971).

To preserve the moral-ethical dimension of socio-political life, Habermas advances a two-level theory of society grounded on a distinction between 'labour', on the one hand, and 'interaction', on the other. Labour signifies the material reproduction of our species, our attempt to dominate and harness nature, while interaction signifies our social reproduction, the linguistic co-generation of a shared way of life. As separate ways of relating to lived existence, labour and interaction correspond to Habermas's basic division between 'instrumental' and 'communicative action' (Habermas 1973, pp. 168–9). When acting instrumentally, we reason in terms of the criteria of efficiency and success as to the best means to our individual ends, viewing objects and people as means to those ends. Communicative action, in contrast, is steered by the internal end of mutual understanding, where actors reason dialogically in accordance with intersubjective validity claims—truth, rightness, and truthfulness—with the aspiration of arriving at 'rationally motivated assent' (Habermas 1984, pp. 287, 329).

Based on this division between action types, Habermas distinguishes two forms of world-historical development, 'lifeworld' and 'systemic' rationalization. By 'lifeworld' he intends the intersubjective horizon in which human beings live, act, and interact. Lifeworld rationalization entails that the symbolic achievements of cultural knowledge transmission, social integration, and identity formation, the core elements of a genuinely human life, increasingly issue more from 'communicatively achieved understanding' than from custom or 'traditionally certified interpretations immune from criticism' (Habermas 1984, p. 340). Systemic rationalization, by contrast, refers to the accelerating material productivity and formal organization of social orders, the defining feature of which is not communication but rather the 'complexity' of institutions that function according to an instrumental, impersonal logic (Habermas 1987a, p. 173). As Habermas sees them, both forms of rationalization represent major civilizational advances—lifeworld rationalization enabling freer, more accountable ways of intersubjective life, systemic rationalization bringing greater productivity and organizational efficiency—yet they remain irreducible to one another, operating in accordance with distinct principles.

A key aim of Habermas's social theory is thus to illuminate how in modernity, 'system' fused into domains of 'norm-free sociality' that split off or 'uncoupled' from the 'lifeworld' institutions of the family, civil society, and the public sphere (Habermas 1987a, pp. 154, 171). In accounting for this uncoupling, Habermas makes very strong claims. Propelled by a depersonalized strategic rationality working behind the backs of actors, the sub-systems of the capitalist market economy and bureaucratic state are now, he maintains, 'regulated only via power and money'. Indeed, within these spheres the 'norm-conformative attitudes and identity-forming social memberships' definitive of the lifeworld 'are neither necessary nor possible', being instead rendered 'peripheral' (Habermas 1987a, p. 154). For Habermas, the fact of 'norm-free sociality' is not in itself problematic, since systemic rationalization is functionally necessary, the modern market and bureaucratic state being the sole means by which to facilitate economic exchange and to coordinate policy. Yet systemic imperatives become damaging when they reach into and alter lifeworld structures, transforming citizens into 'clients' and individuals into 'consumers'. This systemic 'colonization' has detrimental effects because communal and individual life are then no longer shaped by communicative intersubjective will and are instead experienced as uncontrollable and alien (Habermas 1987a, pp. 332–78). A critical politics should seek to render systemic imperatives less destructive of lifeworld relations, but as a result of uncoupling this politics must nonetheless be self-limiting and respect the inner workings of the capitalist market economy. Rather than attempting to democratize or humanize system 'from within', which is no longer possible, the goal should be to curb or channel it toward an 'equilibrium' with lifeworld spheres (Habermas 1992, p. 444).

The narrative woven by Habermas is prompted by real concerns. Marx, for example, assuredly erred in reducing self-transformative human activity to social labour—a reduction which fails to register the plurality of ways in which human beings relate to their world—and it is likewise wrong to equate social emancipation with technological progress and increasing material prosperity. Habermas's colonization thesis also rightly highlights the dangers posed to individual freedom and the fabric of interpersonal relationships by the creeping expansion of market and bureaucratic imperatives into social life. However, the manner in which Habermas addresses these concerns remains very much questionable, not least on account of his claim that the economic realm represents a realm of 'norm-free sociality'. For with this claim, the ideal of meaningful work disappears entirely from our normative vocabulary, and this for two reasons. Most obviously, in identifying labour and economic life with instrumental action and the manipulation of nature, Habermas relegates work to a means-end category whose value resides solely in the products or commodities produced. He thus disregards from the outset that work might have intrinsic value as well, either as a source of ethical aspiration or as a mode of activity through which individual identities are formed.[5] This foreshortening finds reinforcement, in addition, from a dualistic separation of lifeworld from system—the former sphere of human existence governed by communicative reason and moral-ethical norms, the other by a strategic rationality wherein moral-ethical norms appear at best 'peripheral'—that results in economic life as a whole being denied any immanent ethical content.

Of course, Habermas's instrumental vision of work and of the economy as a whole hinges on the plausibility of his 'norm-free sociality' thesis, which we have very good reason to doubt. As argued by John Sitton and others, the problem with this thesis is that, in casting the economic order as largely norm-free, it 'distorts the actual workings of the capitalist economy' by failing 'to recognize the multiples ways in which the economy is "anchored" in the lifeworld' via moral-ethical norms and expectations.[6] The normative anchoring or enmeshment of the economy in lifeworld structures is in fact apparent on a number of levels. The most basic concerns norms that enable and underpin economic exchange. If Habermas is to be believed, economic exchange is primarily coordinated by the delinguistified medium of money, whose imperatives operate unperceived behind the backs of actors. Yet this is belied by the market's dependence on these actors exhibiting and expecting from each other determinate normative attitudes and behaviours. Durkheim (1964 [1893]), for example, made clear that the mechanisms of contract and exchange are impossible without trust and a widespread sense of responsibility, which together sustain the shared belief that agreements will be kept. In turn, trust and a sense of responsibility are secured not only by coercive legal enforcement, since such enforcement would be of limited efficacy on its own, but also by 'feelings of solidarity' that, ideally at least, 'precede all contracts and obligate economic actors to treat each other fairly and justly' (Honneth 2014, p. 181).

Although often in practice breached, the moral-ethical underpinnings of market exchange are nonetheless real, providing key criteria by which individuals judge each other's actions in economic matters. Their reality points to a deeper, cultural level at which the market economy can again be said to rely upon lifeworld discourses and norms. The scheme of social conventions and mores that helps make capitalist exchange relatively stable and predictable renders it desirable and normal as well, transforming it over time into the 'natural' or 'appropriate' order of things. This supportive 'enterprise culture', a culture in which personal initiative, exchange, and profit-making are deemed worthy in themselves, partly explains why the market as an institution for determining equivalences between different goods and capitalism as an economic order are not subject to endemic disruption. Moreover, the enterprise culture central to modern capitalism did not just arise from functional systemic imperatives, but was also motivated by moral-ethical arguments, in particular the claim that market societies, unlike earlier household-based societies defined by rigid status hierarchies, allow for greater individual freedom and well-being. For classical liberal advocates of market societies, as clarified by Booth (1994, p. 661), the 'mode of producing and distributing the means of human sustenance embodied in the market is expressive not of a human propensity to truck, trade, and barter ... but of a moral redrawing of the community and of the place of the economy within it'. Far from being norm-free, then, every economy is at base a *moral economy*.

Sharply distinguishing system from lifeworld, Habermas is led to neglect the normative foundations of capitalism and, concomitantly, to veil important arguments against this economic order, one, of course, being that under capitalism, or specific variants thereof, the productive capacities of human beings are unnecessarily stunted and deformed. What resultantly recedes from view in Habermas's social theory is the truth that the economic realm, along with other spheres of human life, is a prime site for the formation of character, for the fostering of and conflict between rival visions of the 'good person'. Yet it is only by attending to the conflict between these rival visions that we can understand, for instance, the recent history of economic enterprises and the legitimating ethos of what Boltanski and Chiapello (2007) have dubbed the 'new spirit of capitalism'. Displacing the normative consensus definitive of the mid-twentieth century 'second spirit' of capitalism—a consensus in which the ideal employee was committed to long-term service, accepting of rational hierarchy, and secure in his position within the firm—the ideal employees of the new 'third spirit' of capitalism in evidence from the 1980s onwards are 'those who succeed in working with very different people, prove themselves open and flexible when it comes to switching project, and always manage to adapt to new circumstances' (Boltanski and Chiapello 2007, p. 92). What this history tellingly reveals is that the endurance of capitalism through time depends, again contra assertions of 'norm-free sociality', in no small part on recurrent attempts to recraft the ethical ideals people aspire to, the values they endorse, and, ultimately, their very sense of who they are.

3   Narratives of Impossibility

Together, the above observations provide sufficient grounds for asserting the intrinsic ethical salience of economic activity. Doing so, they likewise provide reasons for rejecting narratives of effacement and for thus insisting upon the significance of demands for meaningful work.

The claim that meaningful work is no longer possible clearly differs from the claim that it lacks ethical significance. Under narratives of impossibility, the demand for meaningful work is recognized as important, but deemed, given the reality of contemporary conditions, unrealizable for all but a small minority of people. A vivid statement of this view appears in the concluding pages of Weber's *The Protestant Ethic and the Spirit of Capitalism*, where 'the tremendous cosmos of the modern economic order ... [and] the technical and economic conditions of machine production' are said now to govern the lives of men and women 'with irresistible force'. What Weber laments in those pages is the extension of the detailed division of labour into all forms of work and socio-economic activity, with the result that individuals are increasingly condemned to 'mechanized petrification', to a meaningless, inhuman 'iron cage' (Weber 1992, pp. 123–4). The tragedy, for Weber, is that this 'iron cage' is an unavoidable consequence of modernity and, above all, modern capitalism, the underlying ethic of which has degenerated into a barbarous celebration of technical specialization and hedonistic consumerism.

A similarly pessimistic vision of the present is advanced by Alasdair MacIntyre in his magnum opus, *After Virtue* (1985). Unlike the case with Habermas, however, the value of work in ordinary people's lives figures prominently within MacIntyre's thought. Indeed, the idea of 'practices' underpinning his ethical and social theory has proven a valuable resource both for thematizing the conditions and features of meaningful work and for furnishing criteria in terms of which we can analyse existing work arrangements.[7] In proving so, it has also lent additional credence to the contention that the opportunity to enjoy meaningful work is a reasonable expectation.

The range of activities identifiable as 'practices' is broad, including sciences, arts, games, and childrearing, as well as occupations such as farming, manufacture, and construction. Yet not all activities can be so identified—filing invoices, kitchen portering, line assembly, and so forth—since they lack the internal structure definitive of practices, properly viewed. As defined by MacIntyre, a practice is:

> any coherent and complex form of socially established cooperative human activity through which goods internal to that form of activity are realized in the course of trying to achieve those standards of excellence which are appropriate to, and partially definitive of, that form of activity, with the result that human powers to achieve excellence, and human conceptions of the ends and goods involved, are systematically extended (MacIntyre 1985, p. 187).

The key terms here are 'cooperative human activity', 'goods internal', and 'standards of excellence', terms which further illuminate the sui generis goods of meaningful work discussed above. As cooperative human activities, practices represent communal endeavours involving not merely the participation of individuals, but also their engagement in a 'tradition' or history that informs and directs their actions. All practices, from architecture to carpentry, are therefore inspired by principles, standards, and bodies of expertise transmitted from one generation to another. Furthermore, each practice has particular 'internal goods' that should not be confused with generic 'external goods'. The external goods of money, power, and status are goods attainable through any activity—whether monotonous drudgery or the opportunistic manipulation of others—whereas internal goods are specific to individual practices and can be achieved only through sustained immersion in these practices themselves. The 'aim internal to productive crafts' is 'never only to catch fish, or to produce beef, or to build houses' in the hope of becoming wealthy or powerful. Instead, it is to strive 'in a manner consonant with the excellence of the craft', so that 'not only is there a good product, but the craftsperson is perfected through and in her or his activity' (MacIntyre 1994, p. 284). These internal goods of quality products and of the gradual perfection of practitioners require, in turn, attentiveness to shared standards of excellence that establish the goal of a practice, its ultimate purpose, and regulate how it is carried out. And such attentiveness presumes, over and above deference to established standards, the cultivation of personal virtues—honesty in conceding one's limitations, justice in acknowledging the achievements of others, and courage in experiencing failure—which sustain trust and enable future progress within that practice.

In this account, the goods of self-determination, self-realization, and the development of a professional identity characteristic of meaningful work are central. Experienced as a practice, work requires intelligence and judgement in reflecting upon standards of excellence, necessitates the acquisition and exercise of considerable skill and knowledge, and involves a basic transformation of character, the movement from novice to master practitioner through an extended educational process undergirded by shared values. Attending to these integral features of practice-like work, we can appreciate the ethical complexity of this activity and, hence, realize the basic error of Habermas's instrumental conception of labour.

Yet, for MacIntyre in *After Virtue* at least, the 'work done by the vast majority of the inhabitants of the modern world cannot be understood in terms of the nature of a practice with goods internal to itself'.[8] A major reason for this is the historic movement from premodern production within the household to modern production within the disembedded capitalist economy. With the household economy, work was an essential part of a broader practice of sustaining families and their communities. But as it moved outside the household and was 'put to the service of impersonal capital', it became 'separated from everything but the service of biological survival and the reproduction of the labor force, on the one hand, and that of institutionalized acquisitiveness, on the other'. This is is so because, under modern capitalism, the erstwhile vice of '*pleonexia*', avarice, gradually came to be seen as a virtue, with the necessary yet perverse result that ruthless competition rather than cooperation, short-term profit seeking rather than long-term commitment to a craft or profession, are now presumed commendable. As exemplified by production line assembly, modern work is primarily driven, for workers as well as their managers, by a concern with the external good of money, the chance for meaningful work having retreated 'to the margins of social and cultural life' (MacIntyre 1985, p. 227). Consequently, if we hope to locate and foster genuine examples of practice-like work, we need to look to local communities and associations that stand outside the capitalist order and reject its assumptions.[9]

This is a decidedly bleak view. If an accurate portrayal, then for most people in modern societies the hope of enjoying meaningful work would seem chimerical. In such circumstances, anyone who claimed otherwise would be guilty of dishonesty, of masking the alienated nature of work in the modern economy and deceiving others as to this truth. However, the accuracy of MacIntyre's view depends on whether his answers to two underlying empirical questions are also accurate. Should these answers be moot, then the hope for wider enjoyment of meaningful work might not appear self-deluding.

The first question concerns his general understanding of premodernity and modernity and what happened in the move from one to the other. MacIntyre's main claim here is that with the move to production outside the household, the availability of practice-like work substantially diminished. This claim seems to hinge, in part, on the historical expansion of the detailed division of labour in modern industries as documented by Ruskin and, later, Weber. But while the growth of the detailed division of labour in modernity is undoubtedly real, it gives us little ground for believing either that household economies were more favourable to practices or that their availability in the modern present is less than in premodern times. A first point to recognize is that the principles underpinning the detailed division of labour are not uniquely modern, but have roots stretching back to classical antiquity, as forcefully demonstrated by James Bernard Murphy (1993, p. 24) in his analysis of the social division of labour articulated in Plato's *Republic*. Thus, while the tendencies towards the degradation of work may have accelerated in modernity, these are venerable Western tendencies observable in premodern cultures, too. An additional, more telling, reason for questioning the privileging of premodernity over modernity concerns the unjust status hierarchies prevalent in household economies. It is certainly true that some forms of work, such as manufacture, experienced by many today as alienating had once a practice-like character, but it is also true that whole categories of people—women, serfs, the poor—were denied access to them by institutions such as the medieval guild. Much of the work undertaken by premodern people would therefore not have been practice-like, indeed quite the contrary. We should acknowledge here, as well, that with its rejection of premodern status hierarchies in the name of universal freedom and equality and the gradual extension of educational provision to all citizens, modernity, albeit very imperfectly, allowed for and enabled the widespread flourishing of many other practices, including science, engineering, and the arts (Miller 1994, pp. 258–60). Given this, it would not be altogether mistaken to believe the modern age, despite the spread of the detailed division of labour in various occupations, more receptive to the ideal of meaningful work than the ages preceding it.

The second question relates to MacIntyre's understanding of capitalism. Extrapolating from his discussion in *After Virtue*, that understanding fits most closely with capitalism as found within the 'liberal market economies' (LMEs) of, for instance, the USA, Britain, and Canada. In LMEs, capitalism is defined, roughly speaking, by shareholder concern with the short-term profitability of firms ('impatient capital'), tight managerial control of internal governance and production, competition rather than cooperation between firms, and employees' possession of generic, rather than industry-specific, skills (Hall and Soskice 2001). Because preoccupied with profitability, allowing lesser levels of discretion for workers in comparison to managers, and tending to foster transferable skills not specific to any one profession, capitalism in this guise can readily be thought unconducive to practice-like work. But it is essential to recognize that liberal market capitalism is only *one* form of capitalism and that there are other institutional forms which may be more favourable to maintaining work as a practice. This argument has been made by Russell Keat in relation to capitalism as organized in the 'coordinated market economies' (CMEs) of Germany and other continental European states. The defining features of CMEs, in contrast to LMEs, are shareholder concern with firms' long-term prospects ('patient capital'), shared internal governance between management and workers via supervisory boards and work councils, competition tempered by cooperation between firms within sectors, and the provision of industry-specific vocational training through professional associations.[10] This combination of factors, Keat (2008a, pp. 80–6; see also Chap. 7) persuasively shows, helps explain the focus on product quality, the relatively high levels of worker skill and workplace autonomy, and the strong sense of professional identity—all aspects of work when experienced as a practice—in evidence in CMEs. The salutary lesson worth learning from the differences between LMEs and CMEs is not just that capitalism is protean or varied, but also that the possibility of meaningful work depends greatly on the institutional contexts at hand and that these contexts, since partly created through conscious choice, are not impervious to positive change.

We have good reason, therefore, to question some of the empirical assumptions impelling MacIntyre's—and Weber's—account of the present, and it is important, practically, that we do question them. For although otherwise at odds, the narratives offered by Habermas and MacIntyre have a similarly disempowering effect, since both screen from view opportunities for transforming the present. In Habermas's case, this arises from his denial of the ethical content of economic life, whereas with MacIntyre, it results from a totalizing vision of modernity. A less jaundiced perspective reveals scope for preserving practice-like work and for reordering occupations that had previously succumbed to the detailed division of labour. Even in that occupation cited by MacIntyre as an exemplar of degraded work, production line assembly, it has proven possible to reconfigure work processes in ways ensuring and requiring considerable levels of worker discretion and vocational skill, as the innovations in Volvo's Uddevalla automotive plant show (Berggren 1992; Breen 2012). Thus, while it may eventually turn out that meaningful work is not feasible within the modern economic order, we are not yet at that juncture or anywhere near it.

4   NARRATIVES OF EXCLUSION

The argument that the ideal of meaningful work represents an unacceptable concern of public policy neither denies the ethical significance of that ideal nor takes a stance on its current viability. Instead, it rests on the normative claim that this ideal ought not to be a policy concern for the reason that ethical ideals, or 'conceptions of the good', in general ought to be excluded from public decision-making and justifications of state action in societies purporting to respect individual liberty and value pluralism. This principled exclusion of ethics is the core tenet of the 'neutralist liberalism' advocated by Will Kymlicka (2002) and provides the basis for his dismissal of meaningful work as a political issue.[11] Here I briefly set out Kymlicka's neutralist liberal theory and understanding of the good of meaningful work. I then move to explain why we should reject that theory and understanding.

According to neutralist liberals, what is distinctive about liberalism as a political philosophy is that it precludes people, in their role as citizens and legislators, from employing governmental powers to support any one 'conception of the good' or view of what has value in human life. Conceived as attention to questions of the good life, ethical debate is an ineliminable part of the human condition and entirely appropriate within interpersonal relationships and 'the cultural marketplace of civil society' (Kymlicka 2002, p. 248). Within those relationships and that marketplace, individuals can, in line with the liberal principle of self-determination or autonomy, decide for themselves what their good consists in. However, regard for the principle of self-determination also furnishes, Kymlicka argues, the reason why we should eschew political perfectionism and 'endorse a "neutral state"' that excludes ethics from politics. Such a state respects individual autonomy and freedom of choice insofar as it 'does not justify its actions on the basis of the intrinsic superiority or inferiority of conceptions of the good life, and ... does not deliberately attempt to influence people's judgements of the value of these different conceptions' (Kymlicka 2002, p. 217; see also Dworkin 1978, p. 127). States that disregard this injunction and act upon ideals of the good both offend against the principle of autonomy and fail to treat all citizens equally in favouring some conceptions of the good over others. To protect freedom and equality, governmental action and political discourse should thus be limited to issues of justice or 'the right'—individual rights and liberties, equality of opportunity, fair distributions of resources, et cetera—and scrupulously avoid pronouncing on what makes life worth living.

It is through this normative demarcation of the appropriate boundaries of political action and deliberation that Kymlicka considers the good of meaningful work. He acknowledges meaningful work as a human good and source of value for many people. Yet the key point, he insists, 'is not whether unalienated labour is a good, but whether it is an overriding good, a good which is necessary to any decent life, and which outweighs in value all competing goods' (Kymlicka 2002, p. 192). Against Marx and those who accord unalienated labour evaluative primacy, meaningful work should not be thought an overriding good, but instead simply as one good among a plurality of human goods contending for our allegiance. Given the reality of value pluralism, 'I may value unalienated labour, yet value other things even more, such as my leisure. I may prefer playing tennis to unalienated production' (Kymlicka 2002, p. 191). Furthermore, we may quite reasonably wish to sacrifice the opportunity for meaningful work in order to satisfy preferences of greater consequence to us in our lives. There is nothing objectionable, Kymlicka contends, in people carrying out monotonous work in exchange for higher wages so as to facilitate their interest in consumer goods and services, whether fine cuisine or expensive holidays. A perfectionist politics seeking to promote the good of meaningful work through a coercive 'prohibition on alienated labour' would therefore 'unfairly privilege some people over others', casting their preferences as less worthy than those endorsed by the state, and represent 'an illegitimate restriction on self-determination' (Kymlicka 2002, pp. 193, 214).

The preference for meaningful work is, then, just one preference among many and ought not to be advantaged over alternative preferences. Kymlicka nonetheless thinks that democratic institutions do have certain responsibilities in relation to the world of work, for under capitalism many people who desire meaningful work are, through no fault of their own, unable to enjoy that good, being forced by circumstances to engage in uninteresting, and often poorly remunerated and demeaning, jobs. Yet the '"solution to this problem is not to privilege anybody's preferences ... but to tinker with the distribution of resources that individuals bring to market trading"' (Kymlicka 2002, pp. 194–5, citing Arneson 1987, p. 537). In other words, as regards the workplace the only duty we as political agents have is to ensure that jobs are at least minimally just or decent and that all individuals possess the material and related resources necessary for them to compete equally in the pursuit of their varying preferences and goals.

The worries motivating Kymlicka's defence of the principle of state neutrality are genuine worries. With him, we have grounds to fear the oppression and discrimination that result when extreme perfectionist ideologies harness state agencies to enforce compliance with their visions of the good. Similarly, value pluralism is not merely a fact of human existence, but also a desirable aspect of that existence to be preserved against those who would claim there is only one worthy mode of life. However, neither point justifies state neutrality over the good or the claim that the good of meaningful work lies beyond the bounds of political deliberation. This is because Kymlicka's narrative of exclusion stands open to criticism on three counts: for misappreciating the import of work in contemporary societies, for failing to register the links between the experience of work and individual autonomy, and for courting inconsistency in denying the appropriateness of perfectionist considerations in political decision-making.

As regards the first criticism, Kymlicka, we saw, regards work and the desire for unalienated labour as merely one activity and preference, of no greater import than the preference for various forms of leisure or consumption. However, while we may agree that meaningful work is not an overriding good, since there is no one overriding good, we should nevertheless recognize that work has features, neglected by Kymlicka, which clearly differentiate it in significance from leisure and consumption activities. One obvious differentiating feature is that work in contemporary societies is an activity in which nearly all adults, so as to support themselves and their dependents, *have* to engage. Unlike the discretionary activity of playing tennis, as made clear by Roessler (2012, p. 79; see also Veltman 2015, p. 738), work can thus be said to be 'special and necessary at least in this sense: we can have preferences for different forms of work, but we cannot have the preference not to work'. A related differentiating feature concerns how work is typically viewed in our societies. We often admire those who excel in their hobbies, praising their volley shot or sophisticated appreciation of wine, but it would be odd for us to think they are obligated to partake in these hobbies. Yet this is precisely what most of us do think as regards the activity of work. Few people, and even fewer political philosophers, 'regard the willingness to work as a mere preference', considering it instead as 'a kind of social obligation', a duty based on the idea that one should play one's part in a mutually beneficial 'system of social cooperation' (Muirhead 2004, pp. 17–8). The widely shared belief that participation in work fulfils a social duty is one reason why work tends to carry more normative weight than leisure pursuits in our assessments of others. It also explains the centrality of the work we do—or do not do—in our self-assessments and estimation of own worth.[12]

If most people must work, if we generally think work is something we ought to engage in, and if working activity figures centrally in our judgements of our peers and of ourselves, then it would not be unreasonable to suggest that the nature and content of the work people must and should do is an appropriate subject of political deliberation. An even more telling ground for thinking this, and which underpins the second complaint against Kymlicka, relates to the formative role of work in terms of our personalities and wider lives. Numerous empirical studies confirm Adam Smith's and Ruskin's insight that the experience of work under the detailed division of labour has a deleterious impact upon workers' psychological and physical well-being, this impact affecting their prospects and relationships in other spheres of life.[13] Kymlicka (2002, p. 191) endorses those findings, declaring 'the "degradation of labour" which capitalism has imposed on many people' to be 'abhorrent, an unconscionable restriction on their ability to develop their human potential'. And yet he fails to recognize the implications of that endorsement for reflection upon the value of work and for his own normative position. As pointed out by Adina Schwartz (1982, pp. 637–8; see also Roessler 2012, pp. 81–5), the conclusion empirical research guides us to is that a fundamental problem with work which affords individuals 'almost no opportunities for rationally framing, adjusting, and pursuing their own plans' is that it gradually causes these individuals 'to lead less autonomous lives on the whole'. In short, alienated labour not only restricts human potential, our capacity for self-realization, but also hinders our capacity to lead a self-determined life, and it is this latter capacity, of course, which lies at the heart of Kymlicka's liberalism.

The threats posed by meaningless work to autonomous personhood thus provide additional reason to believe we, as political agents, have a legitimate interest in the content of work. We should acknowledge, however, that that interest requires more than equality of access or resources for all individuals in the play of 'market trading', since if left to its own devices the market may very well yield insufficient opportunities for people to take up meaningful work (Keat 2009, pp. 134–7). Instead, it requires attention to and promotion of institutional structures that are conducive to meaningful work.

The need to promote institutional structures conducive to meaningful work brings us to the third criticism of neutralist liberalism as defended by Kymlicka. Although hostile to perfectionism, he does concur with Joseph Raz's (1986, pp. 162, 369–99) claim that a precondition of being able to exercise our autonomy at all is having meaningful options or 'valuable forms of life' to choose from. He concurs, as well, that we cannot simply rely on the interplay of the 'cultural marketplace' to satisfy this precondition, but must instead task public bodies with the responsibility of ensuring 'people have a valuable range of options' (Kymlicka 2002, p. 247). But averring that we have a political responsibility to safeguard valuable options destabilizes Kymlicka's neutralist stance on meaningful work and rejection of political perfectionism in two ways. First, if meaningful work is a valuable option, which it assuredly is, and if the liberal state should intervene to guarantee the availability of valuable options, then the ethical preference for meaningful work is one that should in some way be advantaged by the state over options deemed trivial or less valuable, though not over options deemed similarly valuable. This clearly sits ill with Kymlicka's contention that no ethical preference or conception of the good ought to be intentionally privileged by governmental action. Second, ensuring the existence of a 'valuable range of options' necessarily requires prior consideration of the comparative value of candidate options for that range, that is, deciding between those options which warrant inclusion and those which do not.[14] But if this is so, then perfectionist considerations as to 'the intrinsic superiority or inferiority' of different preferences—what is good, what is not, what should be promoted, what should not—cannot be excluded from political deliberation, and ethics, contra neutralist liberalism, cannot therefore be excluded from politics.

These arguments against the neutralist liberal narrative of exclusion may not be conclusive, but they do go some way to lessen its plausibility. Its plausibility is further weakened once we recognize the exaggeration involved in claiming that the perfectionist promotion of meaningful work necessarily threatens unfair treatment of citizens and the coercive imposition of one conception of the good. Far from being unfair, the promotion of meaningful work aims to augment people's freedom by increasing the availability of a relatively scarce and yet important social good. And far from coercively imposing one way of life, the moderate perfectionism underlying that aim simply seeks to reduce the incidence of alienated labour in our societies.[15]

5 CONCLUSION

My goal here has been to challenge assertions to the effect that the call for meaningful work is not a significant, a feasible, or an acceptable focus for public policy. Beyond this, a lot more remains to be said. I have said very little about how we might go about fostering the good of meaningful work: what tasks the state might undertake, what tasks should be left to non-state institutions, the role of background cultures and different educational systems in supporting this good, and so forth. Nor have I addressed other reasons some might cite in dismissing arguments for institutionalizing meaningful work, including the suspicion that these arguments are vulnerable to cooption by employers and managers with the intention of getting workers to work ever harder. Yet, despite these limitations, I hope to have shown that the scope for reflecting upon and institutionally facilitating meaningful work is greater than sometimes supposed.[16]

NOTES

1. On the various dimensions of meaningfulness attaching to work, see Yeoman (2014, pp. 8–38). On the distinction between 'external' and 'internal goods', see MacIntyre (1985, pp. 187–197) and Sect. 3 below.
2. See Smith's (1979 [1776], pp. 13–24) analysis of pin production for a classic account of the detailed division of labour.
3. It is worth distinguishing the demand for meaningful work from the demand for 'decent work', that is, work characterized by proper remuneration, safe

working conditions, fair employment practices, et cetera (see ILO 2015). Although these demands are related, they remain distinct: one can have decent work that provides little scope for autonomy or individual flourishing, and meaningful work that is poorly remunerated and undertaken in dangerous environments.

4. In this section I draw on earlier analyses of Habermas (Breen 2007, 2015).

5. Indeed, Habermas repeatedly rejects the view that labour or work has a normative significance comparable with that of the ideal of communicative action (see Habermas 1987a, p. 340, 1987b, pp. 63, 82, 341–49, 1991, pp. 33–4, 38).

6. Sitton (1998, p. 81). For related arguments, see Honneth (1995) and McCarthy (1991).

7. See, for instance, the discussions in Breen (2007), Keat (2000), and Muirhead (2004).

8. MacIntyre (1985, p. 227). Notice my focus here is mainly on *After Virtue*, where MacIntyre excoriates the capitalist present but denies the prospect of any wide-ranging transformation of 'the new dark ages which are already upon us' (MacIntyre 1985, p. 263). In later texts he strikes a more hopeful, and to my mind welcome, chord, arguing the capitalist economic order 'can be successfully resisted and even changed' (MacIntyre 2015, p. 17).

9. The local communities MacIntyre (1999, p. 143) refers to include New England fishing villages, Mayan towns in Mexico and Guatemala, and Welsh mining communities.

10. In comparing LMEs and CMEs, Keat (2008a, p. 80) clarifies 'that the term 'Liberal', in 'LMEs', is used in its economic [primacy of free market relations], not its political, sense'. This is an important clarification because CME societies, with regard to their support for civil rights and liberties, are politically no less liberal than LME societies.

11. I concentrate on Kymlicka for reasons of space, though he himself draws extensively upon fellow neutralist liberals, including Dworkin (1978), Arneson (1987), and Rawls (1971). My argument in this section is indebted to Keat's (2008b, 2009, 2011) critique of the attempt to exclude ethics from politics and political economy.

12. On work's role in both engendering and hindering self-esteem, see Gomberg (2007) and Lane (1991).

13. See, for instance, Hauser and Roan (2007), Kohn and Schooler (1983), and Kornhauser (1964).

14. Against the assumption (Kymlicka 2002, p. 247) that neutrality can be maintained in such decisions, Chan (2000, p. 19) makes it clear that in 'providing and supporting options, the state cannot avoid evaluating the intrinsic merit of the options'.

15. It is essential to note here that 'not all perfectionist action is a coercive imposition of a style of life. Much of it could be encouraging and facilitating action of the desired kind, or discouraging undesired modes of behaviour' (Raz 1986, p. 161). It is this moderate, liberty-preserving, perfectionism, not a coercive perfectionism, that is endorsed by most defenders of a right to meaningful work (see Keat (2011), Muirhead (2004), and Roessler (2012)).

16. I am grateful to Allyn Fives, Russell Keat, Cillian McBride, Paddy McQueen, Geoff Moore, Fabian Schuppert, and Ruth Yeoman for their discussion of the themes addressed in this chapter.

References

Arneson, R. (1987). Meaningful work and market socialism. *Ethics*, 97(3), 517–545.

Berggren, C. (1992). *The Volvo experience*. New York: ILR Press.

Boltanski, L., & Chiapello, E. (2007). *The new spirit of capitalism*. London: Verso.

Booth, W. J. (1994). On the idea of the moral economy. *American Political Science Review*, 88(3), 653–667.

Braverman, H. (1998). *Labor and monopoly capital*. New York: Monthly Review Press.

Breen, K. (2007). Work and emancipatory practice. *Res Publica*, 13(4), 381–414.

Breen, K. (2012). Production and productive reason. *New Political Economy*, 17, 611–632.

Breen, K. (2015). Freedom, democracy, and working life. In A. Azmanova & M. Mihai (Eds.), *Reclaiming democracy* (pp. 34–49). New York: Routledge.

Chan, J. (2000). Legitimacy, unanimity, and perfectionism. *Philosophy & Public Affairs*, 29(1), 5–42.

Durkheim, E. (1964 [1893]). *The division of labor in society* (G. Simpson, Trans.). New York: Free Press.

Dworkin, R. (1978). Liberalism. In S. Hampshire (Ed.), *Public and private morality* (pp. 113–143). Cambridge: Cambridge University Press.

Gomberg, P. (2007). *How to make opportunity equal*. Oxford: Blackwell Publishing.

Habermas, J. (1971). *Toward a rational society*. London: Heinemann.

Habermas, J. (1973). *Theory and practice*. Boston: Beacon Press.

Habermas, J. (1984). *The theory of communicative action: Vol. I. Reason and the rationalization of society*. Cambridge: Polity Press.

Habermas, J. (1987a). *The theory of communicative action: Vol. II: System and life-world—A critique of functionalist reason*. Cambridge: Polity Press.

Habermas, J. (1987b). *The philosophical discourse of modernity*. Cambridge: Polity Press.

Habermas, J. (1991). What does socialism mean today? The revolutions of recuperation and the need for new thinking. In R. Blackburn (Ed.), *After the fall* (pp. 25–46). London: Verso.

Habermas, J. (1992). Further reflections on the public sphere. In C. Calhoun (Ed.), *Habermas and the public sphere* (pp. 421–461). Cambridge, MA: MIT Press.

Hall, P., & Soskice, D. (2001). An introduction to varieties of capitalism. In P. Hall & D. Soskice (Eds.), *Varieties of capitalism: The institutional foundations of comparative advantage* (pp. 1–68). Oxford: Oxford University Press.

Hauser, R. M., & Roan, C. L. (2007). Work complexity and cognitive functioning at midlife. *CDE Working Paper No. 2007–08*. Retrieved July 20, 2015, from http://www.ssc.wisc.edu/cde/cdewp/2007-08.pdf.

Honneth, A. (1995). Work and instrumental action. In A. Honneth (Ed.), *The fragmented world of the social* (pp. 15–49). New York: SUNY Press.

Honneth, A. (2014). *Freedom's right*. Cambridge: Polity Press.

Hsieh, N.-H. (2008). Justice in production. *Journal of Political Philosophy*, 16(1), 72–100.

International Labor Organization (ILO). (2015). Decent work agenda. Retrieved July 20, 2015, from http://www.ilo.org/global/about-the-ilo/decent-work-agenda/lang--en/index.htm.

Keat, R. (2000). *Cultural goods and the limits of the market*. Basingstoke: Palgrave Macmillan.

Keat, R. (2008a). Practices, firms and varieties of capitalism. *Philosophy of Management*, 7(1), 77–91.

Keat, R. (2008b). Social criticism and the exclusion of ethics. *Analyse und Kritik*, 30(2), 291–315.

Keat, R. (2009). Anti-perfectionism, market economies and the right to meaningful work. *Analyse und Kritik*, 31(1), 121–138.

Keat, R. (2011). Liberalism, neutrality and varieties of capitalism. In N. H. Smith & J.-P. Deranty (Eds.), *New philosophies of labour* (pp. 347–370). Leiden: Brill.

Kohn, M., & Schooler, C. (1983). *Work and personality*. Norwood, NJ: Alex Publishing.

Kornhauser, A. (1964). *Mental health of the industrial worker: A Detroit study*. New York: John Wiley & Sons.

Kymlicka, W. (2002). *Contemporary political philosophy: An introduction* (2nd ed.). Oxford: Oxford University Press.

Lane, R. E. (1991). *The market experience*. Cambridge: Cambridge University Press.

MacIntyre, A. (1985). *After virtue: A study in moral theory* (2nd ed.). London: Duckworth.

MacIntyre, A. (1994). A partial response to my critics. In J. Horton & S. Mendus (Eds.), *After MacIntyre: Critical perspectives on the work of Alasdair MacIntyre* (pp. 283–304). Cambridge: Polity Press.

MacIntyre, A. (1999). *Dependent rational animals: Why human beings need the virtues.* London: Duckworth.

MacIntyre, A. (2015). The irrelevance of ethics. In A. Bielskis & K. Knight (Eds.), *Virtue and economy* (pp. 7–21). Farnham: Ashgate.

McCarthy, T. (1991). Complexity and democracy: or the seducements of systems theory. In A. Honneth & H. Joas (Eds.), *Communicative action* (pp. 119–139). Cambridge: Polity Press.

Miller, D. (1994). Virtues, practices and justice. In J. Horton & S. Mendus (Eds.), *After MacIntyre: Critical perspectives on the work of Alasdair MacIntyre* (pp. 245–264). Cambridge: Polity.

Muirhead, R. (2004). *Just work.* Cambridge, MA: Harvard University Press.

Murphy, J. B. (1993). *The moral economy of labor.* New Haven: Yale University Press.

Rawls, J. (1971). *A theory of justice.* Oxford: Oxford University Press.

Raz, J. (1986). *The morality of freedom.* Oxford: Clarendon Press.

Roessler, B. (2012). Meaningful work: Arguments from autonomy. *Journal of Political Philosophy,* 20(1), 71–93.

Ruskin, J. (2007 [1853]). *The stones of Venice: Vol. II. The sea stories.* New York: Cosimo.

Schwartz, A. (1982). Meaningful work. *Ethics,* 92(4), 634–646.

Sitton, J. F. (1998). Disembodied capitalism: Habermas's conception of the economy. *Sociological Forum,* 13(1), 61–83.

Smith, A. (1979 [1776]). *The wealth of nations.* Oxford: Oxford University Press.

Veltman, A. (2015). Is meaningful work available to all people? *Philosophy and Social Criticism,* 41(7), 725–747.

Weber, M. (1992 [1930]). *The protestant ethic and the spirit of capitalism.* London: Routledge.

Yeoman, R. (2014). *Meaningful work and workplace democracy.* Basingstoke: Palgrave Macmillan.

CHAPTER 9

Working from Both Ends: The Dual Role of Philosophy in Research Ethics

Allyn Fives

Philosophers engage with public matters in a number of ways. Increasingly, philosophy has come to play a public role in research ethics, and in particular, the ethical review of research proposals in Universities and other institutions. On University Research Ethics Committees (RECs), also referred to as Institutional Review Boards (IRBs), academics and lay members are tasked with deciding whether research protocols involving human subjects and animals can be given ethical approval. In forming an REC, it is common practice to 'include at least one member who is knowledgeable in ethics' (AREC 2013, p. 15) or require 'member(s) with training in ethics (e.g. ethicist, philosopher, theologian)' (ICB 2004, p. 10). Therefore, philosophical reflection is considered legitimate, even vital, for the rigorous ethical evaluation of research proposals. However, philosophers themselves disagree over precisely what form such philosophical engagement in public matters can and should take.

So as to explore the general question of what role philosophers should play in research ethics, in this chapter, I address the more specific issue of how philosophers can evaluate the ethical permissibility of randomized

A. Fives
School of Political Science and Sociology and the UNESCO Child and Family Research Centre, at the National University of Ireland, Galway, Republic of Ireland

© The Editor(s) (if applicable) and The Author(s) 2016
A. Fives, K. Breen (eds.), *Philosophy and Political Engagement*,
DOI 10.1057/978-1-137-44587-2_9

controlled trials (RCTs) in social settings. The example discussed in some detail is the RCT evaluation of a volunteer reading programme for disadvantaged children in first and second grade experiencing delays in acquiring literacy, Wizards of Words (WOW) (Fives et al. 2013b).

This chapter first examines the two main positions in the debate on RCTs. It will be argued that in both instances, there is a failed attempt at moral simplification, that is, the removal of moral conflict. In both *the difference position* (Miller and Brody 2003, 2007; Veatch 2007) and what I will refer to as *the argument from equipoise* (Freedman 1987, 1990; Freedman et al. 1996; Miller and Weijer 2006, 2007), the relevant authors contend there is no irresolvable moral conflict between the professional's duty of care to individual clients (e.g. the physician's duty of care to her patients) and other moral duties, in particular, the duty to respect the autonomous choices of others (e.g. the autonomous choice to enrol in an RCT) and the duty to maximize good consequences for all affected (e.g. the probable benefits to the wider public of a scientifically promising and worthwhile RCT).

It will be argued that the difference position fails to show that the duty of care is irrelevant to RCTs, while the argument from equipoise fails to show that, as the duty of care is relevant, it will have priority over all other competing moral considerations. In addition, in both positions, there is insufficient appreciation of the possibility for moral conflict in the analysis of RCTs. The second half of the paper then explores ways to resolve such moral conflicts. I will argue against bottom-up (i.e. inductive), as well as top-down (i.e. deductive), approaches on the grounds that neither sufficiently acknowledges moral conflict. The alternative approach presented here is to work through moral dilemmas by a process of practical reasoning that owes much to John Rawls's account of political reasoning. I will argue that the type of moral reasoning required to arrive at shared decisions involves offering *public* reasons, that is, reasons appropriate to others who may reasonably disagree about fundamental moral commitments.

This chapter is intended to illustrate philosophy's dual role in research ethics and to reveal that it can work from both ends and combine two different but related tasks. Through abstract and general theoretical reflection, which requires a significant degree of disengagement, we can examine such issues as whether moral conflicts arise in our ethical evaluation of research protocols. Through practical reasoning, which requires ongoing, direct involvement, we can pursue agreement on public matters, including cases where we are faced with moral dilemmas.

1   WHEN ARE RCTS PERMISSIBLE?

RCTs are conducted in various fields of enquiry. Much of the debate on the ethics of RCTs has addressed clinical trials, and the terminology employed reflects this medical context. However, many of the same issues arise concerning social trials, and in this chapter I will be concerned with social trials in the field of education. The starting point in the ethical evaluation of RCTs is the recognition that a trial involves two different and perhaps incompatible roles. In clinical trials, this is referred to as the 'dual role of clinician and investigator' (Beauchamp and Childress 2009, p. 317). If the attending clinicians are not also the investigators, at the very least they are aware of their patients' enrolment in the study. Dual roles also arise in social trials, and, generally speaking, this issue concerns the dual role of professional service provider, on the one hand, and scientist, on the other.

In clinical practice, physicians use therapeutic criteria to assign treatments to patients. All other things being equal, patients are to receive the treatment that will best meet their needs, and this represents the assumption that physicians have a professional duty of care to the specific individuals that they treat (Miller and Weijer 2006). Similarly, in the delivery of educational programmes, the relevant professionals (teachers, tutors, school principals, and so on) have a duty of care to ensure their students receive the programme best suited to their needs.

However, in an RCT, treatments are assigned randomly and certain treatments are withheld from some subjects (Altman 1991; Boruch et al. 2009; Jaded 1998). Although there are numerous RCT study designs, in the WoW study, the intervention group received regular treatment (normal classroom teaching) plus an innovative treatment (WoW), while the control group received only regular treatment. Whatever the study design, subjects receive treatments based on a random process and not because of clinical judgements and the application of therapeutic criteria. Random allocation is necessary for methodological reasons, because the absence of systematic differences between the two study conditions (i.e. control versus intervention) *prior* to the treatment being received is instrumental in establishing a relation of causality between study condition and outcomes *after* treatment. It is believed that such a trial can be justified if 'patient-subjects give comprehensive informed consent' and also if 'the trial is designed as a crucial experiment to determine which therapeutic alternative is superior and shows scientific promise of achieving this result' (Beauchamp and Childress 2009, p. 323).

In both professional practice and in science, a number of ethical principles are relevant, three of which I want to focus on here. Consequentialist principles 'identify the maximizing of good consequences and/or the minimizing of bad ones as right-making characteristics of actions' (Veatch 1995, p. 200). If I am a physician, I have a *duty of care* to my patients, and I am expected to act from the principle of Hippocratic utility, which is a consequentialist principle that 'limits relevant benefits and harms to the individual patient with whom one is interacting' (Veatch 1995, p. 200). In addition, as a physician, in medical practice and/or in clinical studies, I have a *duty to promote the utility of all those affected by my actions*, which is another consequentialist duty, but one that 'considers the benefits and harms for all parties affected by an action or rule' (Veatch 1995, p. 200). I also have to acknowledge non-consequentialist principles, such as respecting the autonomous choices of others. This is one reason why, in clinical trials, physicians/scientists must ensure patients/subjects are fully informed and give voluntary authorization for the treatment/trial.

Given that the duty of care requires professionals to prioritize the interests of each of their clients, how can professionals justify their involvement in trials where treatments are assigned randomly and treatments are withheld? According to the seminal text on biomedical ethics, clinicians' involvement in RCTs can be ethically permissible if 'true clinical equipoise exists in the community of relevant medical experts' (Beauchamp and Childress 2009, p. 323). Equipoise is defined as follows:

> On the basis of the available evidence, members of the relevant expert medical community are equally poised between the treatment strategies being tested in the RCT, because they are equally uncertain about, and equally comfortable with, the known advantages and disadvantages of the treatments to be tested (or the placebo being used). No patient, then, will receive a treatment known to be less effective or more dangerous than an available alternative (Beauchamp and Childress 2009, p. 320).

When there is equipoise, professionals can support the enrolment of their own clients as subjects in clinical trials, where treatments will be assigned randomly and treatments will be withheld, without violating their duty of care to those clients.

Although Beauchamp and Childress believe that equipoise is a threshold requirement for the ethical permissibility of RCTs, in the debate in applied philosophy, the concept itself is contested:

1. *The difference position*: some believe there is a strong distinction between the ethics governing professional practice and research ethics. The duty of care is irrelevant in an RCT, it is argued, as the underlying purpose of an RCT is scientific rather than therapeutic. For that reason, it is argued, equipoise is unnecessary in an RCT. Scientists must not exploit participants, and to that end they need only ensure that the study is a vital trial and scientifically promising and also that participants provide fully informed consent (Veatch 2007; Miller and Brody 2003).

2. *The argument from equipoise*: others have argued that RCTs are permissible only if there is equipoise, and this is the case because the duty of care is normatively binding in RCTs (Miller and Weijer 2006). They have argued also that equipoise is 'the same' as the requirement that the study is scientifically rigorous (Freedman et al. 1996, pp. 252–53). If a trial is a crucial experiment, scientifically promising, and based on fully informed consent, it is argued, then, it must also be the case that professionals are equally poised between treatments.

In the debate in applied philosophy, therefore, there is considerable disagreement over the question of if, and under what conditions, an RCT in a social setting is morally permissible. In the first instance, we will address this debate purely as a matter of argumentative rigour, and what we find is that both arguments are questionable. In particular, they fail in their efforts to show that moral conflicts of a particular kind do not arise in the ethical evaluation of RCTs, namely, that the duty of care does not come into conflict with the duty to respect autonomous choices of others and/ or the duty to promote the utility of all those affected.

2   THE INCONCLUSIVE DEBATE ON RCTS IN APPLIED PHILOSOPHY

Let us start with the argument from equipoise. Freedman et al. argue that the Helsinki Declaration prohibits any compromise of a patient's right to medical treatment by enrolling in a study, but also:

> the same concern is often stated scientifically when we assert that a study must start with an honest null hypothesis, genuine medical uncertainty concerning the relative merits of the various treatment arms included in the trial's design (Freedman et al. 1996, pp. 252–53).

This could be described as an attempt at moral simplification, that is, the removal of moral conflict. It runs together or conflates the duty of care (i.e. a client's right to a professional service) and equipoise (i.e. genuine uncertainty in the relevant expert community), on the one hand, with, on the other hand, the duty to promote the utility of all those affected through putting in place a scientifically rigorous trial, one requirement of which being an honest null hypothesis.

However, there are strong grounds to argue that an honest null hypothesis and equipoise are *not* the same. On the one hand, an honest null hypothesis is a hypothesis of no effect, that is, that no statistically significant differences between the two arms of a study will be observed after completion of the trial. A null hypothesis is *honest* when the researchers do not have evidence strong enough to predict which study arm will be more beneficial to participants. Scientists must start from an honest null hypothesis if their study is to be worthwhile and therefore maximize good consequences for all those affected. This scientific uncertainty also must be clearly and fully communicated to potential subjects, so that their decision to enrol in the trial can be fully autonomous. On the other hand, the community of relevant experts is in equipoise if, based on the duty of care to subjects, there is no decided preference in the community for either of the two arms of the study, or any other relevant treatment that is available, but not part of the study design. In Beauchamp and Childress's terms, no patient will receive a treatment known to be less effective or more dangerous 'than an available alternative' (Beauchamp and Childress 2009, p. 320). That the two are not *the same*, and that a conflict between the two requirements is possible, can be illustrated by the following example (see Fives et al. 2015).

In the WoW study, the control group were to receive standard treatment (regular classroom teaching only) and the intervention group were to be withdrawn from class to receive an innovative treatment (one-to-one reading tuition with a trained volunteer) as a supplement to regular classroom teaching. The intervention group were to receive their 30-minute WoW sessions approximately three times per week. There are good reasons to believe the expert community was *out of equipoise* here: in Ireland and the UK, policy documents and reports strongly suggest the education community did have a decided preference for programmes very similar to WoW, namely, structured, targeted, one-to-one reading support programmes, including those delivered by trained and well-supported volunteers drawn from the community (Brooks 2002; NESF 2005).

However, this was not incompatible with an honest null hypothesis. The innovative program was *promising*, but nonetheless *not known* to be beneficial. Other studies had shown that one-to-one reading programs delivered by highly trained and well-supported volunteers were effective in reducing the number of children at risk of reading failure (Meier and Invernizzi 2001; Pullen et al. 2004; Rimm-Kaufman et al. 1999). However, WoW is unlike other programs, as it is based on an innovative programme model and mode of implementation, neither of which had been evaluated previously (Barnardos 2008). There was no evidence for its effectiveness as a programme, and so the scientists did have an honest null hypothesis at the outset of the trial. Therefore, while teachers and school principals, based on a duty of care, had a decided preference for programmes like WoW, it could be argued that an RCT evaluation of WoW was justified by its possible good consequences for all those affected and by the fact that participants could autonomously enrol in such a trial.

So far we have addressed one attempt to minimize moral pluralism in the debate on RCTs, which runs together or conflates the duty of care and equipoise with the duty to promote the utility of all those affected. A separate attempt to minimize moral pluralism is evident in the difference position, where it is claimed that the duty of care is simply irrelevant in research ethics. While a physician's duty is to the patient and his/her interests, 'the investigator has the interests of future patients at heart' (Miller and Brody 2003, p. 26).

Miller and Brody do insist on a favourable risk-benefit ratio. A trial can be justified only if the risks to study participants are minimized and the benefits to future patients are maximized, which is required by the duty to promote the utility of all those affected. However, there should be no reference to equipoise in research ethics. The danger of viewing trials through a 'therapeutic lens', it is argued, is that this may foster 'the therapeutic misconception among research participants—that is, the tendency of participants to confuse clinical trials with medical care' (Miller and Brody 2003, p. 25). The therapeutic misconception undermines informed consent, and therefore the principle of respect for the autonomous choice of others, if potential participants are unaware that the trial is aimed 'not at their own ultimate benefit, but at discovering new knowledge to help future patients' (Miller and Brody 2003, p. 25).

However, this line of argument is unsatisfactory, as the duty of care *is* relevant to research ethics. Even when an RCT is compatible with our duties to promote the utility of all those affected and the duty to respect autonomous choices, if participants do not receive an available treatment that is considered beneficial to them, this raises independent ethical questions about the permissibility of the trial. This is the case because an investigator, who has no pre-existing professional relationship to them, nonetheless has a duty of care to the subjects of a study. For that reason, an application for ethical approval to an REC must satisfy the principle of 'non-maleficence', which requires that 'any possible harm must be avoided or at least mitigated by robust precautions' (AREC 2013, p. 5). If the investigator is aware that professionals from the expert community have good reasons to believe that one arm of the study is likely to be harmful to some subject or deny a benefit to some subject, then, in the first instance at least, the investigator has a duty to ensure the subject gets the beneficial treatment and/or does not receive the harmful treatment.

Therefore, attempts to reduce the plurality of moral principles and to remove conflicts between those principles in the debate on RCTs have been unsuccessful. This is the case because a dilemmatic conflict of principles is possible where to do what is required by the first principle (the duty of care) means being unable to do what is required by other principles (the duty to respect autonomous choices and the duty to promote the utility of all those affected). A moral dilemma is a case 'where there is a conflict between two moral judgments that a man is disposed to make relevant to deciding what to do', and more precisely, where 'it seems I ought to do each of two things, but I cannot do both' (Williams 1965, p. 108). In some instances, it may be relatively unproblematic to resolve such a dilemma, for example, if a trial is scientifically promising, but there is a high probability of causing harm of a significant magnitude. In such a case, we should refuse to approve the trial, and in doing so give priority to the duty of care. In other studies, however, the conflict between principles may be harder to resolve. For instance, in the WoW evaluation, the study was scientifically promising, was of high social importance, and was based on informed consent. However, the relevant expert community was not in equipoise. How do we resolve such a moral dilemma?

3   How to Deal with Moral Dilemmas (I): 'Bottom-up' Accounts of Moral Justification

A central issue in the debate on RCTs is whether the duty of care can come into conflict with the researcher's duty to conduct rigorous trials based on informed consent. This points to the methodological issue of moral justification, and, more specifically, to how we are to deal with what appears to be a plurality of, at times, conflicting moral requirements.

Casuistry is an example of a *bottom-up* approach to ethical justification, as it builds up inductively *from* cases and intuitions *to* justified moral beliefs. As Albert Jonsen and Stephen Toulmin discovered from their work on a committee to develop 'recommendations to protect the rights and welfare of human subjects of research', 'the development of ethical principles to govern research, was performed at the end ... after it [the committee] had proposed recommendations for many specific cases of research' (Jonsen 1995, p. 239; Jonsen and Toulmin 1988). Their starting point was attention to circumstances, the particularities of the case, and 'the nature of the practice or institution that gives rise to the case' (Jonsen 1995, p. 246).

Pragmatism, another bottom-up approach to moral judgement, has been applied by Joffe and Miller and others, both to clinical practice and research ethics (Joffe and Miller 2008; Fins et al. 1997, p. 140). As pragmatists, they contend the two settings call for different ethical considerations. They propose a 'conception of clinical research ethics based on a scientific orientation ... without making any appeal to the therapeutic norms governing the physician-patient relationship' (Joffe and Miller 2008, p. 32). This is the case because clinical research, 'as a scientific activity ... is governed by a series of *internal norms*' (Joffe and Miller 2008, p. 32; emphasis in original).

For Joffe and Miller and others, equipoise is irrelevant when we judge the ethical permissibility of a trial for the reason that clinical trials should be judged on the basis of norms *internal* to the relevant practice or institution, in this case, scientific enquiry. However, those who, in contrast, insist that equipoise *is* a moral requirement of clinical trials, also do so on the basis of considerations internal to what they believe to be the relevant practice or institution, that is, clinical practice. Benjamin Freedman has concluded that the argument from equipoise is:

> grounded in the normative nature of clinical practice, the view that a patient is ethically entitled to expect treatment from his or her physician – an entitlement that cannot be sacrificed to scientific curiosity (Freedman 1990, p. 5).

The limitations of a bottom-up methodology for the resolution of moral conflicts are illustrated by the debate on RCTs. Proponents on both sides of the debate believe they have shown there to be no conflict of moral duties, or no irresolvable conflict. Freedman (1990) presents

the duty of care as the fundamental moral requirement of clinical practice, and so it is given priority when it comes into conflict with other
duties. Joffe and Miller (2008) and others judge the duty of care to
be irrelevant in research ethics, and therefore believe there can be no
dilemmatic conflict between it and other duties in an RCT study. The
question is whether such a bottom-up approach is adequate for research
ethics. The evidence would suggest that it is not. As they build upwards
from what are understood to be mutually exclusive starting points
(the clinical context and the scientific context), they arrive at mutually
incompatible conclusions. Rather than help resolve the disagreements
in research ethics concerning RCTs, the bottom-up approach is responsible for the emergence of multiple, conflicting conclusions concerning
the same moral issue.

4   HOW TO DEAL WITH MORAL DILEMMAS (II): 'TOP-DOWN' THEORETICAL APPROACHES

How are we to resolve moral dilemmas in research ethics? A second
approach is to start from a single moral principle, and apply it in a *top-
down* fashion to decide between competing moral considerations.

One version of this approach is to give non-consequentialist principles
lexical priority over consequentialist principles. As we saw, Robert Veatch
argued that equipoise is irrelevant in research ethics. Rather, 'what was
morally critical was the willingness of some group of potential research
subjects to be randomized after having enough information about the
alternatives' (Veatch 2007, p. 167). Elsewhere, Veatch has argued that
consequence-maximizing principles are secondary to non-consequentialist
principles, which include respect for persons (which, in turn, includes the
principles of autonomy, veracity, fidelity, and avoidance of killing) and justice. The duty to promote good consequences and the duty to do no harm
'by themselves can never justify breaking a promise, telling a lie, violating
autonomy, killing another, or distributing goods unjustly' (Veatch 1995,
pp. 211–12).

According to this line of thought, if there *appears* to be a conflict between
the duty of care to individual clients and the duty to promote the utility of
all those affected, it can be resolved by applying the non-consequentialist
duty to respect autonomous choices. Therefore, in an RCT, if the expert
community has a decided preference for one arm of the study, subjects
should be informed of this fact, so as to satisfy the principle of respect for

autonomous choices, but the study remains ethically permissible for those subjects who continue to give their informed consent. However, if preliminary results show statistically significant differences between the two arms of the study, then the study should be terminated. This is the case, because not only would continuing with the trial be of no further benefit to society (the duty to promote the utility of all those affected), but more importantly, it would require that investigators, at the very least, withhold information from participants and therefore violate the respect owed to them as persons.

An alternative top-down approach to resolving moral dilemmas is to give consequentialist principles lexical priority over non-consequentialist principles. According to R.M. Hare, there are two levels of moral reasoning (Hare 1981). The intuitive level involves appeal to everyday moral intuitions, such as respect for autonomous choices and the duty of care. This is necessary for 'economy of thought' and usually will be sufficient in that it will yield 'correct conclusions' (Donagan 1993, pp. 17–18). In contrast, the critical level of moral reasoning is one 'at which the shortcomings of the intuitive stage for complex and difficult cases are removed by recourse to utilitarian calculation' (Donagan 1993, p. 18). Therefore, difficult cases create only the *appearance* of dilemma, as any conflict can be resolved by utilitarian calculation: namely, we sum the benefits and burdens of all those affected by the proposed course of action and choose the one that best promotes utility. According to this line of thought, if the likely benefits to the wider society from an RCT are sufficiently large, this would justify any smaller sacrifices made by study subjects, but also it may justify violation of the duty to respect autonomous choices, such as lying to and withholding information from participants.

In both, the consequentialist and the non-consequentialist positions above, it is argued that moral conflicts are only apparent rather than real (de Haan 2001). Philippa Foot agrees, and argues that if it is possible for two moral judgements about our duties to be in conflict, it follows that one or both of these represents merely a *prima facie* (i.e. at first sight) duty, and that, all things considered, only one of these can be considered an actual moral duty. Because it is a logical contradiction, it is *not possible* that we 'ought to do X' (i.e. that X is the best thing to do) and that we 'ought not to do X' (i.e. that X is not the best thing to do) (Foot 2002, p. 183). We can resolve moral conflicts in this way only if we can establish what is right, all things considered. Foot states that her position is one of 'absolute moral prohibitions', such that 'each and every torturer acts wrongly', moral absolutes that are part of the Aristotelian and Catholic traditions of thought (Foot 2002, p. 188).

Consequentialists, non-consequentialists, and moral absolutists provide very different ways in which to establish what is right, all things considered. Should we give priority to a utilitarian calculation in resolving moral conflicts, or instead make utilitarian calculations secondary to non-consequentialist principles, or instead appeal to Aristotelian and Catholic moral absolutes? A great deal may seem to turn on this question. However, what I want to emphasize is that at present, after many centuries of effort, philosophers have not arrived at an agreed answer to this question. Therefore, if we are tasked with making a decision on the ethical permissibility of an RCT, we do not have philosophical licence to insist that we should resolve all value conflicts through utilitarian calculation (or alternatively through appeal to non-consequentialist values or moral absolutes). This would suggest that we must try to resolve such conflicts by some other means.

5   How to Deal with Moral Dilemmas (III): Offering Public Reasons

In this section, I look at attempts to resolve moral dilemmas through the use of practical reason. It may be wondered why practical reasoning can resolve moral dilemmas where they could not be resolved through theoretical reflection. However, we should note the following. Although a theorist can attempt to resolve moral dilemmas in a solitary fashion as an intellectual exercise, it is in practice and it is with others that we try to resolve such dilemmas by making decisions. This is the case when working with others in conducting research and/or when sitting on a research ethics committee where the permissibility of such studies is assessed. What these experiences suggest is that it is possible to reach ethical decisions together about such studies, but to that end we must do the following:

1. Marshal the relevant moral considerations;
2. illustrate the current state of the research domain in question; and
3. work together towards resolving the moral conflicts that have arisen and do so with considerations that should be acceptable to others as participants in a public debate.

Marshal the Relevant Moral Considerations

When the members of a research ethics committee review a proposed RCT, there is a variety of relevant moral principles to consider. In such a review, it is not assumed that one moral principle has priority (AREC 2013, p. 5). The conclusion of a review may be that an application is deferred or rejected because of serious concerns relating to one consideration only: for example, that the proposed informed consent procedure shows insufficient respect for autonomous choices. That does not entail any a priori assumptions about the status of this consideration in relation to others. Also, an application will be found wanting if any one of the relevant considerations is not addressed satisfactorily. It is therefore necessary to marshal a plurality of moral considerations.

Beauchamp and Childress list the relevant moral conditions for the permissibility of RCTs as follows:

1. True clinical equipoise exists in the community of relevant medical experts.
2. The trial is designed as a crucial experiment to determine which therapeutic alternative is superior and shows scientific promise of achieving this result.
3. An IRB or its functional equivalent has approved the protocol and certified that no physician has a conflict of interest or incentive that would threaten the patient-physician relationship.
4. Patient-subjects give comprehensive informed consent.
5. Placebos cannot be used if an effective treatment exists for the condition being studied, if that condition involves death or serious morbidity, and if a new treatment is promising.
6. A data and safety monitoring committee will either end the trial when statistically significant data displace clinical equipoise or will supply physicians and patients with significant safety and therapeutic information that is relevant to a reasonable person's decision to remain in or to withdraw from a trial.
7. Physicians have the right to recommend withdrawal and patients have the right to withdraw at any time (Beauchamp and Childress 2009, p. 323).

We have already discussed the conditions in Beauchamp and Childress's list. The first condition represents the duty of care; the second the duty to promote the utility of all those affected; and the fourth, the duty to respect autonomous choices. The fifth, sixth, and seventh conditions specify how the first, second, and fourth conditions are to be balanced in different ways. The third condition is simply the requirement of REC (or IRB) approval. In the first section of this paper, I engaged with these moral considerations at the level of general and abstract philosophical reflection. What I argued there was that efforts to remove moral conflicts have failed and that there is no philosophical licence to insist that we can resolve all moral conflicts by giving priority to one moral doctrine or one moral duty.

Illustrate the Current State of the Research Domain in Question

As we shall see below, the critics argue that RCTs in social settings are ethically impermissible. The two main objections are that (a) equipoise cannot be established and/or (b) RCTs cannot be scientifically promising. Therefore, if we are to evaluate the ethical permissibility of any one RCT, it must be possible to come to a conclusion on whether the study is a crucial experiment that shows scientific promise and also whether the relevant expert community is, or need be, in equipoise. For that reason, we require detailed practical knowledge of the field of study.

Some have argued that in many, if not most cases, an RCT in a social setting cannot be scientifically promising (Bonell et al. 2011; Ghate 2001; Morrison 2001; Stewart-Brown et al. 2011). A study is internally valid when the differences between the two study conditions observed at the completion of the treatment (i.e. at post-test) can be ascribed to the different treatments (along with random error) and not to other variables (Juni et al. 2001). Although critics acknowledge that RCTs can generate evidence of causality in appropriate contexts, they also believe that, unlike the controlled environment of biomedical studies, very often the fluid and dynamic context of social interventions is not appropriate for RCTs.

The following are just some of the threats to the internal validity of an RCT (Shadish et al. 2002): Random allocation may be undermined, leading to *selection bias*, if investigators influence the allocation of treatments. There may be *confounding*, where there is an overlap between study condition (i.e. control or intervention) and some other variable that may be the cause of the observed changes. The control group may receive additional supports or services (*compensatory equalization*); or they may receive the same treatment as the intervention group (*treatment diffusion*).

The critics argue that such threats to internal validity arise in social settings and in many, if not most, cases generate insurmountable methodological obstacles to RCTs. However, these threats to internal validity must be addressed in clinical trials as well as in social trials. As shown elsewhere in more detail (Fives et al. 2013a, 2015), in the WoW study, the investigators protected against these threats to validity in the following ways: random allocation of participants helped protect against both selection bias and confounding, and ongoing thorough monitoring of the treatments received by participants protected against compensatory equalization and treatment diffusion.

Therefore, RCTs can be scientifically promising if the investigators are aware of the threats and have planned sufficiently to minimize them. However, these are highly technical matters of research methodology and study design, and so detailed knowledge of the field of study is necessary so as to be aware of these facts. It is for this reason that good practice requires REC committees to include 'members with a broad experience of and expertise in the areas of research regularly reviewed by the REC, and who have the confidence and esteem of the research community' (AREC 2013, p. 15). As explained above, it is in practice and it is with others that we try to resolve dilemmas by making decisions. What we have now seen is that philosophical knowledge is necessary yet insufficient, as the ethical evaluation of social trials requires expert knowledge of study design and quantitative (and qualitative) methodology.

The second major issue to address when evaluating a proposed RCT is equipoise. The critics have argued that social trials cannot be justified, because in social settings, equipoise will be fleeting at best. Individual professionals are likely to come to a conclusion about which study arm would be most beneficial to their clients, thereby disturbing any equipoise that may have existed (Hammersley 2008). However, this critique rests on an outdated understanding of equipoise. While the earliest uses of the term presented equipoise as a matter of each individual's preference in respect of each subject's treatment (Fried 1974), in more recent formulations, it is the decided preference of the community of experts that is considered relevant (Miller and Weijer 2006). At the level of the expert community, it is possible for there to be a relatively stable state of equipoise. However, as I have argued, the duty of care, from which the requirement of equipoise is derived, is but one of a number of moral considerations, and it can come into conflict with other moral duties. We are therefore left with the task of resolving such dilemmas.

*Work Towards Resolving the Moral Conflicts that Have Arisen
and Do So with Considerations that Should Be Acceptable to Others
as Participants in a Public Debate*

It is not unusual for REC committee members to be faced with indecision due to a conflict of values. How would we then resolve such a conflict? This is not simply an issue of *convincing* others through rhetorical devices of what is *known* to be the case through some other means. Rather, what is being looked for are moral reasons that are *binding*, that is, reasons that others ought to accept and reasons that justify the proposed judgement. What kinds of reasons are they?

Let us start with an example. I may say to fellow members of an REC that the duty of care must always have priority over other duties, and for that reason, a proposed RCT must be stopped if the relevant expert community is out of equipoise. However, the committee members would be failing in their duties if they did not ask me to *give reasons* for my conclusion (that the proposed RCT must be stopped), independent of the theoretical ones just mentioned. In such an instance, my colleagues are looking for reasons why they should agree with me, and this has not been provided by my insisting that the duty of care must always have priority. What would happen if another committee member, a utilitarian say, simply insisted that the duty to promote the utility of all those affected had priority, and for that reason, the proposed RCT may proceed even in the absence of equipoise?

Why is it inappropriate to simply state we should reach conclusion X because it follows from the duty to promote the utility of all those affected? It is inappropriate, because there is no overwhelming reason why everyone else should accept that this duty has priority over other duties: that is, there is no overwhelming reason why everyone should be a utilitarian. We have already seen that trained philosophers disagree about the relative importance of moral duties in the debate on RCTs, and that they disagree about whether consequentialist or non-consequentialist principles or moral absolutes should always have priority in research ethics. In addition, if we live in a society where individuals are permitted to freely use their powers of reasoning, it is to be expected that they will come to different conclusions about which moral principles are more important when they try to answer moral questions and make moral decisions.

In a context such as this, where we wish to debate a moral issue with others who are also free to use their powers of reason independently of us, what type of reasons is appropriate? I want to argue that the type of reasons appropriate to this moral debate is the *public* reasons of *political* reasoning. Reasonableness 'involves a readiness to politically address others of different persuasions in terms of public reasons' (Freeman 2000, p. 401). And *public* reasons are considerations 'we might reasonably expect that they, as free and equal citizens, might also accept' (Rawls 1999b [1997], p. 579; see also Scanlon 2002). Public reasons do not presuppose the truth of any one moral doctrine, such as utilitarianism, Catholicism, Kantianism, and so on.

So public reasons are considerations that you and I can share, and you and I can arrive at a shared decision on the basis of those considerations, even though we disagree about moral fundamentals, such as whether or not the ultimate moral considerations are consequentialist. In proceeding in this way, we can hope to come to an agreement that is morally justified because it has proceeded reasonably, that is, from a commitment to view others as our moral equals. It is assumed that a reasonable agreement is the appropriate goal of moral debate in the public sphere. The public sphere of a free society is composed of those whose freedom to reason about such moral issues is protected. We could attain consensus on the truth of one moral doctrine (for instance, utilitarianism), but it would require the use of coercion (Rawls 1999a [1987], p. 425, n. 7).

Others will argue that political reasoning is problematic on at least two fronts. First, we should not bracket moral and philosophical questions, such as what moral duty has priority, but rather welcome profound disagreements about such questions into our public discourse, so as to deepen our mutual respect and create a more robust public life (Raz 1990). Second, this account of political reasoning actually presupposes certain truths it claims to bracket, in particular Kantian or liberal ideas that moral justification is based on consent or contract, and that a morally worthwhile life must be an autonomous life (Dryzek and Niemeyer 2006; Thunder 2006). These are important counter arguments, which I have attempted to address in more detail elsewhere (Fives 2013a, b).

In reply to the first objection, I can say here that a political approach to public debate is one that requires mutual respect of a deep kind, namely, respect for the other as a free and equal fellow citizen. It is viewing others as our moral equals that gives moral weight to subsequent agreements. That is, such agreements are not merely the outcome of a bargain and binding only insofar as they are beneficial to each party, but rather are morally binding even when not beneficial to the individual (Rawls 1999b [1997],

p. 578). In reply to the second objection, a distinction should be made between justifications *of* morality and justifications *in* morality. It may well be that there are Kantian, liberal substantive moral commitments beneath and behind this approach to practical reason, while alternative philosophical doctrines provide competing justifications *of* morality. However, justification *in* morality is a common feature of all moral doctrines, as all assume we can be held to account and should be willing to give an intelligible account of ourselves. Political reasoning is offered as one such approach, and the case for it as a better approximation of justification *in* morality is its requirement that we view others as free and equal fellow citizens.

Returning to our example, is it possible to offer public reasons to help resolve the moral dilemma in the WoW study? In trying to come to a shared decision about the permissibility of the trial, we should recall that there is a plurality of moral principles and no unquestionable reason why one should be considered more fundamental than others. One is the duty to maximize good consequences for all affected. If there is strong evidence that the investigators are aware of possible threats to internal validity, and have in place strategies to minimize those threats, from the moral point of view this counts in favour of the trial. In addition, there is the duty to respect autonomous choices. An important factor is the need to avoid a therapeutic misconception as a result of poorly informed participants. However, while this requires that all potential participants be aware that treatments will be randomly allocated, and so they are not guaranteed any one treatment, it does not entail that investigators have no duty of care to participants.

In fact, it is not inconsistent with any of the above to argue that the duty of care requires that investigators consider how to minimize risks of harm to participants. In an RCT, this can be done in a number of ways. In the WoW study, a *wait list control* and an *active controlled non-inferiority* trial design were used. In a wait-list control study, some or all of those assigned to the control group will graduate into the intervention group after the data collection period is completed for them; and in an active controlled non-inferiority trial, the control group receive standard treatment (rather than a placebo) and the intervention group receive an innovative treatment. Therefore, without giving up the experimental approach, it is possible to minimize risks to participants. These adaptations are still compatible with the requirement to promote utility for all those affected, as every effort should be made to ensure the study is worthwhile, and therefore to rigorously maintain the controlled nature of the trial. This means there are strong ethical grounds to randomly allocate in the first instance, but also to rigorously enforce the results of the allocation process and so exclude participants from treatments they have not been assigned to receive.

6 Conclusions

The contributors to this book explore how philosophical reflection can be combined with practical engagement about public matters. If philosophical reflection requires disengagement from the everyday world so as to better call into question the taken for granted, will philosophy therefore be ill-suited to play a public or political role? Will philosophy and philosophers be ill-informed about the issues under consideration, or too distant from those who need to be persuaded, or will it lack credibility among decision makers? While some have urged caution, and restricted philosophy to a theoretical role of conceptual analysis, others have been more expansive and ascribed to philosophy a role in actively resolving public matters. This chapter has sought to show the need for and the benefits of combining the disengagement characteristic of philosophical reflection with an active engagement in public matters.

This chapter also explored the general question of what role philosophy should play in research ethics, and the more specific issue of the ethical permissibility of RCTs in social settings. I have tried to illustrate philosophy's dual role in research ethics. Through abstract and general theoretical reflection, we can examine such issues as whether moral conflicts arise in our ethical evaluation of research protocols. Through practical reasoning, we can pursue agreement on public matters, including cases where we are faced with moral dilemmas.

Acknowledgments I would like to thank the anonymous reviewers for their comments on an earlier draft of this chapter. I would also like to thank Keith Breen, in particular, for his critical insights. I have written on this topic elsewhere, including a number of joint-authored papers with colleagues in the UNESCO Child and Family Research Centre at NUI Galway. I would also like to acknowledge the importance, for my own understanding of this field, of the work of colleagues on the NUI Galway Research Ethics Committee, including Heike Schmidt-Felzmann, Brian McGuire, and Saoirse Nic Gabhainn. Finally, I would like to thank Joseph Mahon for starting my formal education in this area.

REFERENCES

Altman, D. G. (1991). Randomization: Essential for reducing bias. *British Medical Journal*, 302(6791), 1481–1482.

Association of Research Ethics Committees (AREC). (2013). *A framework of policies and procedures for university research ethics committees.* Retrieved July 20, 2015, from http://s3.spanglefish.com/s/21217/documents/independent-membership/12-11-13-framework-complete.pdf.

Barnardos. (2008). *Wizards of words' manual for volunteers.* Dublin: Barnardos.

Beauchamp, T. L., & Childress, J. F. (2009). *Principles of biomedical ethics* (6th ed.). Oxford: Oxford University Press.

Bonell, C. P., Hargreaves, J., Ciousens, S., Ross, D., Hayes, R., Petticrew, M., & Kirkwood, B. R. (2011). Alternatives to randomisation in the evaluation of public health interventions: Design challenges and solutions. *Journal of Epidemiology and Community Health*, 65(7), 582–587.

Boruch, R., Weisburd, D., Turner, H. M., III, Karpyn, A., & Littell, J. (2009). Randomized controlled trials for evaluation and planning. In L. Bickman & D. J. Rog (Eds.), *The sage handbook of applied social research* (2nd ed., pp. 147–181). London: Sage.

Brooks, G. (2002). *What works for children with literacy difficulties? The effectiveness of intervention schemes.* London: Department for Education and Skills. Retrieved July, 20, 2015 from http://www.dcsf.gov.uk/research/data/uploadfiles/RR380.pdf.

de Haan, J. (2001). The definition of moral dilemmas: A logical problem. *Ethical Theory and Moral Practice*, 4(3), 267–284.

Donagan, A. (1993). Moral dilemmas, genuine and spurious: A comparative anatomy. *Ethics*, 104(1), 7–21.

Dryzek, J. S., & Niemeyer, S. (2006). Reconciling pluralism and consensus as political ideals. *American Journal of Political Science*, 50(3), 634–649.

Fins, J. J., Bacchetta, M. D., & Miller, F. G. (1997). Clinical pragmatism: A method of moral problem solving. *Kennedy Institute of Ethics Journal*, 7(2), 129–143.

Fives, A. (2013a). Non-coercive promotion of values in civic education for democracy. *Philosophy and Social Criticism*, 39(6), 577–590.

Fives, A. (2013b). *Political reason: Morality and the public sphere.* Houndmills: Palgrave.

Fives, A., Russell, D., Kearns, N., Lyons, R., Eaton, P., Canavan, J., Devaney, C., & O'Brien, A. (2013a). The role of random allocation in randomized controlled trials: Distinguishing selection bias from baseline imbalance. *Journal of MultiDisciplinary Evaluation*, 9(20), 33–42.

Fives, A., Kearns, N., Devaney, C., Canavan, J., Russell, D., Lyons, R., Eaton, P., & O'Brien, A. (2013b). A one-to-one programme for at-risk readers delivered by older adult volunteers. *Review of Education*, 1(3), 254–280.

Fives, A., Russell, D., Kearns, N., Lyons, R., Eaton, P., Canavan, J., Devaney, C., & O'Brien, A. (2015). The ethics of randomized controlled trials in social settings: Can social trials be scientifically promising and must there be equipoise? *International Journal of Research & Method in Education*, 38(1), 56–71.

Foot, P. (2002). Moral dilemmas revisited. In P. Foot (Ed.), *Moral dilemmas and other topics in moral philosophy* (pp. 175–188). Oxford: Clarendon Press.

Freedman, B. (1987). Equipoise and the ethics of clinical research. *New England Journal of Medicine*, 317(3), 141–145.

Freedman, B. (1990). Placebo-controlled trials and the logic of clinical purpose. *IRB: A Review of Human Subjects Research*, 12(6), 1–6.

Freedman, B., Glass, K. C., & Weijer, C. (1996). Placebo orthodoxy in clinical research: II. Ethical, legal, and regulatory myths. *Journal of Law, Medicine & Ethics*, 24(3), 252–259.

Freeman, S. (2000). Deliberative democracy: A sympathetic comment. *Philosophy & Public Affairs*, 29(4), 371–418.

Fried, C. (1974). *Medical experimentation: Personal integrity and social policy.* New York: American Elsevier.

Ghate, D. (2001). Community-based evaluations in the UK: Scientific concerns and practical constraints. *Children and Society*, 15(1), 23–32.

Hammersley, M. (2008). Paradigm war revived? On the diagnosis of resistance to randomized controlled trials and systematic review in education. *International Journal of Research and Method in Education*, 31(1), 3–10.

Hare, R. M. (1981). *Moral thinking: Its levels, method, and point.* Oxford: Oxford University Press.

Irish Council for Bioethics (ICB). (2004). *Operational procedures for research ethics committees: Guidance 2004.* Dublin: Irish Council for Bioethics.

Jaded, A. (1998). *Randomised controlled trials: A user's guide.* London: BMJ Books.

Joffe, S., & Miller, F. G. (2008). Bench to bedside: Mapping the moral terrain of clinical research. *Hastings Center Report*, 38(2), 30–42.

Jonsen, A. R. (1995). Casuistry: An alternative or complement to principles? *Kennedy Institute of Ethics Journal*, 5(3), 237–251.

Jonsen, A. R., & Toulmin, S. (1988). *The abuse of casuistry: A history of moral reasoning.* Berkeley, CA: University of California Press.

Juni, P., Altman, D. G., & Egger, M. (2001). Assessing the quality of controlled clinical trials. *British Medical Journal*, 323(7303), 42–46.

Meier, J., & Invernizzi, M. (2001). Book buddies in the Bronx: Testing a model for America reads. *Journal of Education for Students Placed at Risk*, 6(4), 319–333.

Miller, F. G., & Brody, H. (2003). Therapeutic misconception in the ethics of clinical trials. *Hastings Center Report*, 33(3), 19–28.

Miller, F. G., & Brody, H. (2007). Clinical equipoise and the incoherence of research ethics. *Journal of Medicine and Philosophy*, 32(2), 151–165.

Miller, P. B., & Weijer, C. (2006). Fiduciary obligation in clinical research. *Journal of Law, Medicine & Ethics,* 34(2), 424–440.

Miller, P. B., & Weijer, C. (2007). Equipoise and the duty of care in clinical research: A philosophical response to our critics. *Journal of Medicine and Philosophy,* 32(2), 117–133.

Morrison, K. (2001). Randomised controlled trials for evidence-based education: Some problems in judging "what works". *Evaluation and Research in Education,* 15(2), 69–83.

National Economic and Social Forum (NESF). (2005). *Early childhood care and education, Report 31.* Dublin: NESF.

Pullen, P. C., Lane, H. B., & Monaghan, M. C. (2004). Effects of a volunteer tutoring model on the early literacy development of struggling first grade students. *Reading Research and Instruction,* 43(4), 21–40.

Rawls, J. (1999a [1987]). The idea of an overlapping consensus. In S. Freeman (Ed.), *John Rawls: Collected papers* (pp. 421–448). Cambridge, MA: Harvard University Press.

Rawls, J. (1999b [1997]). The idea of public reason revisited. In S. Freeman (Ed.), *John Rawls: Collected papers* (pp. 573–615). Cambridge, MA: Harvard University Press.

Raz, J. (1990). Facing diversity: The case of epistemic abstinence. *Philosophy & Public Affairs,* 19(1), 3–46.

Rimm-Kaufman, S. E., Kagan, J., & Byers, H. (1999). The effectiveness of adult volunteer tutoring on reading among 'at risk' first grade children. *Reading Research and Instruction,* 38(2), 143–152.

Scanlon, T. M. (2002). Reasons, responsibility, and reliance: Replies to Wallace, Dworkin, and Deigh. *Ethics,* 112(3), 507–528.

Shadish, W. R., Cook, T. D., & Campbell, D. T. (2002). *Experimental and quasi-experimental designs for generalized causal inferences.* Boston, MA: Houghton Mifflin Company.

Stewart-Brown, S., Anthony, R., Wilson, L., Wintsanley, S., Stallard, N., Snooks, H., & Simkiss, D. (2011). Should randomised controlled trials be the "gold standard" for research on preventive interventions for children? *Journal of Children's Services,* 6(4), 228–235.

Thunder, D. (2006). A Rawlsian argument against the duty of civility. *American Journal of Political Science,* 50(3), 676–690.

Veatch, R. M. (1995). Resolving conflicts among principles: Ranking, balancing, and specifying. *Kennedy Institute of Ethics Journal,* 5(3), 199–218.

Veatch, R. M. (2007). The irrelevance of equipoise. *Journal of Medicine and Philosophy,* 32(2), 167–183.

Williams, B. (1965). Ethical consistency. *Proceedings of the Aristotelian Society,* 39(Suppl.), 103–124.

PART III

The Justification of Power and Resistance

CHAPTER 10

Three Mistakes About Democracy

Philip Pettit

This chapter addresses three claims that are often made among contemporary policy-makers, political scientists, and political theorists about democracy. The claims, in my view, are false and, indeed, revealingly false: they display a serious misunderstanding of the nature and appeal of democracy. As we see why they are false, we will come to appreciate dimensions of democracy that easily escape notice. Hence the title of the chapter.

I name the mistakes after outstanding thinkers who have made them. The first I describe as Berlin's mistakse, finding it in the work of the Anglo-Russian philosopher, Isaiah Berlin. The second I describe as Schumpeter's mistake, naming it after the Austrian-American banker, economist, and political thinker, Joseph Schumpeter. And the third I describe as Riker's mistake, associating it with William Riker, the American political scientist famous for his distinction between liberalism and populism. All three played important roles in promulgating the mistakes that they endorsed, though Riker probably made a smaller mark than the other two.

In indicting these thinkers, I do so from the perspective of the republican tradition that emerged in classical Rome, came to life again in the

P. Pettit
Princeton University, Princeton, NJ, USA,
and Australian National University, Canberra, Australia

© The Editor(s) (if applicable) and The Author(s) 2016
A. Fives, K. Breen (eds.), *Philosophy and Political Engagement*,
DOI 10.1057/978-1-137-44587-2_10

187

Italian cities of the high middle ages, fuelled the Dutch and English republics of the seventeenth century, and inspired various eighteenth-century revolutions, including the American, the French, and, indeed, the Irish.[1] That tradition is built around a conception of freedom as non-domination, to be elucidated later in the text. And it requires a rich conception of democracy of a kind that the mistakes charted here would cause us to overlook (Pettit 2012).

1   BERLIN'S MISTAKE

Isaiah Berlin is best known for his work on the concept of freedom, in particular, for his 1958 inaugural lecture in Oxford on 'Two Concepts of Liberty'. In that lecture, Berlin insisted that individual freedom was constituted by nothing more or less than the absence of interference: primarily, the absence of any willful obstruction or penalization or misrepresentation of a choice, whether by a private individual or group, and whether done covertly or openly. This led him to think that every law, insofar as it holds out the coercive threat of penalty, is an infraction of freedom, albeit one that may prevent more interference that it perpetrates. 'Law is always a fetter', he says, 'even if it protects you from being bound in chains that are heavier than those of the law, say some more repressive law or custom, or arbitrary despotism or chaos' (Berlin 1969, p. 123).

If law is always a form of interference, and takes away your freedom of choice in some measure, then it follows that a democratically enacted law is going to have this effect, just as much as a law imposed by a tyrannical government. And so Berlin argues that the cause of freedom is quite distinct from the cause of democracy and gives us no reason in itself to want democracy; 'there is no necessary connexion', he says, 'between individual liberty and democratic rule' (Berlin 1969, p. 130). He even goes so far as to suggest, indeed, that democracy might do worse by the cause of freedom than a non-democratic, even an autocratic regime: 'Just as a democracy may, in fact, deprive the individual citizen of a great many liberties which he might have in some other form of society, so it is perfectly conceivable that a liberal-minded despot would allow his subjects a large measure of personal freedom'. Illustrating the point, he says that 'it is arguable that in the Prussia of Frederick the Great or in the Austria of Joseph II men of imagination, and creative genius, and, indeed, minorities of all kinds, were less persecuted and felt the pressure, both of institutions and custom, less heavy upon them than in many an earlier or later democracy' (Berlin 1969, pp. 129–30).

Berlin admits, in making these points, that he is following in the steps of Jeremy Bentham, who had written to similar effect in the late eighteenth century on the basis of what he called 'a kind of discovery I had made', that freedom is nothing more or less than 'the absence of restraint' (Bentham, in Long 1977, p. 54). Bentham (1843, p. 503), too, had concluded, on the basis of this equation between freedom and non-interference, that law is inherently opposed to freedom: 'All coercive laws ... are, as far as they go, abrogative of liberty'. And so it was accepted in his circle that freedom had little or nothing to do with democracy. Thus his close associate, William Paley (2002, p. 314), could write in 1785 on the same lines as Berlin that 'an absolute form of government' might be 'no less free than the purest democracy'.

The point in tracing Berlin's attitude back to Bentham and Paley—the utilitarian, unwitting founders of what became classical liberalism or libertarianism—is that they, unlike him, were very conscious of maintaining a novel, even outrageous position in severing the connection between freedom and democracy. The reason why Bentham thought that his idea of freedom as non-interference was 'a kind of discovery' is that he was aware of rejecting the more traditional idea of freedom associated over nearly two millennia with the republican way of thinking. This was familiar to him and his contemporaries from the writings of Polybius and Cicero and Livy in the Roman Republic, as well as the writings of the Renaissance republicans of northern Italy—in particular, Machiavelli's *Discourses on Livy*—and the supporters of the cause of American independence.

On that more traditional conception, freedom is not equivalent to the absence of interference, but rather to the absence of what the Romans called *dominatio*: the absence of subjection to the will of another, in particular the will of a would-be *dominus* or master (Pettit 1997; Skinner 1998). On this approach, you could be dominated by another and lacking in freedom without actually suffering interference: the fact that another stood ready to interfere, should they take against you, meant in itself that you were under the control of their will. And on this approach, you could be interfered with by another—for example, interfered with by the law—and yet not be dominated by that interference and not rendered unfree. This possibility was associated with non-arbitrary interference, as it was generally called: that is, interference that you controlled and that did not impose an alien will or *arbitrium* in your life. When Ulysses was held to the mast by his sailors, on this way of thinking, he was not dominated by their interference, because they were acting only on terms that he had laid down. They were not imposing an alien will in the practice of such interference but merely channeling his own will, as that had been expressed in his instructions to them.

I propose that we should recover this way of thinking about freedom, for reasons I cannot detail here in full (Pettit 2014). And I want to point out that once we begin to think of freedom as equivalent to non-domination, not non-interference, we can bring back the connection between democracy and freedom that Berlin and Bentham unfortunately denied.

Democracy requires, as its etymology suggests, that the *demos* or people enjoy *kratos* or power over the government that imposes coercive laws on them, thereby interfering in their lives. But to the extent that people share equally in the exercise of such power over government, as they are supposed to do in most democratic theories, they are going to determine at least the broad shape of the laws under which they live. And to that extent, those laws are not going to represent an alien will or *arbitrium* in their affairs; the laws are going to constitute a non-dominating form of interference akin to the interference of Ulysses's sailors in his life. This is the reason why there is, indeed, a deep and intimate connection between the idea of freedom and the idea of democracy. If it works well, the point and value of democracy lies in the fact that it offers us a way of having a coercive government that guards us against private domination without perpetrating public domination.

The first dimension of democracy that I wish to emphasize, then, is the freedom dimension. Democracy can allow people to live under a coercive law, without being dominated by that law and made unfree by its imposition. It can ensure that the law under which they live is enacted, administered, and adjudicated on terms that they play an equal part in imposing and can therefore see as an expression of a shared will (Pettit 2012).

Before leaving this first dimension, it may be worth remarking that one salient way in which the freedom associated with democracy can be flouted is via the colonial or quasi-colonial control of a foreign power. It is interesting in that regard that those who stood by the American colonies in their war of independence always stressed the fact that any colonial power, even one that is wholly beneficent, will dominate those on whom it imposes laws and taxes and deprive them of their freedom. They will not have any control over the shape of those laws and taxes, not even the control that would come of being able to force law-makers to live under the laws they form. The eminent chemist, Joseph Priestley (1993, p. 140), had fastened on this point in discussing the cause of the American colonists:

'Q. What *is* the great grievance that those people complain of? A. It is their being taxed by the parliament of Great Britain, the members of which are so far from taxing themselves, that they ease themselves at the same time'.

By contrast with the anti-colonialism—and, indeed, the support for democracy—that the republican conception of freedom led Priestley and others to embrace, it is worth noting that the opponents of the American cause used Bentham's new conception precisely to argue that colonialism was not so bad—as, indeed, Berlin had been accused of suggesting in the 1950s. This observation is particularly interesting for anyone concerned with issues of international relations.

A friend of Bentham's, John Lind, made the pro-colonialism case quite openly. He argues in a pamphlet directed against Richard Price, another British defender of the American cause, that freedom requires, not non-domination, but non-interference; it is 'nothing more or less than the absence of coercion', whether coercion of the body or the will (Lind 1776, p. 16). British law may interfere in the lives of the Americans, he says, imposing compliance and levying taxes, since 'all laws are coercive'. But the law interferes in the lives of the British, too, and the Americans, therefore, have no particular grounds for complaint (Lind 1776, pp. 24, 114). So what, he asks, is all the fuss about?

Richard Price, a well-known mathematician in his own right, was quite clear about the reason to fuss. Given the republican conception of freedom as non-domination, he argues that to be subject to a master is enough to make you unfree, even when the master does not impose harshly—even when he imposes only in the modest manner of the Stamp Act of 1765. Individuals may be lucky enough to find kindly masters, he says, but they 'cannot be denominated free, however equitably and kindly they may be treated'. And this lesson, he insists, applies in the relation between societies—in particular, Great Britain and its colonies—not just in the relation between persons: it 'is strictly true of communities as well as of individuals' (Price 1991, pp. 77–78).

2   SCHUMPETER'S MISTAKE

The discussion of Berlin's mistake suggests that the demands of freedom, understood as freedom as non-domination, make a strong case for the value of democracy. Or at least that they do so to the extent that democracy gives people equal access to a system of popular power or control over government. But now, we are positioned to see a further mistake in how contemporary thinkers conceive of democracy. This is the mistake of taking democracy to require something less than a system of popular power or control over government. The mistake must be forever associated with Joseph Schumpeter, since he built it into the model of democracy that he developed in his classic book of 1942, *Capitalism, Socialism and Democracy*. He popularized the model to such an effect that it remains the standard image of democracy among many mainstream political scientists. As part of the model, Schumpeter (1984, p. 272) argues that democracy does not enable the people to 'control their political leaders', holding instead that all it gives them is a wayward form of influence.

In order to understand this claim, it is important to understand the distinction between influence and control. Imagine the effect you will have on the traffic at a busy intersection if you play police officer and give hand signals in the usual manner, inviting the cars to ignore the lights. In all likelihood, some cars will take their lead from your signals, others not; and among those that do not, some will try to drive quietly by, others protest with honking horns or exasperated gestures. You will certainly have an influence in such a case, making a difference to how the cars behave; you will probably create utter chaos. But will you have control? Not on the assumption that you wanted the cars to follow your signals, as they might follow the signals of a police offer. You will have made a difference to how the cars behave, but not a difference that imposes any desired direction or pattern—not a difference that serves any identifiable end or goal.

What will be required in order for your influence to give direction to a process like the flow of cars in this example? The influence must give rise to a recognizable pattern in the process and that pattern must be one that you seek. The influence, in other words, must control for the appearance of a desired pattern. There will be a range of ways in which you can vary your input to the process, since there are different hand signals you can give. And for each of those inputs there will be a corresponding output: the traffic will alter in response to your signals. In the case where you take the police officer's place at the intersection, this condition will not be fulfilled: there will be a more or less random correlation between how you move your hands and how the cars adjust. Were a police officer to be in your place, however, then things would certainly be different. The officer's hand signals would reliably generate, now this sort of effect, now that; as we say, they would control for how the traffic moves.

If the *demos* or people are to share equally in exercising *kratos* or power over government, and if the power they share is to mean that the coercive laws of government are not arbitrary and dominating—not the imposition of an alien will—then what they exercise has to constitute control, not just influence. The people might have influence on government without this impressing any particular shape or pattern on the acts of government; it might be an influence as wayward and random in its effects as the influence of the weather. That the people had such an influence would not give us any reason to think that the laws and decrees passed by government are passed on terms that they dictate, as the actions of Ulysses's sailors are performed under terms that he dictates.

What Schumpeter did in his influential book is to persuade the generations following him that democracy cannot be expected to do anything more than have an influence of a more or less pattern-less, direction-less kind on those who are in government and on how they enact and enforce the law. He assumes, reasonably, that any plausible democratic system is going to involve open, periodic, electoral competition, with different parties seeking to attract enough support to win office. Such a system is undoubtedly better than one of dynastic or chaotic succession, but Schumpeter is skeptical about the possibility that the results of such a democratic process would be 'meaningful in themselves—as for instance the realization of any definite end or ideal would be'. The people do not form systematic views that they might impose on leaders; under the influence of popular pressure and party propaganda, he says, they display only 'an indeterminate bundle of vague impulses loosely playing about given slogans and mistaken impressions' (Schumpeter 1984, p. 253). And even if they did form such views, they would not be able to impose them. The political decisions produced from 'the raw material of those individual volitions', as he puts it, might take any of a variety of forms, depending on the initiatives of the party boss and the party machine. Parties and leaders are primarily committed to keeping a hold on office, not to representing any standing principles, and no matter what the input from the electorate, 'the pyrotechnics of party management and party advertising' will deliver whatever response promises to serve best in 'the competitive struggle for political power' (Schumpeter 1984, pp. 254, 83).

I cannot go into any detail on the issue of how a democratic people might impress a pattern or shape on the doings of government, holding it to terms that they dictate. But let me set out some basic assumptions that I make (Pettit 2012). The system of popular influence that democratic institutions establish must be one that all can equally access. And that system of popular influence must serve to impose a direction on government that all are disposed to find acceptable. The most plausible way in which a democratic system might achieve this result is by imposing such electoral and other constraints on those in power that they have to respect community-wide standards in what decisions they make and in how they make them. The policies in any domain of decision-making that breach those standards must be put out of court, off the table. And the processes for deciding between the remaining candidates in any domain must be equally put out of play, if they breach such standards. The processes I have in mind here might vary from popular referendum to parliamentary vote, to referral to a court, an independent commission, or a citizen assembly.

Are there community-wide standards of the kind that democracy might serve to impose in this way on government? I believe that in any society that recognizes the equal status of all its citizens, and that opens citizenship fairly to newer residents, such standards are bound to emerge and evolve in the wake of public discussion, whether discussion in centralized forums or across the different venues of public space, from workplace to café to seminar. When people debate about policy in different areas, inevitably building dissensus as well as consensus, they have to do so on the basis of some common points of reference, some shared terms of argument; else the debate gives way to something akin to war. And when the debate continues over time in the public space of claim and counter-claim, proposal and contestation, those standards are more or less bound to have an impact on what and how things are done by government. Or at least they will do so in the absence of special lobby groups who achieve hidden or deceptive modes of influence on those in power.

If this is right, then the main effect of a well-ordered democracy will be to make an infinite number of policies or processes simply unthinkable. The *demos* that keeps tabs and checks on government may exercise *kratos*, not in causing this or that is done, or to be done by this or that procedure, but in ensuring that a myriad of other policies and processes never get a look-in. Think about how in the classic western, the cowboy controls his cattle as he rides along behind them, not taking any initiative in particular. He rides herd on the animals, as we say, controlling them just by being there, ready to take action if one of them should chance to go off track. That may offer the best image of how the people in a functioning democracy can exercise control over those in government. They ride herd on the proposals and decisions of those they elect, making sure that the authorities don't ever go off track and being ready to blow the whistle—to make democratic trouble—if they do. It may have been this pattern that traditional republicans had in mind when, in a phrase made famous by the Irish eighteenth-century lawyer, John Philpot Curran, they endorsed the idea that the price of liberty is eternal vigilance—that is, eternal, democratic vigilance.

3 Riker's Mistake

On the emerging view of democracy, its main role is to give the people control over government, enabling them to impose community-wide standards on the policies adopted and on the processes followed in adopting them. The point of democracy, on this view, is to ensure that the people are not dominated by the interference of government associated with its imposition of laws and decrees and taxes. Whatever measures the government imposes, it imposes on terms that the people equally endorse and play an equal role in enforcing. The authorities channel the popular will, as we might put it—if you like, Rousseau's general will—not the will of an alien agency. Like Ulysses's sailors, they act as servants, not as masters.

It is important in this image of democracy that the people are said to exercise control and that the question is left open as to which channels of control—which channels of directed influence—serve the required purpose; that is an issue for more detailed institutional design. The third common mistake about democracy is not to leave this question open, but to equate democracy with an electoral mechanism of influence and control, holding that the use of other mechanisms is undemocratic. This mistake is found in the many authors who think that democracy is present wherever there is a system of open, periodic, and competitive election, and absent wherever there is no such system. I believe that an electoral system is necessary for democracy, at least in a world where it is only regular elections that are likely to prompt robust public discussion and contestation, the assertion and reinforcement of free speech, and the effective identification of shared standards. But I think it is a serious mistake to think that an electoral system is sufficient for democracy and that other systemic devices are irrelevant or inimical to the cause of popular, democratic control.

I associate this mistake with William Riker (1982), because he provides a formulation that has proven very influential. In his account of things, elections give people all the control they can hope to have over government, and other devices—in particular, the devices we associate with constitutional constraints—have nothing to do with advancing such control; on the contrary, he suggests, they represent constraints that shackle popular will rather than implementing it. He describes electorally imposed restrictions on government as populist in character, where this is not meant to have pejorative overtones, and the constitutionally imposed restrictions as liberal. And he casts the advanced democracies as being democratic insofar as they are populist, undemocratic insofar as they are liberal.

According to the account sketched here, a society is going to be democratic to the extent that the people are able to impose community-wide standards on how the government forms its decisions and on what it actually decides. And there is absolutely no reason to think that the people will have this power only in virtue of their electoral impact on who is in government and on how they behave. There is equal reason to think that the people may impose their terms on government in a variety of other ways; for example, via the constraints that they uphold within the constitution of their society. Via the actions of unelected personnel who are appointed under such constraints; these will include the official ombudsman, auditor, and statistician, as well as those who wield authority in the central bank, in the electoral commission, and, of course, in the courts of law. And, perhaps most important, via their own readiness to challenge and contest, whether individually or collectively, and in formal or informal forums, in ways that the constitution makes possible.

It goes without saying that the constitutional guidelines that set up the electoral system—and that are required for this purpose (Ely 1981)—must not themselves be undemocratic in character. They should generally be subject to democratic contestation and amendment—although constitutions do often err in making amendment too difficult. The same goes, of course, for the constraints that establish the basic rights of citizens, ensuring another aspect of popular control. They should themselves be imposed under a system of popular control, staying in place only insofar as they are not exposed to democratic challenge and amendment.

What should we say about the various unelected authorities who are going to play a role in the governance of a society, under any plausible constitution or arrangement? Do they have to be regarded as a foreign imposition on the people and, unlike elected deputies, not representative of popular will? I argue not.

Suppose that I am asked to nominate someone for a position on a committee. I might select someone whom I can require to consult with me and adopt my instructions on how to vote. Let us call such an appointee a responsive representative. But equally I might select someone whom I cannot consult with or instruct on the grounds that the person is of a similar mind to me and is likely to act as I would act. Being someone whose decisions are indicative of what I would decide on the committee, we might describe this person as an indicative representative.

When we appoint ombudsmen, statisticians, and auditors, the members of central banks, and electoral commissions, and the judges who determine the interpretation and application of the law, we can appoint them under such tight constraints and with such precise briefs that they count as our indicative representatives. Unlike elected deputies, these authorities will not be particularly responsive to popular demand; that is how we set things up. But if they operate in fidelity to their constraints and briefs, as popular scrutiny and vigilance can ensure that they do, then their decisions ought to conform to the terms we encode in their protocols of appointment and office. And to the extent that they do this, they will act in a way that is indicative of how we, the people—we, who are ultimately responsible for the constraints and briefs that guide them—would want them to act in their various positions. Like elected deputies, who are responsive representatives, they will be forced to act in a manner that conforms to the community-wide standards we impose.

Not only should we want a democracy that gives people control over government, ensuring that the government does not dominate its citizens and deprive them of their freedom. The upshot of these final observations is that we should also want a democracy that is not just electoral but, in a broad sense, constitutional: a democracy that implements popular control by the non-electoral means of constitutional constraints and constitutionally appointed authorities. To establish a constitutional democracy is not to establish a democracy and then to make it constitutional, as if that were something extra. It is hard to imagine what a democracy would be like if it did not function under the constraints of a constitution—written or unwritten—as well as under electoral pressures.

4   CONCLUSION

While this has been a mainly critical essay, I think that the upshot is fundamentally positive. Berlin's mistake derives from not seeing that, identified in the traditional manner with non-domination, freedom requires the democratic control that would render government interference undominating. Schumpeter's mistake consists in thinking that the most that democracy can achieve is popular influence, not popular control. And Riker's mistake consists in not recognizing that democracy, in the sense in which it involves popular control, requires a constitutional, contestatory set of institutions, not just devices of an electoral kind.

The upshot is a case, strengthened in each round of critique, for a republican or neo-republican conception of democracy. Under this conception, the role that democracy should play is that of ensuring that government, even a government that protects people against private domination, should not itself perpetrate public domination; it should be forced to operate on the people's terms, responding to desiderata that they impose. The democracy I envisage would aim, not just at giving people influence, enabling them to make a difference; it would aim at giving them a form of influence that enables them to make a systematic difference, imposing their shared standards on government. And it would deploy a range of institutions and offices in the course of activating this control, not restrict the tools at its disposal to electoral measures alone. The neo-republican approach behind these lessons does not offer us a ready blueprint for democratic organization. But it challenges us to work at elaborating the institutions that would advance republican aims and guard us against the usurpation of political power by those with special interests and a factional agenda.[2]

NOTES

1. For an elaboration of the republican view, see Pettit (1997, 2012, 2014). And, more generally, on the republican tradition of thinking about liberty, see Skinner (1998), Honohan (2002), Viroli (2002), Laborde and Maynor (2007), and Lovett and Pettit (2009).
2. This chapter is based on a presentation to the President of the Swiss Confederation, Micheline Calmy-Rey, and her Departmental colleagues in Berne, September 2011.

REFERENCES

Bentham, J. (1843). Anarchical fallacies. In J. Bowring (Ed.), *The works of Jeremy Bentham* (Vol. II, pp. 489–534). Edinburgh: W. Tait.
Berlin, I. (1969). *Four essays on liberty.* Oxford: Oxford University Press.
Ely, J. H. (1981). *Democracy and distrust: A theory of judicial review.* Cambridge, MA: Harvard University Press.
Honohan, I. (2002). *Civic republicanism.* London: Routledge.
Laborde, C., & Maynor, J. (Eds.). (2007). *Republicanism and political theory.* Oxford: Blackwell.
Lind, J. (1776). *Three letters to Dr Price.* London: T. Payne.

Long, D. C. (1977). *Bentham on liberty.* Toronto: University of Toronto Press.

Lovett, F., & Pettit, P. (2009). Neo-republicanism: A normative and institutional research program. *Annual Review of Political Science,* 12, 18–29.

Paley, W. (2002). *The principles of moral and political philosophy.* Indianapolis: Liberty Fund.

Pettit, P. (1997). *Republicanism: A theory of freedom and government.* Oxford: Oxford University Press.

Pettit, P. (2012). *On the people's terms: A republican theory and model of democracy.* Cambridge: Cambridge University Press.

Pettit, P. (2014). *Just freedom: A moral compass for a complex world.* New York: W.W. Norton and Company.

Price, R. (1991). *Political writings.* Cambridge: Cambridge University Press.

Priestley, J. (1993). *Political writings.* Cambridge: Cambridge University Press.

Riker, W. (1982). *Liberalism against populism.* San Francisco: W.H. Freeman and Company.

Schumpeter, J. A. (1984). *Capitalism, socialism and democracy.* New York: Harper Torchbooks.

Skinner, Q. (1998). *Liberty before liberalism.* Cambridge: Cambridge University Press.

Viroli, M. (2002). *Republicanism.* New York: Hill and Wang.

CHAPTER 11

Karl Marx After a Century and a Half

Allen W. Wood

1 THE PARADOX OF MODERNITY

The modern world is in contradiction with itself. Since the industrial revolution in the middle of the nineteenth century, there has been an incredible expansion of the capacity of the human species to understand, control, and make use of nature to satisfy human needs. There has also been an incredible increase in the extent and complexity of the network of forms of cooperation, especially in the kinds of skill developed and the division of human labour, and in the degree of coordination, both actual and potential, among human beings. In all these ways, there has also been an incredible expansion in the capacity human beings have for leading satisfying and fulfilling lives, developing the abilities that matter to themselves and to one another. Human abilities that were earlier conceived of only as the result of magic or divine influence—the capacity to fly like the birds, to explore the depths of the ocean, to be cured of fatal diseases and healed of crippling injuries—have now been put within people's reach as a result merely of their knowledge and their developed natural capacities.

A.W. Wood
Indiana University, Bloomington, IN, USA

© The Editor(s) (if applicable) and The Author(s) 2016
A. Fives, K. Breen (eds.), *Philosophy and Political Engagement*,
DOI 10.1057/978-1-137-44587-2_11

201

There has also been an incredible expansion in their capacities for human community and in the potential for the enrichment of the lives of all human beings, and not only the lives of a privileged few, beyond what was possible in previous ages. The capacity for human cooperation and interdependency is worldwide. Resources and commodities from one continent regularly serve the needs of people halfway around the globe, from another climate, another culture, previously from another world.

This has gone hand in hand with the growth of certain ethical conceptions pertaining to the form this human community should have. Human beings, all human beings, all human lives, are regarded as having dignity. The capacity of people to choose how to lead their lives, to shape their own lives through free choice, is widely regarded as a human right. People have come to think that justice requires that all, and not merely a privileged few, should have this freedom, that every human being has a right to it. At the same time, it has come to be accepted that human beings ought to address one another on terms of equality and mutual respect. No human being should be in a position of servitude to another, differences between human beings should not be constituted by relations of superiority and inferiority, women should not be the chattels of men, differences of skin colour and religion should not matter. These changes in ethical evaluation and perception have taken hold at the same time that the technological, economic, and social capacities of the species to realize them have expanded to an extent hitherto unknown or even undreamt of.

Yet there has been a painful and even an astonishing gap between, on the one hand, these aspirations and also our capacities to realize them and, on the other, the degree to which human beings have actually achieved health, happiness, comfort, both individual and collective freedom, and the fulfilment of the lives of all. Although those in what it pleases us to call 'the developed world', or at least a privileged minority of them, lead lives of relative safety, prosperity, and comfort, the vast majority of human beings who live outside this world are still scourged with hunger and disease. They lack food, clean water, a healthful environment, even minimal education.

Even in the relatively prosperous world, the uneven distribution of resources and freedoms and the inequalities in wealth and life prospects are shocking in their extent and degree, and in the past half century, these inequalities have been steadily growing and even accelerating. The USA is generally considered the most prosperous of all nations on earth, but it is also the most unequal: the 400 wealthiest individuals possess more than the bottom 150 million Americans. The 1 % of wealthiest individuals possess over one third of all the wealth, more than the combined wealth of the lowest 95 %. They own 42.7 trillion dollars, more than the bottom three billion residents of earth.[1] The political system is firmly under the control of wealthy individuals and corporations, who use their political power to increase their power over the rest of society and to accelerate the rate at which their superiority is growing.

By most measures, these inequalities, and the domination exercised by the privileged over the disadvantaged, are greater now than in the mid-nineteenth century, when Karl Marx wrote in revolutionary protest against class rule and class domination. This is the *paradox of modernity*.

2   Marx's Materialist Conception of History

Marx was not the first to see the incredible gap between the human potential of modernity and its ideals, on the one hand, and the actual achievements and social dynamics, on the other. Jean-Jacques Rousseau perhaps deserves credit for being the first to focus on the contradictions of modernity. Others were painfully aware of them. Kant, for example, wrote that 'Rousseau was not so wrong when he preferred to [modern civilization] the condition of savages, as long, namely, as one leaves out this last stage to which our species has yet to ascend' (Kant 1902 [1784], p. 26). Fichte divided the history of the species into five ages, of which the present age is the third: it is a time of liberation, but also maximum corruption, yet eventually to be redeemed by future progress (Fichte 1971b [1804]). Fichte looked forward to a future age in which the powers of nature, comprehended by science, would be subjugated to the human will, and in which human beings would constitute 'an association in which one cannot work for himself without working at the same time for others, nor work for others without working for himself' (Fichte 1971a [1794], p. 321).

Marx, however, was the first to attempt to use the science of political economy to understand these workings and gain a theoretical grasp of them. He is still the thinker who achieved the most developed understanding of the paradox of our planet and our species, whose capacities and aspirations seem to go in one direction, and whose actual lives and achievements have gone in the opposite direction. He attempted to comprehend the dynamics of history scientifically by understanding the genesis and the 'laws of motion' of modern society, which he conceptualized under the name of 'capitalism'. Marx developed a speculative theory of historical change through which modern capitalism had arisen, and through which its future could also be projected.

The fundamental tendency of this history was the constant development of the productive forces of society. The application of these forces, as well as their further development, are determined and constrained by the structure of social practice. This practice constitutes a set of relations of production and relationships of cooperation, but also of dominance and subjection, between social classes. It gives some effective control over the means of production and subordinates others to their class rule. The superficial legal form of this rule consists in rights of property, and the political form of this rule, through which people are governed, consists in state coercion. The economic structure of society also manifests itself in the way people think about themselves and their relations to one another. Class society, seen clearly for what it is, could not be tolerated, especially by those subjected to its oppression, but even by those who play the role of oppressors. Thus, ideological forms of consciousness serve the needs of the social system. The demands of social practice create the institutions and forms of consciousness that enable them to function in accordance with the economic structure of the society that has created them.

As productive forces develop, the demands of social practice undergo change, and the power relations between classes shift. Conflicts emerge between ideological forms and political movements representing the clashing interests of social classes. That class emerges as dominant whose interests correspond to the emerging state of the productive forces. This is the way Marx understands the genesis of modern capitalism.

Marx sees the instability of modern society, its vulnerability to economic crises, generated not by any unstable human relation to nature but by the dynamics of capitalist society itself, as a sign that bourgeois society is only a transitional form, destined to pass over—like Kant's present stage of 'civilization' or Fichte's 'third age'—into something higher, in which humanity will take control of the productive powers capitalism has placed within its grasp, and begin to organize society according to the modern conception of human individuals as beings destined for freedom rather than servitude, and for relations with one another on terms of cooperation, mutual valuation, and mutual caring. The vehicle of this change is the class oppressed by the bourgeoisie, the class of wage labourers, the modern proletariat, or working class. This class, consisting of the vast majority of society, will find the conditions of capitalism increasingly intolerable, and will inevitably find a way to a new, higher, and freer social order. Marx thought that the contradictions of modern society must eventually resolve themselves, and that they would do so not through the condescending moral generosity or sense of justice of the privileged, but instead through the self-development of the exploited. Marx's political activities were directed to organizing and developing, through scientific understanding, the capacities of the working class to fulfil the mission his understanding of history would assign them.

3 HAS MARX'S THOUGHT BEEN DISCREDITED?[2]

Clearly, things have not gone as Marx thought they would. As I have already said, modern society now displays an even larger chasm between human potentialities and their realization than it did in Marx's day. We are even farther than we were then, from appropriating scientific understanding, technology, and human cooperation for the uniform enhancement of human life. The inequalities between rich and poor and the oppression of those who labour by those who own are even greater. The fate of Marx's own ideas—especially as they were interpreted and appropriated by others, and then acted on—has had a complex role to play in this process. In considering these facts, we need to reflect both on the ways Marx seems to have been wrong and on the ways others—both his self-appointed followers and his enemies and critics—have been wrong about Marx.

It is now often said that Marx's ideas have been discredited. This is often stated as if it were the report of a fact, but more often it functions more as a performative utterance, whose illocutionary force is: 'Our minds are hereby closed to Marx's ideas'. The connection between the two is provided by the sociological truth that as regards the political influence of an idea, it is sufficient for it actually to be discredited, that it be widely believed to be discredited. When it is said that Marx's ideas have been discredited, however, there is also the implication that they now lack intellectual merit, that their evidential support or cogency has been removed by either empirical facts or sound reasoning. Such claims are false and highly misleading. We can see this if we consider the converse phenomenon: an idea that has no intellectual merit or evidential support whatever cannot be considered discredited in this political sense, as long as it is being promulgated with some success by a powerful propaganda machine. This is true, for instance, of the idea, utterly rejected by the community of climate scientists, that there is no climate disruption due to human-made global warming, but that climate disruption is a hoax perpetrated on us by a leftist conspiracy.

Sometimes, it is claimed that the collapse of the Soviet Union and its empire has discredited Marx's ideas in this latter sense. Sometimes, the thesis is that they have been discredited by the moral unacceptability of the institutions in the Soviet Union and other self-described Marxist states. As G.A. Cohen has cogently argued, if Marx's theory of history is properly understood, then it will be seen that this theory would not predict that a successful working-class revolution could occur in Russia under the conditions in which the Russian Revolution occurred in 1917 (Cohen 2000, pp. 389–95). Marx did, in fact, encourage his Russian correspondents to make a socialist revolution, but he expected them to be successful only if their revolution were part of a more general upheaval in capitalist society that was centred on the more developed capitalist societies of Western Europe, such as France, England, and Germany. If events in Russia and Eastern Europe challenge Marx's theories, they do so mainly by showing that something like a socialist revolution could occur, and persist for a number of decades, even under conditions where Marx's theory implies that such a revolution would be impossible.

The most flagrantly false idea now widely disseminated about Marx is that he offered a utopian programme for a communist or socialist utopia, which was then put into practice in Russia and elsewhere, and then proved to be not only unsuccessful economically and politically, but also highly objectionable morally. Marx, in fact, offered no such vision, contemptuously refusing to offer 'recipes for the cook-shops of the future' (*Capital*, 1, p. 99) and stating bluntly that 'everyone will have to admit to himself that he has no exact idea what the future ought to be' (*CW*, 3, p. 142). Communism, declares the *German Ideology*, 'is not an ideal to which reality has to adjust itself. We call communism the real movement which abolishes the present state of things' (*CW*, 5, p. 49). Marx studied capitalism intensively; about socialism, he wrote almost nothing.

Sometimes a connection is made between Marx and later totalitarian regimes that called themselves 'Marxist', based on the *Communist Manifesto*'s use of the phrase 'the dictatorship of the proletariat'. But the term 'dictatorship' in the mid-nineteenth century did not mean what it came to mean in the twentieth. As Marx wryly points out in the *Eighteenth Brumaire*, ancient Rome, especially the Rome of the republic, was the source of much nineteenth-century verbal and conceptual vocabulary in political matters (*CW*, 11, pp. 110–1). This is true of both the terms 'dictatorship' and 'proletariat' in his own writings. In the Roman republic, a 'dictator' was a *magistratus extraordinarius* who, in times of emergency or transition, was empowered to perform tasks beyond the authority of ordinary magistrates. The *Communist Manifesto*'s reference to the dictatorship of a *class* (the proletariat) indicates that this transitional power, as Marx and Engels conceive it, would not reside in a single individual, but would be shared by an entire class. Viewed in its historical context, the term 'dictatorship of the proletariat' is not an endorsement, even temporarily, of the despotic rule of an autocrat, much less advocacy of the more or less permanent totalitarian regime that such despots, later called 'dictators', were able to set up under early twentieth-century political conditions.

The *Communist Manifesto* does list a series of ten steps Marx and Engels think would likely be taken after a communist revolution (*CW*, 6, p. 507). But they emphasize that these steps are not a utopian programme, but only tentative predictions. In any case, some of them (such as universal free public education) do not any longer even sound radical. Clearly, these measures were intended to describe a necessary response to the potential chaos of any revolutionary transition. Marx was not, in general, an advocate of state power, and in his later comments on the Civil War in France, he advocated the decentralization of state power. Marx was, of course, also supposing that after the communist revolution, the state would be in the hands of the working class (the vast majority of society), rather than under the control of either the traditional aristocracy or the bourgeoisie. He was, in general, resistant to state power as it was wielded in capitalist society. Within the working-class movement, Marx did oppose the anarchists, who favoured the immediate and total abolition of the state. This is still sometimes seen as ominous—evidence that he would support Stalinist totalitarianism. But it should rather be seen as an indication that he recognized some need for a public legal order, even during a period of revolutionary transition, and also that he wanted to dissociate the movement from the terrorist tactics adopted by some of Bakunin's Russian followers. Resistance to terrorism need not be an endorsement of totalitarianism.

4   Soviet 'Marxism'

Sometimes, when it is pointed out that Marx criticized the environmental pollution of industrial capitalism, the immediate response is that such pollution was even worse in the Soviet Union than in most capitalist nations. Here we see operative a transition in thought, so automatic that an intervening inference does not seem to be involved, that the Soviet Union was simply the practical expression of Marx's ideas. If there were an inference here, then there might also be the possibility of seeing how deeply questionable it is.

The Soviet Union did not come into being until over three decades after Marx's death. It is preposterous, in light of this, that people should assume without question that he is to blame for the Soviet system, or that it resulted from a correct application of Marx's ideas.[3] No doubt the Soviet leaders persuaded themselves that they were being faithful to 'Saint Marx', and even believed their own propaganda when they claimed to represent the working-class movement called for by his theory. But those who associate Marx's thought with the deeds of the Soviet Union would never accept Soviet propaganda at face value on any other subject. Why do they do it here? Because it lends support to their pre-existing prejudices and keeps them imprisoned within their complacent circle of illusion. In this respect, they merely mimic what was most deplorable about the mindset of Soviet dogmatism itself.

We all know that the revolution did not occur where Marx expected it, in the nations of Western Europe where capitalism was most fully developed, but instead in Russia and in other countries with political traditions favouring repressive absolutism. It is all too predictable that the new political system would perpetuate—perhaps in a revolutionary crisis, even intensify—the most abominable aspects of the old regime. We have seen the same political tendencies in Russia since the fall of the Soviet system. Marx's writings contain no advocacy of the tyranny of Stalin, any more than they do the tyranny of Tsar Nicholas II or of Vladimir Putin and his oligarchs (or, as we might call this procession, the Cossacks, the commissars, and the crooks).

Much of what was wrong with Soviet 'Marxism' had to do with its quasi-religious character. It is as if Marxism itself became a sort of outrageous caricature of that religious view of the world, whose critique Marx himself always regarded as the starting point for all criticism (CW, 3, p. 175). Marx never encouraged others to treat his writings as sacred texts. Marx never thought of the working-class movement as something that ought to bear his name, like a corporate logo. I suggest that this nevertheless happened, partly because it soon became unclear where the working-class movement cited by Marx was to be found, or even uncertain that there still was such a movement. Those who needed to believe in its existence took the dogmatic adherence to the letter of Marxist texts (as authoritatively interpreted), as a substitute for evidence of the existence of the actual movement itself.

I do not lack sympathy with those whose hopes were concentrated on such a movement and the revolution it was supposed to bring. But sympathy with their hopes should not blind us to the ways in which their faith was tragically misplaced. It is not always easy to apportion our beliefs to the objective evidence, but failure to do so has had disastrous historical consequences for the working-class movement in which Marx believed. Twentieth-century 'Marxism' subverted the political practice for which Marx was hoping, causing it (at least for the time being) to dead end in a rubbish heap.

Karl Marx was, above all, an empirical researcher. He devised the materialist conception of history based on the historical evidence as he saw it, and he used this conception as a guide to further empirical inquiry. To those who read his writings without seeing them through the lens of some pernicious dogmatism (either Marxist or anti-Marxist), it can be seen that Marx was not closed to new evidence, or imprisoned by a rigid ideology. Marx saw his role in history as advocating for the working class, and also helping it develop the intellectual tools it would need to understand the workings of the capitalist system and fulfil its mission of human liberation. Chief among Marx's achievements was developing the capacity to see through the illusions promulgated by the bourgeoisie, as well as the illusions of practical life itself that capitalist society inflicts on those subject to it—such as the 'fetishism of commodities' or the view that capitalists are in some way rightfully 'entitled' to the profit they gain from exploiting workers. The intended effect of his writings was always to open people's minds, never to close them.

Marx often changed his mind over the years. His writings can be viewed, as they recently have been by historian, Jonathan Sperber (2013), as a series of highly contextualized responses to the precise and changing series of political conditions under which he wrote. Marx's confident predictions of an imminent working-class revolution, and his occasional declaration that such a revolution is inevitable, should always be seen not as doctrines that follow from his theories, but instead, as hopeful political acts designed to bring about what was being predicted and being declared 'inevitable'. Engels later candidly admitted that he and Marx were simply wrong about the revolutionary potential of the events of both 1848 and 1870 (*CW*, 27, pp. 510–3).

Even on matters of important economic doctrine, Marx changed his mind. To cite one example: in early writings such as *Wage Labour and Capital* and even the *Communist Manifesto*, he seems to have believed in what was then called the 'wages minimum' doctrine—the proposition that under capitalism, wages naturally tend to fall to the point where workers can barely survive on them. Later, however, in *Capital*, he came to see that the level of wages in a country depends on other factors—including historical traditions and customs—and that it involves a 'historical and moral element' (*Capital*, 1, p. 275). In *Critique of the Gotha Program*, Marx roundly rejects the Lassallean 'iron law of wages', which is merely Lassalle's name for the 'wages minimum' doctrine (*CW*, 24, pp. 91–3).

Marx was never in a position to censor or suppress anything, and never showed any tendency to do so. He was himself a victim of political repression, and an ardent defender, both in print and in court, of freedom of the pen and the right of political dissent. When Marx thought the International Workingmen's Association was heading in directions he could not approve, the only measure available to him was to dissociate himself from it and dissolve it. Later, when his German followers formed an alliance with the Lassalleans of which he disapproved, he could only communicate to them his criticisms of the programme on which they were agreed, registering his political impotence, both ironically and humorously, with his final Biblical valediction: *Dixi et salvavi animam meam* (*CW*, 24, p. 99; see *Ezekiel*, 3: 18–9).

5   WHERE DID MARX GO WRONG?

Let us consider two common answers to this question.

The Revolution Has Not Occurred

Many people may say that the most obvious point on which Marx was wrong is simply that capitalism still exists, that there has been no successful working-class revolution—none that established the higher form of society for which Marx was hoping, and which he declared to be inevitable. In my view, however, it would fly in the face of a higher wisdom to expect Marx to have been right about this, namely, the wise saying that 'prediction is difficult, especially about the future'.[4] Human life is subject to contingency and chance, more than it is to any determinate trends or laws of motion. Little or nothing in human history is inevitable, and even less is inevitable that people have any reason to hope for (perhaps the only thing truly inevitable is that sooner or later we will all die).[5]

Marx's materialist conception of history presents a pattern, according to which the economic development of society exerts an influence on other features of social life, and he makes a good case that this pattern can be seen in modern European society, with the rise of capitalism. His prediction that an analogous pattern would show itself in the decline and fall of capitalism may have been a reasonable guess at the time he wrote. I cannot fault him for it, except for his overconfidence in any prediction he (or anyone else) might make about the course of history on a large scale. I would sooner direct intellectual criticism towards those who think it a serious shortcoming in Marx's thought that his overconfident predictions have not been fulfilled.

Marx Has Been Rendered Redundant by Progress in Economic Science

Some charge Marx with adhering to the outdated 'labour theory of value', just as more precise mathematical models were about to render economics more 'scientific'. Those economists who study and report on actual facts may deserve to be called 'scientists'. But so-called 'neoclassical economics' should not be considered a science. Classical political economy in the tradition of Smith, Ricardo, and Marx, with its grounding of value on socially necessary labour time, was an intellectually well-motivated social theory. It produced a more realistic analysis of the modern economic order, as that order existed in its time, than most of what has since been achieved by neoclassical abstractions.[6] Neoclassical economics was devised precisely to offer an ideological counter-weight to Marx and other critics of capitalism. Its precise mathematical models describe reality only by way of idealized approximation; they predict very little and explain virtually nothing. Their main influence has been to distort people's perceptions of social life. Those who reproach Marx, for not having predicted the course of history a century in advance, should reflect on the fact that our economists cannot predict sizable crises in the economy, such as occurred in 2008, even a few months before they happen.

Political economy has never been, probably never will be, probably never *ought* to be, a *science* in the sense in which physics is a science. It will always be a species of social philosophy, in the sense in which that last terms implies something uncertain, open to dispute, and even discreditable—at least in the eyes of those who lack the wisdom and courage to live in a permanent condition of doubt and controversy. Marx himself always described his work not as political economy but as a contribution to the *critique of political economy* (this was the title of his 1859 work (*CW*, 29, pp. 257–420), and also the subtitle of *Capital*). The best economic science will always be that which is critical in the Kantian sense of the term, aware of the limits of science.

6   MARX'S CRITIQUE OF RIGHT AND MORALITY

My own work on Marx is perhaps best known for its emphasis on one particularly philosophical—and also particularly radical—aspect of his views, namely, his reductive or deflationary treatment of standards of morality and justice, and his consequent refusal to condemn capitalism for its injustice to workers, its violation of their rights, or its violation of any alleged principles of equality (Wood 2004, pp. 125–62, 242–64; 2014, pp. 252–73). This feature of Marxian doctrine is radical, in some ways, perplexing and even forbidding. Many who want to agree with Marx about most things wish these views were not there or even attempt to interpret them away. I understand why, but I think the texts are clear, and the views (even if we don't like them and don't regard them as defensible) are clearly there in Marx along with a body of doctrine and argument to back them up. They belong to the side of Marx that is hostile to the political state and thinks of its abolition or transcendence as on the agenda of the working-class revolution.

Concepts like right and justice, Marx thinks, belong to the realm of law and politics, the legal and political superstructure. The proper standards for them consist in correspondence to the prevailing mode of production and do not transcend any given mode of production. Thus, to the Gotha Program's demand for 'a just distribution', Marx responds with a series of pointed rhetorical questions:

> Do not the bourgeois assert that the present distribution is 'just' [*gerecht*]? And is it not in fact the only 'just' distribution on the basis of the present day mode of production? Are economic relations regulated by concepts of right [*Rechtsbegriffe*], or do not, on the contrary, relations of right arise out of economic ones? (*CW*, 24, pp. 85–6).

Of course, the bourgeois do assert that the present distribution is just. Marx agrees with them that it is the only just distribution on the basis of the present-day mode of production, because the materialist conception of history says that economic relations are not regulated by concepts of right, but, on the contrary, that relations of right arise out of economic relations.

More generally, Marx rejects all moral standards that claim to rest on universal principles or values. Here, he agrees to a surprising extent with the radical *individualism* of Max Stirner (1995 [1844]), who regards all universal moral values as belonging to the 'hegemony of thoughts' from which individuals must liberate themselves (on this connection, see Wood 2014, pp. 262–7). Marx rejects Stirner's 'egoism'; he does not think that self-interest is any more natural or rational than promoting the interests of others. He thinks that for healthy human beings, living for oneself and living for the community are not opposed orientations: 'Only within the community has each individual the means of cultivating his gifts in all directions; hence personal freedom becomes possible only within the community' (*CW*, 5, p. 78).

Like Fichte, Marx thinks that the truly human society will be one in which one will not work for oneself without also working for others, nor work for others without working for oneself. Yet Marx also accepts Stirner's idea that free human beings will not govern their lives by universal moral standards, but instead will merely live as the social individuals they are. He interprets all conceptions of general interests or universal values as only the masquerades worn by class interests. This is just as true of the values put forward by the proletariat as by those of other classes. The difference, Marx thinks, is that proletarians will still be able to devote themselves to the cause of the working class while not succumbing to such illusions, but seeing working-class interests only for what they are. For free human beings, one's own good, the good of others, the interests of one's class, none of these will need to wear the false masks of morality. When the *Communist Manifesto* considers the bourgeois objection that communism does away with all morality instead of founding it anew, its response is simple and blunt: 'The Communist revolution is the most radical rupture with traditional property relations; no wonder that its development involves the most radical rupture with traditional ideas' (*CW*, 6, p. 504). The abolition of morality is simply part of this radical rupture.

Marx's 'anti-moralism' (as one might call it), as well as his materialist critique of justice, is clearly an element in Marx's thought that is difficult to accept. Even Marx admits that there will have to be standards of right and justice governing distribution in the early phases of communist society (*CW*, 24, pp. 85–7), but he gives (and can consistently give) no positive account of their normativity, except to say that they must correspond to the mode of production. While I find Marx's radical rejection of right and morality fascinating, even in some respects appealing, I do not think it is an acceptable philosophical position (this is why so many who are sympathetic to Marx have been so eager to interpret it away).

7   THE 'JUST' SOCIETY

The concept of 'right', especially the right of private property, if seen in historical perspective, can be used to articulate Marx's most basic and enduring insight about capitalism, and at the same time, to explain why Marx himself was so hostile to the use of this concept in social criticism. If we look at the concept of natural or human rights in the thought of such modern thinkers as Locke, Rousseau, Kant, Fichte, and Hegel, we see that 'right' is the term used to capture the value of individual freedom in the sense of self-government and independence from the arbitrary will of another who might deprive you of the ability to govern yourself. Private property was defended by all these philosophers as a way of ensuring this kind of freedom: my private property is what I have acquired through my own labour and make use of for my own ends, as a self-governing rational being. What Marx saw, however, was that under capitalism, private property had come largely to take the form of one person's (or class's) ownership of the conditions of life for another person (another class). It had ceased to be a protection of individual liberty, and had instead become the chief threat to it. This Marxian insight remains true of capitalism today. But, in Marx, the insight was articulated in part through his hostility to the very concept of right, which he viewed as a bourgeois pretext for denying freedom to many by asserting it for a few.

Contrary to his own intentions, Marx's penetrating analysis of capitalist society can be used to argue that capital violates the rightful freedom of workers, and that this constitutes a set of powerful reasons why capitalism must not continue. The critique of capitalism can be combined with acceptance of standards of right and justice based on the human right to freedom (as defended by Kant, Fichte, and others in what Marx would call the tradition of bourgeois thinking about right and morality). This is one point on which I think that agreement with Marx on one important point is helped along if we disagree with him on another. A just society, by these standards, would be one in which all have the right to live freely and with modest comfort based on their own labour, and in which no one is in a position to deprive anyone else of this right because they are in possession of the means of production that other persons need in order to work and live. The role that property rights might have in such a society is unclear, but they could not include the right to exploit the labour of others.

A just society, in which no one's opportunity to earn their livelihood is dependent on the property of others, would no doubt feel like 'totalitarianism' to some, because it would take away their freedom to exploit the labour of others. Perhaps someday, as Marx speculated, society will be able to leave behind the concepts of rights and justice entirely, and write on its banner Louis Blanc's slogan: 'From each according to his abilities, to each according to his needs'.[7] But this is not a distribution that could be enforced coercively through right and the state. Marx did not think we were yet close to that form of society, and until then we need the concepts of right and justice, despite Marx's own attempts to deflate them away.

8   WHERE MARX MOST WENT WRONG

It has taken me a long time to realize that my deepest disagreement with Marx is about capitalism itself, of which his opinion was *far too favourable*.

This may strike us as a paradox, but it is obviously true. Just look at Section I of the *Communist Manifesto* (*CW*, 6, pp. 482–96). It is a paean of praise directed at capitalism and its bourgeois protagonists, who, Marx says, have created the means of production capable of liberating humanity, forced the human species at last to see clearly the nature of its social relations, and even brought into being the class that will liberate humanity once and for all. Marx saw the inherent economic instability and periodic crises of capitalism as signs that it was only a transitory social order, which was soon to pass from the scene and give humanity the opportunity to create a higher and freer social order. He was confident that the human species could not long perpetuate a social order that was so wasteful of human potential and that purchased the comfort and freedom of a few at the cost of the misery and servitude of the vast majority.

We now know, however, that capitalism—unstable, wasteful of human potential, hostile as it is to the freedom of the vast majority—nevertheless possesses a resilience that Marx did not appreciate. The extreme inequalities of wealth and power that go with the capitalist social order do not necessarily undermine it. Capitalism has been very successful in exploiting jealousies and divisions among workers. No doubt: '*El pueblo unido jamás será vencido*'. But when were the people ever united? The ideology of capitalism, blared at us through the mass media, even persuades many workers to accept their position of degrading servitude to capital as the price they must pay for living in a 'free' society.

Capitalism, instead of being a merely transitory social order, leading inevitably to something higher and freer, may instead be a quicksand or trap from which the human race, unable or unwilling to free itself, will be destined to perish in misery, or to survive only in a condition of misery, due precisely to the unsustainability of the technological control over nature which Marx thought was capitalism's great liberating gift to humanity. Marx could not bring himself to believe that our species is so stupid and inept as to tolerate indefinitely a society that benefits so few, based on the oppression and misery of so many.

9   The Fragile Prospects for Marx's Hopes

What are the prospects for liberating social change today? Our political institutions present themselves to us as 'democratic': each person is supposed to have a vote, and the outcome of our political system is supposed to be the will of the people. Marx knew that even the system closest to this, the 'bourgeois republic', had been carefully crafted to give power to wealth and privilege and to keep it away from the great masses, of whose potential power all those who designed all our modern republican constitutions were deathly afraid. Working-class movements of the nineteenth and twentieth centuries, or the recent Occupy movement in the USA, have never managed to get a firm grip on the levers of political power, even though they represent the will and the interests of the vast majority of society. But this is the way our political institutions were designed.

We leftists must face these facts, and devise realistic strategies for using the existing political system. We must avoid disillusionment with our politicians, who inevitably represent interests adverse to our aims. We must not opt out of the political system in a mood of despondency, or think we can compel our political allies to represent the interests of the majority, just by threatening to opt out. This merely plays into the hands of those who hold power and privilege, for whose benefit the system has from the first been devised. Do not forget that in the 1848 turmoil, Marx favoured aligning the proletarian movement with the interests of the bourgeoisie. Leftist politics today must be resolute and persistent, but also patient, realistic, and open to compromise in the short run, for the sake of gaining more influence in the long run.

There is no short, easy, or obvious way for a progressive revolution to be made under modern political conditions. Our political institutions were never designed to be 'democratic', if that means 'responsive to the interests or the will of the vast majority'. The false pretence that we have such institutions is an important part of the modern system of oppression. We have never seen political institutions that were democratic in this sense. We still do not even know what such institutions would look like. Marx was aware of this, and we should be, too. There is nothing inevitable about a revolution on behalf of the vast majority or about its victory in the struggle against its oppressors. If Marx thought otherwise, then that was another of his errors.

But is such an assessment too hasty, and too pessimistic? Does the enormous expansion of social inequality in the past half century portend a social revolution such as Marx predicted, even perhaps leading to a 'Marxist phoenix', a workers' revolution that will rise from the ashes finally to fulfil Marx's hopes (see Smith 2014)? We must continue to hope so, because we ought to do what we can to make it happen. But I will believe it only when I see it, and at my age I do not expect to live that long.

What we can already see, however—if we have eyes to see—is that Karl Marx was the historical thinker who best understood the agonizing paradox of modernity. Marx still poses to us the challenge to overcome the yawning gap between the modern world's wondrous potentiality for freedom and the oppression that is its terrible actuality.

NOTES

1. On these facts and figures, see Inequality.org (2012). There is a huge literature on this topic, but see, for example, Collins (2012), Pogge (2002), and Stiglitz (2012). The big book right now is, of course, Thomas Piketty's (2014) *Capital in the Twenty-First Century*.
2. In the following, *CW* is used as an abbreviation in references to *Marx Engels Collected Works* (1975) and *Capital* in references to *Capital: A Critique of Political Economy* (1977–1981). Numerical textual references in each case are to volume and page number.
3. We humans do a lot during our lives for which we should be held accountable. We should not also be held accountable for what others do in our name long after we are dead. To look in Marx for evidence that he would support totalitarianism is like looking in the Gospels for evidence that Jesus would have supported the Inquisition. I have sometimes heard it suggested that the polemical tone Marx took in many of his writings about other leftists is evidence that he would have supported the totalitarian repression and intellectual unfreedom that prevailed in the Soviet system. I regard such suggestions as ridiculous. Even if true, this would be only an *ad hominem* observation about Marx's personality; it could not pertain to the content of his doctrines, or show that *they* advocate totalitarianism. Engels reports that Marx denied being a 'Marxist' (for example, *CW*, 46, p. 126; 49, p. 10).

One of Marx's most repeated claims is that the modern working class, in the course of its development, has made mistakes and will make more of them, from which it must learn (see *CW*, 11, pp. 106–7; 22, pp. 328–35). Rigid adherence to 'Marxist' dogmas could never be part of that learning process.

4. This statement is a 'Yogiism': one of the many assertions so stupid they are brilliant, attributed to the Hall of Fame catcher, Yogi Berra. It has also been attributed to Niels Bohr. But Bohr never said: 'It's *déjà vu* all over again'. That is a Yogiism that could well be applied to twenty-first-century capitalism.

5. Benjamin Franklin said that the only things inevitable are *death* and *taxes*. But US corporations, with the help of the Republican party, have definitely proven him wrong about taxes. See McIntyre et al. (2014).

6. The notion that Marx's claim that capital exploits labour depends on this theory of value seems to me clearly false, as I have argued in Chap. 16 of my book *Karl Marx* (2004).

7. Blanc (2012 [1851], p. 108, cited in *CW*, 24, p. 87). When Marx quoted this slogan in *Critique of the Gotha Program*, his audience knew its source and would not have associated it with Marx himself.

REFERENCES

Blanc, L. (2012 [1851]). *Plus de Girondins*. Boston: General Books.

Cohen, G. A. (2000). *Karl Marx's theory of history: A defence* (expanded ed.). Princeton: Princeton University Press.

Collins, C. (2012). *99 to 1: How wealth inequality is wrecking the world*. San Francisco: Berrett-Koehler.

Fichte, J. G. (1971a [1794]). Some lectures concerning the scholar's vocation. In I. H. Fichte (Ed.), *Johann Gottlieb Fichtes sämmtliche Werke, Band VI* (pp. 291–346). Berlin: W. De Gruyter.

Fichte, J. G. (1971b [1804]). Characteristics of the present age. In I. H. Fichte (Ed.), *Johann Gottlieb Fichtes sämmtliche Werke, Band VII* (pp. 4–256). Berlin: W. De Gruyter.

Inequality.org—Institute for Policy Studies. (2012). Facts and figures in 99 to 1. http://inequality.org/99to1/facts-figures/. Accessed 20 July 2015.

Kant, I. (1902 [1784]). Idea for a universal history with a cosmopolitan aim. In H. Maier (Ed.) *Kants gesammelte Schriften, Akademie Ausgabe, Band VIII* (pp. 17–31). Berlin: W. De Gruyter.

Marx, K., & Engels, F. (1975). *Marx Engels collected works*. New York: International Publishers.

Marx, K. (1977–1981). *Capital: A critique of political economy* (Vol. I–III, B. Fowkes & D. Fernbach, Trans.). New York: Vintage.

McIntyre, R., Gardner, M., & Philips, R. (2014). The sorry state of corporate taxes: What fortune 500 firms pay (or don't pay) in the USA and what they pay abroad—2008 to 2012, citizens for tax justice. http://www.ctj.org/corporatetaxdodgers/sorrystateofcorptaxes.php. Accessed 20 July 2015.

Piketty, T. (2014). *Capital in the twenty-first century* (A. Goldhammer, Trans.). Cambridge, MA: Harvard University Press.

Pogge, T. (2002). *World poverty and human rights.* Cambridge: Polity Press.

Smith, M. E. G. (2014). *Marxist phoenix: Studies in historical materialism and Marxist socialism.* Toronto: Canadian Scholars Press.

Sperber, J. (2013). *Karl Marx: A nineteenth-century life.* New York: Norton.

Stiglitz, J. (2012). *The price of inequality: How today's divided society endangers our future.* New York: Norton.

Stirner, M. (1995 [1844]). *The ego and its own.* Cambridge: Cambridge University Press.

Wood, A. W. (2004). *Karl Marx* (2nd ed.). London: Routledge.

Wood, A. W. (2014). *The free development of each: Studies on freedom, right, and ethics in classical German philosophy.* Oxford: Oxford University Press.

CHAPTER 12

Neither Victims nor Executioners: Camus as Public Intellectual

John Foley

As a public intellectual—a writer who engaged publicly with matters of public importance—Albert Camus made significant contributions to a wide range of critical public debates in post-war France, including the future of socialism in Europe in light of its perceived failure in the USSR, the place of capital punishment in a democracy, the political legitimacy and moral rightness of an independent Algeria, and, perhaps most importantly, the permissibility of violence for political ends. In this essay, I intend touching on these questions to some degree, but the question I want to focus on is somewhat less easily defined, but one I think may constitute his most significant legacy as a public intellectual: his attempt to introduce a moral vocabulary into the principal political debates of his time.

Even the fictional works, for which Camus is best known, are pervaded by a sense of the civic duty of social and political solidarity. For example, his novel *The Plague* is usually read as an allegory of popular French resistance to the Nazis (whom the French called 'la peste brune'). Indeed, the novel is sometimes criticized for what is considered its rather moralizing tone. His plays, such as *Caligula* and *The Just Assassins*, are probably more often understood as moral inquiries into political action than they

J. Foley
National University of Ireland, Galway, Republic of Ireland

© The Editor(s) (if applicable) and The Author(s) 2016
A. Fives, K. Breen (eds.), *Philosophy and Political Engagement*,
DOI 10.1057/978-1-137-44587-2_12

are as plays to be performed. The clearest evidence of Camus as a public intellectual, however, comes from a consideration of his career as an essayist and journalist, and it is upon this that I will focus my attention.

This career began in 1938, when Camus began writing for the left-wing newspaper *Alger républicain* (and later *Le Soir républicain*). Camus published an estimated 150 articles in these newspapers, several of which described the corruption of the colonial judicial system. Perhaps most notable among these articles was a series written in 1939 called 'Misery in Kabylia', in which the 25-year old journalist publicizes and investigates the cause of a famine then ravaging the Kabylia region of Algeria, before attributing the famine to the injustices of the colonial system and calling upon the government to fulfil its responsibilities to all of its people. Clearly, Camus was of the view that colonialism was a system that needed to be fixed rather than dismantled, but in 1939, this placed him at the radical end of the political spectrum in Algeria (indeed, in 1936, Camus's militancy on behalf of Arab and Berber Algerians resulted in his expulsion from the Communist Party).[1] As a result of the kind of modest criticism articulated in 'Misery in Kabylia', the newspaper was shut down in 1940, Camus found himself *persona non grata* in Algeria, and later that year, unable to find employment, he moved to Paris to work on *Paris-Soir* (arriving in Paris about three months before the Nazi occupation began). By 1943, he was active in a French Resistance group called Combat, and became editor-in-chief of its clandestine eponymous newspaper.

1   'NEITHER VICTIMS NOR EXECUTIONERS': CAMUS AND POLITICAL VIOLENCE

Since the ending of the war in France in 1944 and, most particularly, the purge of alleged collaborators that followed it (which he came to consider 'odious'), Camus had begun to argue fervently for a moral dimension to political discourse—one which, in particular, would confront the degree to which contemporary history and politics were pervaded by violence, most especially the ideologically weighted legitimizations of violence articulated on both sides in what became known as the Cold War. In October 1944, for example, he declared that the intention of *Combat* would be 'to undertake a very limited experiment: to introduce the language of morality into the practice of politics' (Camus 2006a, p. 63).

What this meant for Camus, and the significance of this view of the relationship between politics and morality in the intellectual environment of his time, are illustrated by an entry in his notebook from October 1946, in which he gives an unusually detailed summary of an exchange between himself, Arthur Koestler, and Jean Paul Sartre. Two especially interesting passages are reproduced in quotation marks (suggesting some degree of literal accuracy). The first of these is from Camus, where he affirms his conviction regarding the need to introduce morality into politics:

> Don't you think that we are all responsible for the absence of values? And that if all of us who come from Nietzscheism, from nihilism, or from historical realism said in public that we were wrong and that there are moral values and that in the future we shall do what has to be done to establish and illustrate them, don't you think that this might be the beginning of hope? (Camus 1965a, pp. 145–6, revised translation).

This affirmation of moral value is immediately followed by this assertion attributed to Sartre:

> I cannot turn my moral values solely against the USSR. For it is true that the deporting of several million men is more serious than the lynching of a Negro. But the lynching of a Negro is the result of a situation that has been going on for a hundred years and more, and that represents in the end the suffering of just as many millions of Negroes over the years as there are millions of Cherkess deported (Camus 1965a, p. 146).

The view of the relationship between morality and politics that Sartre is beginning to articulate here was informed by an essay by his friend and colleague, Maurice Merleau-Ponty, entitled 'Le Yogi et le prolétaire' ('The Yogi and the Proletarian'), the first part of which had just been published in their journal, *Les Temps modernes* (and which was, in part, a response to Koestler's novel, *Darkness at Noon*). The essay was of great significance in Sartre's political development: he praised it for having released him from political 'immobility' (Sartre 1965, p. 253). However, as we shall see, it had an equal and opposite effect on Camus.

The purpose of *Humanism and Terror*, the title under which 'Le Yogi et le prolétaire' was published in book form, was to investigate the role of violence in history.[2] Merleau-Ponty argues that despite the evident failings in the USSR, there is no viable political alternative to Marxism's rational account of human history (Merleau-Ponty 1969 [1947], p. 141). And indeed, despite its democratic pretensions, despite the horror it exhibits at the reports of violence perpetrated by the Communists, Western liberal society is also marked by violence—most clearly in its long and bloody history of colonial domination. Given that liberal democracy is pervaded by violence at least to the same extent as that of revolutionary Communism, the task Merleau-Ponty sets himself in *Humanism and Terror* is to examine the question of 'whether communist violence was, as Marx thought, "progressive"'. In order to properly understand violence, he contends, it is necessary to locate it 'in the logic of a situation, in the dynamics of a regime, and into the historical reality to which it belongs, instead of judging it by itself according to that morality mistakenly called "pure" morality' (Merleau-Ponty 1969 [1947], pp. 1–2). This is not, however, to affirm the legitimacy of all action which calls itself revolutionary, since the legitimacy of revolutionary violence depends, he says, on its adherence to the 'logic of development' contained within the Marxist theory of history. It is exactly this 'logic of history' which distinguishes Marxism from other revolutionary ideologies. Revolutionary violence consistent with this 'logic of history', argues Merleau-Ponty, will be vindicated in the future 'by a way of life in which violence will no longer be necessary' (Roth 1988, p. 52). However, as Michael Roth (1988, pp. 52, 54) notes, 'the unasked question whose absence is at the centre of the book' is 'where this logic of history is to be found or derived'. Merleau-Ponty offers no satisfactory response to this question, arguing only that 'all we know is different kinds of violence and we ought to prefer revolutionary violence because it has a future of humanism' (Merleau-Ponty 1969 [1947], p. 107).

Camus's writing for *Combat* culminated in a series of articles published under the collected title of 'Neither Victims nor Executioners' in November 1946, while Merleau-Ponty's essay was still being serialized in *Les Temps modernes*. These articles constituted Camus's most sustained expression of a political perspective articulated in the language of morality. As we shall see, they also, in part, served as a critique of the kind of theoretical defence of violence that Merleau-Ponty's essay exemplified.

The twentieth century, says Camus at the beginning of the first article, is the 'century of fear'. The post-war period has been characterized by a hardening of entrenched positions to a point where dialogue 'in the language of a common humanity' is becoming impossible. The resultant 'conspiracy of silence' has served only to further polarize existing camps: 'You shouldn't talk about the Russian culture purge—it would play into the hands of the reactionaries'; 'Don't mention the Anglo-American support of Franco—it would play into the hands of Communism'. 'We suffocate', says Camus of this political climate, 'among people who think they are absolutely right ... And for all who cannot live without dialogue and the friendship of other human beings, this silence is the end of the world'. While there are many who 'doubt that socialism has been realized in Russia or liberalism in America', and 'who grant each side the right to affirm its truth but refuse it the right to impose that truth by murder [a term Camus uses habitually, and in translation confusingly, to denote political violence]', if this independent critical voice is to be heard, it must clarify what it is that it wants 'and proclaim it directly and boldly enough to make its words a stimulus to action'. In light not just of the industrial slaughter that marked the Second World War but also, more immediately, the theoretical defence of violence exemplified in Merleau-Ponty's essay, the first issue upon which this opposition must achieve clarity, Camus says, is that of the use of violence for political ends (Camus 2006a, pp. 257–60, revised translation).

While the focus of Camus' criticism is the theoretical justification of political violence, this does imply, he says, that violence may never be the appropriate response to a specific state of affairs, and he argues that while it would be 'completely utopian to want people to stop killing people', 'a much sounder utopia is that which insists that murder be no longer legitimised'. Indeed, implicitly rejecting Merleau-Ponty's claim that Marxism was not utopian, Camus claims that both Marxist and capitalist ideologies are utopian, in that they are both 'based on the idea of progress' and are 'both certain that the application of their principles must inevitably bring about a harmonious society', a society in which violence will no longer be necessary. Furthermore, he adds, in their ready use of violence in the cause of an imagined non-violent future, 'they are both at the moment costing us dearly'. In reality, thinks Camus, the struggle of the next few years (between the East and the West) will not be between the forces of utopia and the forces of reality, 'but between different utopias'. Ultimately, then, he says, it comes down to choosing the 'least costly' among competing utopian visions. In this context, the purpose of 'Neither Victims nor Executioners', he says, will be 'to define the conditions for a political position that is modest—i.e., free of messianism and disencumbered of nostalgia for an earthly paradise', which may form the basis of a provisional consensus 'among those of us unwilling to be either victims or executioners' (Camus 2006a, pp. 260–1, revised translation).

Favouring what he calls elsewhere a form of 'liberal socialism', which 'tends to invoke the French collectivist tradition that has always made room for individual freedom and that owes nothing to philosophical materialism', in these articles, Camus aims to articulate a political perspective independent of both US-inspired free-market capitalism and Soviet-inspired Communism (Camus 2006a, p. 121). Such is the problem, Camus argues, that confronts socialists in France—as evinced in the recently concluded Socialist Party Congress, in which the humanism of Léon Blum clashed with the orthodox Marxism of Guy Mollet (Camus 2006a, p. 262). From Camus's perspective, if the Socialists 'reject Marxism as an absolute philosophy, confining themselves to its critical aspect, which is often valuable', they will exemplify the degree to which the post-war era marks 'the end of ideologies [and] absolute utopias', favouring instead 'a more modest and less costly utopia' (Camus 2006a, pp. 263–4, revised translation).

While the Socialist Party in France may offer the greatest hope for a national politics free from interference from either the USA or the USSR, the realization of such a 'modest and less costly utopia' will necessarily occur on an international scale. Camus seems broadly in favour of the United Nations, but he also regards it in its current formation as undemocratic— reflected particularly in the extraordinary powers bestowed upon the five permanent members of the Security Council. Rather than a manifestation of Camus's relative utopia, then, the UN either constitutes, or is in danger of constituting, 'a regime of international dictatorship'. Structured in this way, the UN is ill-equipped to deal with 'the clash of empires which threatens us'—the escalating tension between the USA and USSR. Indeed, Camus (2006a, pp. 268–70, revised translation) suggests, it is becoming increasingly likely that even this epochal ideological battle may be obscured, in the not too distant future, by the demise of colonialism and the concomitant demise in the dominance of the West—another source of rising international tension which the UN cannot address in its present form (not least, one might suppose, because in 1946, the UN comprised just 55 member states).

In the context of such an uncertain political landscape, Camus proposes a number of modest, practical measures which could serve as the basis for effective international cooperation: individuals, he says, must 'draw up among themselves, within frontiers and across them, a new social contract which will unite them according to more reasonable principles'. Such groups could be formed, nationally, on the basis of labour organizations, and, internationally, on the basis of intellectual organizations [communautés de réflexion], whose purpose 'should be to meet the confusions of terror with clear language and at the same time to set forth the values that a world at peace will find indispensable'. The first objective of such a group 'could be to formulate an international code of justice whose first article would proclaim the abolition of the death penalty everywhere and give a clear statement of the principles necessary for any civilisation based on dialogue'. Far from being utopian, such people would be acting in accordance with 'the most genuine realism'. Possessing 'the courage to give up, for the present, some of their dreams, so as to grasp more firmly the essential point, which is to save lives', such people would be acting as 'honest realists' (Camus 2006a, pp. 271–3, revised translation).

The need for such 'honest realism' is certain, Camus says, for, in a clear allusion to Merleau-Ponty, 'we are being torn apart by a logic of history'. Recognizing that 'we cannot escape from history, since we are in it up to our necks', he insists that we can still endeavour to struggle within history to preserve that part of us which is not reducible to history (Camus 2006a, pp. 274–5, revised translation). Parenthetically, it is worth noting that Camus's commitment to such an 'honest realism' was reflected in his own actions in the post-war period: notably in his co-founding of *Groupes de Liaison Internationale* in 1948, short-lived groups of intellectuals that sought to create just the kind of independent intellectual platform that 'Neither Victims nor Executioners' proposes (and which was associated with the Europe-America Groups, established in New York by Dwight Macdonald, Mary McCarthy, and others), and in his support of anarchists and revolutionary syndicalist organizations across Europe (when Camus was awarded the Nobel Prize in 1957, *La Révolution Prolétarienne* reminded its readers of Camus's 'solidarity, a thousand times manifested, with militants from Spain, Bulgaria and Hungary' (in Brisville 1970, p. 202).

While neither Merleau-Ponty nor Sartre responded to 'Neither Victims nor Executioners' directly (Sartre made several indirect criticisms), when it was reprinted in 1947, Emmanuel d'Astier de la Vigerie, a Communist member of the French National Assembly, did. D'Astier directly criticized Camus's desire to introduce moral language into political discourse, accusing him of 'shun[ning] politics and tak[ing] refuge in morality' (D'Astier in McCarthy 1982, p. 236). By refusing violence any theoretical legitimacy, D'Astier (1948) claimed, Camus had committed himself to ineffectual pacifism, thereby becoming an accomplice of the right, an apologist for the status quo.

Responding to D'Astier, Camus reiterated his view that violence was 'inevitable', but that he believed it was still possible to refuse all attempts to theoretically legitimize it, 'whether as an absolute *raison d'Etat* or in defence of a totalitarian philosophy'. While he insists he favours neither non-violence ('which I know to be impossible') nor 'sanctity' (as he had been accused of), 'in a world where people are occupied with opposing arguments defending the use of terror', it becomes necessary to argue for a 'limit to violence', to 'confine it when it becomes inevitable, to limit its terrifying effects by restricting its excesses'. Increasingly, Camus was concerned not only with the scale of modern political violence, but with the ease and certainty with which such violence was being defended by intellectuals:

> I have a horror of comfortable violence. I have a horror of those whose words exceed their actions. It is on this basis that I distance myself from several of our great minds for whose appeals to murder I will cease feeling contempt only when they themselves take up the executioner's gun (Camus 1965b, pp. 355–6).

The vehemence of Camus's response might suggest that he had more than D'Astier in mind. Indeed, the title of Camus's response ('Where is the Mystification?') evokes not so much d'Astier's article as those of Merleau-Ponty and Sartre who, at this time, were suggesting that there was a 'mystification' at the heart of anti-communist liberalism, a mystification which ascribes violence to Marxism and only progress to itself.[3] Addressing precisely this argument, in his response, Camus writes of 'that mystification which aims to convince us that a politics of power, of whatever kind, can lead us to a better society where social freedom will at last be realised'. 'In truth', Camus goes on to argue:

> despite your declarations, justice is no longer at issue. What is at issue is a prodigious myth of the divinisation of mankind, of domination, of the unification of the world through human reason alone. What is at issue is the conquest of totality, and Russia considered the instrument of this messianism without God. Of what significance is justice, the lives of generations, human misery, compared to this monstrous mysticism [*ce mysticisme démesuré*]? (Camus 1965b, pp. 360–2).

Alluding again, perhaps, to Merleau-Ponty's talk of the 'logic of history' in *Humanism and Terror*, Camus suggests that from a certain perspective, these self-declared orthodox Marxists 'are no longer of this world' and exist instead in 'logic'. And it is in the name of this logic, says Camus, that for the first time in the intellectual history of France, writers on the *avant-garde* 'have applied their intelligence to the justification of the executioners [*les fusilleurs*], forsaking protest in the name of those who are clearly the victims [*les fusillés*]' (Camus 1965b, pp. 360–2).

In this way, Camus rejects accusations of pacifism and utopianism, but he also affirms his rejection of Marxism as an 'absolute philosophy', while recognizing the value of its 'critical aspect' (Camus 2006a, p. 264, revised translation). He hoped, he told Roger Quilliot in 1948, that the French Socialists would 'repudiate dialectical materialism as an absolute principle of explication as we are unwilling to accept with light hearts its inevitable consequences', while at the same time affirming that 'the Marxist critique of bourgeois society is our particular arsenal' (Camus 1965b, pp. 1579–80). Accordingly, Ronald Aronson's claim that by this time Camus was asserting that 'Marxism equalled murder but capitalism and colonialism did not' is without justification (Aronson 2004, p. 91). While it may be difficult for us now to imagine the intellectual atmosphere in which 'Neither Victims nor Executioners' appeared, Camus's vision of a moral politics, one shorn of the bankrupt grand narratives of teleological History and so on, yet vibrantly critical and purposeful, is still a standard of intellectual engagement worthy of consideration.

2   ALGERIA I: BETWEEN FREEDOM AND JUSTICE

The kind of moral politics advocated in these post-war articles achieved its fullest expression in the essay *The Rebel* (1956 [1951]), where Camus suggests that political consciousness is inherently moral: he identifies its origin in the move from the personal awareness of suffering as a solitary experience (explored at length in *The Myth of Sisyphus* (1955 [1942])) to the recognition of that suffering as a common experience (which he associates with the image of Prometheus). He likens this recognition of a common human condition to Descartes's *Cogito*, the first principle on which it may be possible to base a moral politics:

> In our daily trials rebellion plays the same role as does the 'cogito' in the realm of thought: it is the first piece of evidence. But this evidence lures the individual from his solitude. It founds its first value on the whole human race. I rebel – therefore we exist (Camus 1956 [1951], p. 22).

Camus argues that political revolution and rebellion tend to manifest themselves as the affirmation of two values: freedom and justice. Much of *The Rebel* (and indeed, indirectly, much of Camus's mature writings) is concerned with exploring what appears to be the incompatibility of these values:

> Absolute freedom is the right of the strongest to dominate. Therefore it prolongs the conflicts that profit by injustice. Absolute justice is achieved

by the suppression of all contradiction: therefore it destroys freedom. The revolution to achieve justice, through freedom, ends by aligning them against each other (Camus 1956 [1951], pp. 287–8).

While the demands for justice and freedom are to be found at the nexus of rebellion, and while the history of revolutions tends to show that the two values conflict, according to Camus, this contradiction only exists insofar as the two are understood as absolute values. *The Rebel* suggests that the history of rebellion has all too often been a history of the forgetting of its origins and that legitimate political action is not characterized by a pursuit of absolute freedom or absolute justice (values which are incompatible and therefore mutually defeating), but a relatively successful accommodation of both. Given the absence of transcendent meaning, if rebellion could articulate a philosophy, 'it would be a philosophy of limits, of calculated ignorance and of risk' (Camus 1956 [1951], p. 289).

Echoing his characterization of the absurd in *The Myth of Sisyphus* as 'lucid reason noting its limits', this idea of a 'philosophy of limits', of a political and moral perspective which acknowledges from the outset its own limitations and the risks it faces in trying to effect change, constitutes the basis of legitimate political action in Camus's estimation (Camus 1955 [1942], p. 44). The rebel opposes injustice:

> not because it contradicts an eternal idea of justice, but because it perpetuates the silent hostility that separates the oppressor from the oppressed. It kills the small part of existence that can be realised on this earth through mutual understanding (Camus 1956 [1951], p. 283, revised translation).

From this perspective, political actions and doctrines are legitimate to the extent to which they refute absolutism and reflect the needs of individuals and communities in relation to their own particular political, social, and economic circumstances. Camus implies that the ideologically inspired pursuit of utopia, witnessed for example in the Soviet Union, is both intolerant of difference, in respect of the ways humans are different, and intolerant of commonality, in respect of the ways humans are the same (i.e., in respect of human nature or, at least, the human condition). Camus's claim is that indeed absolute justice and absolute freedom are unattainable, and all that individuals can aspire to is a more or less accurate approximation to these values. But more radically, he is also suggesting that revolt is not itself a demand for these absolute values. A legitimate revolutionary act, 'a revolutionary action which wishes to be coherent in terms of its origins', must be 'uncompromising as to its means', but will accept 'an approximation as far as its ends are concerned' (Camus 1956 [1951], p. 290).

The Rebel was read with enthusiasm by many, including those who saw in it a defence of libertarian socialism and revolutionary syndicalism (see Marin 2008). However, among Communists and fellow travellers, it was generally interpreted as a hostile attack on the kind of socialism manifest in the USSR. Perhaps most famously, in Sartre's journal, *Les Temps modernes*, the essay was also interpreted as conclusive evidence of Camus's political irrelevance. Interestingly, the focus of Sartre's critique of *The Rebel* was precisely its attempt to introduce the language of morality into politics (a criticism already made, as we have seen, in 1947, by D'Astier): 'Your morality first changed into moralism. Today it is only literature. Tomorrow perhaps it will be immorality' (Sartre 1952, p. 353).[4] Sartre had by this time made distinctly different choices. For him 'ethics became indistinguishable from history and politics', and 'being moral involved acknowledging that we and our world are inescapably violent'. Sartre had:

> finally articulated the framework for an ethics that would satisfy him, namely, that radical political change is the only path for creating a world in which moral human relations are possible (Aronson 2004, p. 112).

The extent to which Camus now insisted that political discourse be rooted in morality, and the extent of the differences between himself and many of his contemporaries, most notably Sartre, became even clearer with the outbreak of war in his native Algeria in 1954, and it is on this, and Camus's response to it, that I wish to devote the remainder of this consideration of Camus as a public intellectual.

Although Camus, a *pied noir* or French Algerian, has been accused of being the beneficiary and defender of a regime of racial apartheid (e.g., by Conor Cruise O'Brien [1970] and Edward Said [1993]) because of his unwavering opposition to Algerian independence, any reasonably thorough consideration of his public writings on Algeria make it clear that this is not the case. From the outbreak of war in 1954, Camus did indeed dispute the legitimacy of the claim by the *Front de libération nationale* (FLN) to political authority in Algeria, but in the previous two decades, he had repeatedly disputed the legitimacy of the political status quo. While the institutional racism of French rule in Algeria is undoubted, it is also clearly not the case that Algeria was divided simply into a disenfranchised Arab and Berber majority and a wealthy French minority. Germaine Tillion points out that of 1.2 million non-Muslims in Algeria in 1958, only about 45,000 constituted 'settlers', in the sense that they or their families were landowners (of whom, by her calculations, a little over 1000 were rich). The remaining European population of Algeria, 'well over a million men, women and children', were 'skilled workers, government officials, office employees, taxi-drivers, garage proprietors, station-masters, nurses, telephone girls, labourers, tradesmen and heads of businesses' (Tillion 1958, pp. 4–5). The young Camus, as the son of a cellar-man who was killed in the First World War and an illiterate cleaning woman, would have found himself at the bottom end of this economic scale. While the poverty among the worst off of the Arabs and Berbers was still far worse than that endured by working-class European Algerians (as Camus had himself attested to in 'Misery in Kabylia'), it is doubtful that Camus, in refusing Algerian demands for independence, was concerned to defend the economic and political status quo, let alone the rights of a parasitic class of wealthy landowners.

While for some, the conflict in Algeria was comparable to the Soviet invasion of Hungary and even the Nazi occupation of France, Camus (who had, in 1947, accused the French army of using torture in Algeria, and compared it to the actions of the Nazis in France), sought to deflate the comparison with Hungary by pointing out the factual differences in a letter to *Encounter*:

> There was not in Hungary, installed for more than a century, more than a million Russians ... whose lives, whose rights (and not merely privileges) the Hungarian revolution menaced. The Hungarian problem is simple: the Hungarians must be given back their liberty. The Algerian problem is different: there, it is necessary to assure the liberties of the two peoples of the country (Camus 1957, p. 68).

In the same article, he also offers a summary of what he proposes as a basis for a resolution of the conflict:

> – Proclamation of the end of colonial status for Algeria

> – A round-table conference, without any preconditions, that would include all the representatives of Algerian parties and groups (an idea approved by numerous trades unions and – more important – by the National Algerian Movement)

– Discussion of the possibility of an autonomous, federated (on the Swiss style) Algeria, which would preserve the liberties of the two peoples who inhabit the country (Camus 1957, p. 68).

The rapid escalation in violence in Algeria and the rapidly polarizing views the conflict provoked led Camus to make a return to full-time journalism after an eight-year hiatus, and in May 1955, he began to publish regular editorials in the liberal-socialist *L'Express*, focussing again on the need for dialogue to replace violence (Camus 1987). He criticized the brutal suppression of the Algerian rebellion by the French Army (particularly their use of indiscriminate 'collective repression' against the civilian population), as well as the violence of the FLN (specifically their targeting of civilians and their attacks on other nationalist groups), and argued that a peaceful future for Algeria required immediate all-party negotiations. Later that year, Camus made what was probably his most significant attempt to introduce moral discourse into an increasingly polarized political debate. Coordinating with European and Arab friends and comrades from the 1930s in Algiers (including Amar Ouzegane who, Camus soon learned, was a member of the FLN), Camus established *The Committee for a Civilian Truce*, and organized, under the title 'Call for a Civilian Truce', a public meeting in Algiers in January 1956, which he hoped would help to create a space in which dialogue between the various parties could take place.

Camus's speech begins by refuting the suggestion that the conflict in Algeria could be reduced to the problem of a homogenous Arab majority subjugated by a small but powerful alien French colonial minority:

> sharing this land are a million Frenchmen who have been settled here for more than a century, millions of Muslims, both Arab and Berber, who have been here for many centuries, and any number of strong and vibrant religious communities (Camus 2013 [1958], p. 153).

As he had in *L'Express*, he asserts that while Algeria's future may look bleak, the basis for fruitful dialogue can still be found if each party would 'make an effort to think about his adversary's motivations'. While a general ceasefire may be inconceivable, 'we can act … on what is odious about the conflict', namely the killing of innocent civilians. Such a 'civilian truce' would not only reduce the number of civilians being killed in the war, it would also create a space for dialogue which, in turn, would serve as 'the groundwork for a more just and nuanced understanding of the Algerian problem' (Camus 2013 [1958], pp. 152–5).

The 'Call for a Civilian Truce' has often been seen, especially by proponents of the post-colonial critique of his writings, as evidence of little more than the irrelevance of Camus's moral politics by this time. For example, Conor Cruise O'Brien, who inaugurated the post-colonial critique of Camus in English, calls the truce Camus's 'one concrete idea', but dismisses it with the claim that when Camus came to Algiers to promote it, he was 'barracked by the Europeans' and 'largely ignored by the Muslims' (Cruise O'Brien 1970, pp. 72–3; see also Taleb Ibrahimi 1973 [1967], p. 176). However, the civilian truce was not as fanciful as Cruise O'Brien suggests. Rather than jeer, right-wing *pieds noirs* made threats against Camus's life, and attempted to hijack the meeting by producing forged invitations, such was their implacable hostility to any policy even resembling negotiation with the FLN. An angry crowd of about 1000 *pieds noirs* congregated outside the hall in which the meeting was held, some shouting slogans such as 'Camus to the wall' and 'Down with the Jews', and making Fascist salutes. Far from being 'largely ignored by Muslims', Camus was joined on the platform by Ferhat Abbas, who was to become independent Algeria's first President (Abbas, though a moderate nationalist, aligned himself with the FLN shortly after the failure of the civilian truce. In 1963, he resigned his presidency when the FLN declared Algeria a one-party state). And, indeed, while the FLN publicly disavowed the appeal, they secretly infiltrated the committee set up to oversee it and made certain that the conference was protected by FLN militants. Mohamed Lebjaoui, a member of the truce committee, informed Camus that he, like Amar Ouzegane, was also a member of the FLN, and claimed that it 'was ready to respect the rules of the civil truce if the French government would' (Lottman 1979, p. 572).[5]

While, from a practical point of view, there may have been difficulties with such a proposal—for example, in a popular guerrilla war, how easy would it have been to differentiate between civilians and combatants?—the most significant problem with the idea of a civilian truce was the absence of political appetite for such a proposal, either in Algeria or in France. Certainly the French government showed no interest. Simone de Beauvoir expressed the view of many leftist intellectuals in thinking that 'Camus's language had never sounded hollower than when he demanded pity for the civilians' (de Beauvoir 1968, p. 354). On the other hand, Germaine Tillion, an ethnologist who began working in Algeria in the 1930s, continued to believe, even in 1958 (two years after Camus's appeal) that such a civilian truce was possible. In July and August 1957, she met the FLN leader, Saadi Yacef, who promised her that if the French ceased executing imprisoned Algerian 'patriots', the FLN would stop targeting civilians. While the French initially showed interest, they continued to execute Algerian prisoners. The FLN, on the other hand, appear to have stopped their attacks on civilians, and did not resume until Yacef himself was arrested that September (Tillion 1961, pp. 22–51).

3   ALGERIA II: THE SILENCE OF THE PUBLIC INTELLECTUAL

In any event, the failure of Camus's truce appeal quickly resulted in his decision to withdraw from public discourse on Algeria: after making one final appeal in favour of the truce, he resigned from *L'Express* in February 1956. The polarization of opinion, which had shocked him when he visited Algeria, and which he evidently blamed for the failure of the truce proposal, convinced Camus that he could no longer have any positive influence on events there. His silence has attracted a fair degree of criticism, and as this pertains directly to the idea of Camus as a public intellectual, this silence deserves some consideration.

Before exploring this silence, however, it is worth examining one of the most controversial statements Camus made about Algeria at this time. For many, conclusive proof of his political obsolescence (or, we might say, the obsolescence of his kind of moral politics) seemed to be provided by Camus himself on the occasion of his Nobel Prize for Literature, awarded in 1957. At an informal question and answer session at Stockholm University, an Algerian student asked Camus why he intervened so readily in defence of Eastern Europe, but never in defence of Algeria. Camus replied that he had been the only French journalist obliged to leave Algeria—his country of birth—because of his militancy in favour of rights for the Muslim majority and that his support for a democratic Algeria was well known. He assured the Algerian questioner 'that some of his comrades were alive today thanks to actions of which the young man was not aware, and Camus was sorry to have to speak about that' (Lottman 1979, pp. 617–8). He continued:

> I have been silent for a year and eight months now, though that does not mean that I have ceased to struggle. I have always been a partisan of a just Algeria, where the two peoples can live in peace and in equality. I have repeatedly called for justice to be done for the Algerian people, that they

be granted a fully democratic regime ... I have always condemned the use of terror. And I must also condemn the use of terrorism which is exercised blindly, in the streets of Algiers for example, and which could one day strike my mother or my family. I believe in justice, but I will defend my mother before justice (Camus 1965b, pp. 1881–2).

For Simone de Beauvoir, and one imagines for a great many of her contemporaries, this statement was proof that while he pretended to be 'above the battle', Camus was in reality 'on the side of the *pieds noirs*'. In fact, for de Beauvoir, the 'humanist' in Camus had in any case 'given way to the *pied noir*' years before (de Beauvoir 1968, p. 362). Conor Cruise O'Brien suggested that the statement amounted to a confession that 'the defence of his mother required support for the French army's pacification of Algeria' (Cruise O'Brien 1970, p. 75). Susan Dunn claimed that the presence of Camus's mother in Algeria 'was sufficient to counterbalance for him the entire colonial situation' (Dunn 1998, pp. 345–6; see also Taleb Ibrahimi 1966 [1959], pp. 67–83). Camus's biographer, Olivier Todd, considers the claim to be regrettable and grounded on 'poor logic' (Todd 1996, p. 700). The editors of the new authoritative collected works of Camus—relying on the 40-year-old memory of his Swedish translator— suggest that Camus was misquoted (in Camus 2008, pp. 1405–6).

However, Camus made the same point on several occasions, and con- sequently, we should be wary of treating it as an unguarded comment, let alone as 'a kind of Freudian slip' (Hargreaves 1986, p. 80).[6] The reference to his mother and justice—far from unfortunate—is rooted in the ideas of relative freedom and relative justice he articulated in *The Rebel* and elsewhere. 1957 saw an escalation in the number of FLN attacks on civilians in Algeria (in June and July, they bombed several tram stops and a casino). While Camus certainly did not believe there was any justice to the French policy of brutal retaliation and *ratissage*, the justice of the FLN's fight was frequently taken for granted (not least by his Algerian ques- tioner), and it was this assumption that he sought to address. Responding then to the question implicit in the student's intervention—why didn't Camus support the FLN, since their cause was just?—Camus's point was that an idea of justice which licences the indiscriminate killing of innocent civilians ('terrorism practiced blindly in the streets') is, in his estimation, a travesty of justice. This kind of violence is indefensible, not because such attacks could conceivably kill Camus's mother, but because the victims of such an attack were inevitably like Camus's mother, that is, innocent civilians. Accordingly, when the *pied-noir* poet, and one-time protégé of Camus, Jean Sénac, complained to Camus that he would 'try to defend my mother and justice together', he displayed only a failure to understand the point being made (Sénac to Camus in Camus 2004, p. 158).[7]

Besides this impromptu statement, Camus did maintain a relative silence over events in Algeria after the failure of the civilian truce, but this silence cannot simply be reduced to exasperation at the failure of what many considered his hopeless political idealism. Rather he found himself in precisely the intellectual environment he had feared in 1946, 'suffocat[ing] among people who think they are absolutely right ... And for all who cannot live without dialogue and the friendship of other human beings, this silence is the end of the world'. Finding himself in a political context where dialogue was no longer possible, he regretfully chose silence. He told Mouloud Feraoun:

> When two of our brothers engage in a fight without mercy, it is criminal madness to excite one or the other of them. Between wisdom reduced to silence and madness which shouts itself hoarse, I prefer the virtues of silence. Yes, when speech manages to dispose without remorse of the existence of others, to remain silent is not a negative attitude (Feraoun, in Lottman 1979, p. 626).[8]

The degree to which Camus may have felt justified in thinking this relative silence to be his best recourse becomes clearer if we consider the alternatives suggested by his critics. Steven Bronner, for example, considers Camus's 'completely impractical politics' morally unjustifiable, arguing that precisely because he was 'disgusted with the fanaticism' on both sides, 'his primary ethical aim should have led him to embrace the side with the best chance of ending the bloodshed', by which he means the FLN (Bronner 2009, p. 114). Bronner calls Camus's belief in the possibility of a 'rational resolution of grievances' a 'liberal presumption' (itself a rather extraordinary presumption), and accuses him of refusing 'to choose between the only serious alternatives available'—he even suggests that his failure to take sides in the conflict '*actually hindered bringing the conflict to a close*' (Bronner 2009, p. 116, emphasis in original). Bronner, of course, isn't criticizing Camus for refusing 'to choose between the only serious alternatives available', because the 'alternative' he suggests to the French surrender of Algeria to the FLN is for the French army to maintain French rule in Algeria by whatever means necessary, which is clearly not a 'serious alternative' at all, least of all for Camus. On the other hand, recent scholar-ship on Algeria could be used in support of just such a realist argument. Since even at the time of Camus's death in 1960, 'France was still winning militarily', it could be said that from a strictly 'realist' point of view, Camus ought to have abandoned all attempts to encourage peaceful negotiation in favour of the French army's use of torture and collective punishment (Schalk 2004, pp. 344–6). So while the attempt to introduce the language of morality into the practice of politics may be judged a failure, it is unclear that realism offers a particularly effective alternative.

Furthermore, Camus's silence regarding Algeria was only ever partial. Based on his long-standing opposition to capital punishment, throughout this period, he wrote numerous petitions on behalf of Algerian militants condemned to death (Jean Daniel and Germaine Tillion estimate there were more than 150 such cases).[9] While this work was done privately, sometimes even on condition of remaining unknown to the public, in 1958, Camus made one final public intervention—he published an anthol-ogy of his writings on Algeria, *Algerian Chronicles*, a book largely ignored in France on publication and not published in English until 2013, a full 55 years after its original publication. Calling the book in its preface 'among other things the history of a failure', it clearly delimited and explained his silence:

> When violence answers violence in a growing frenzy that makes the sim-ple language of reason impossible, the role of the intellectual cannot be to excuse from a distance the violence of one side while condemning the violence of the other ... If the intellectual does not join the combatants themselves, their role ... must be merely to strive to calm the situation so that reason will again have a chance ... It seems that metropolitan France was unable to think of any political solution other than to say to the French in Algeria: "Go ahead and die; that's what you deserve!" or else "Kill them all; that's what they deserve!" That makes two different policies and a single abdication, for the question is not how to die separately but how to live together (Camus 1960, pp. 116–7, revised translation; see also Camus 2013 [1958], pp. 28–9).

Camus justifies his reluctant silence in the context of others' delib-erate silences: on the one hand, the silence of the *pieds noirs* in the face of the use of torture by the French, even after the publication of Henri Alleg's famous exposé, *La Question* (1958), and, on the other hand, the silence of the pro-FLN French in the wake of FLN massacres of *pieds noirs* in Philippeville (1955), and of Arab supporters of the rival *Mouvement national algérien* (MNA) in Melouza (1957). He suggests that the only alternative to silence in such a circumstance is to actually take up arms, and he especially objects to the 'lethal frivolity' with which the French Left adopted the FLN's cause, beating their *mea culpa* 'on someone else's breast' (Camus in Daniel 1973, p. 257; Camus 1960, p. 120). Curiously, both of these criticisms could have been applied to Sartre. In the wake of the Melouza massacre (in May 1957, the FLN massacred 374 inhabitants of the village of Melouza, because they were suspected of supporting the rival nationalist group, the MNA), Sartre, who had called such violence 'an historical necessity' (in Burnier 1988 [1973], p. 42), argued that journalists were mistaken in even reporting the event, arguing that 'Politics imposes a constraint to remain silent about certain things. Otherwise one is a "beautiful soul" and is not acting politically' (in Daniel 1973, pp. 251–2). Similarly, in his famous preface to Frantz Fanon's (1967), *The Wretched of the Earth*, Sartre extols the virtues of revolutionary violence, but, to be sure, from a safe distance:

> to shoot down a European is to kill two birds with one stone, to destroy the oppressor and the man he oppresses at the same time; there remains a dead man and a free man ... The child of violence, at every moment he draws from it his humanity. We were men at his expense, he makes himself a man at ours: a different man, of higher quality.[10]

Camus referred to his writings on Algeria as, in part, the 'history of a failure'. It could be argued that the failure was Camus's own, that his hope for a politics articulated in the language of morality was a hopeless fantasy, and that his silence (such as it was) was the inevitable result. However, even if Camus's attempted accommodation of politics and morality is to be so judged, we may still harbour doubts about the success of those of his contemporaries who attempted to articulate a politics without morality. When he died in 1960, Sartre expressed surprising admiration for Camus's 'stubborn humanism, strict and pure, austere and sensual, [which] delivered uncertain combat against the massive and deformed events of the day'. Associating Camus with the French *moralistes*, he observed that 'by the unexpectedness of his refusals, he reaffirmed, at the heart of our era, against the Machiavellians, against the golden calf of realism, the existence of the moral act' (Sartre 1964, cited in Lottman 1979, p. 673).[11]

Tony Judt, too, argues that Camus should be thought of as a moralist, suggesting that he was not 'in the established sense, "a public intellectual"' at all, and that his writings 'bear copious witness' to 'his unsuitability for any political camp, and to the hyperpoliticised atmosphere of post-war France' (Judt 1998, p. 121).

As useful as this idea of Camus as moralist is, it is not at all clear that it is in any way incompatible with the idea of him as a politically engaged public intellectual. The importance of the writings of Camus I have examined originates precisely, as I have argued, in the way in which they seek to 'introduce the language of morality into the practice of politics'. While this project may be deemed a failure in regard to Algeria, it nevertheless points to Camus's contemporary significance. While his identification of the fraudulence of totalizing ideologies and his promotion of various forms of international cooperation may seem unusually prescient, it could be said that Camus's most important legacy is his identification of the centrality of the problem of political violence in the modern era and his insistence on the need for a moral language with which to address it. In an era marked by a vertiginous rise in civilian casualties (World War One, 5 %; World War Two, 50 %; Vietnam, 90 %, according to one estimate), an era of suicide bombings and drone warfare, this problem cannot be said to have diminished in any way.[12]

NOTES

1. David Carroll (2007, p. 136) argues that Camus's conception of assimilation was, for its time, liberal in the extreme.
2. Merleau-Ponty (1969 [1947], p. 107). 'Le Yogi et le prolétaire' was published in instalments in *Les Temps modernes* in October 1946, November 1946, and January 1947. In July 1947, *Les Temps modernes* printed a related editorial, 'Apprendre à lire' [Learn to read]. A slightly revised version of the three parts of 'Le yogi et le prolétaire' and 'Apprendre à lire' was published in book form as *Humanisme et terreur* (1947).
3. See, for example, Merleau-Ponty (1969 [1947], pp. xiii, xv, xxiii, 21, 93, 104, 125, 155, 177) and Sartre (1967, pp. 90, 211; 2001, pp. 8–9).
4. The original review was written by Francis Jeanson (1952a) under the provocative title 'Albert Camus, or the Revolted Soul'. Camus (1952) responded to Jeanson's review with a letter addressed to Sartre directly. This was published together with replies from both Jeanson (1952b) and Sartre (1952, which is quoted above) in the August issue of the same journal.
5. Lottman's version of events is based on Lebjaoui's own account (in Lebjaoui 1970, p. 43). According to Olivier Todd, Camus did not know that

Ouzegane, Lebjaoui, and the other Muslim members of the civil truce group were also members of the FLN (Todd 1996, pp. 625–6).

6. He made this point in March 1956 to his friend Emmanuel Roblès, and again in the 1958 preface to *Algerian Chronicles*, where he also comments on the 'peculiar commentary' it provoked (see Camus (1965b, pp. 892, 1843; 2013 [1958], p. 25) and Roblès (1988, p. 48)). Camus wrote to the editor of *Le Monde* to clarify a number of points in the published report, but never disputed the accuracy of the comment regarding his mother and justice (Camus 1965b, pp. 1882–3). See also Camus's letter to Jean Amrouche (Camus 1989, p. 238).

7. For details of Sénac's criticism of Camus, see also Le Sueur (2001, pp. 113–115).

8. Mouloud Feraoun was a Kabylie novelist with whom Camus began to correspond after the publication of Feraoun's first novel, *Le Fils du Pauvre*, in 1950. He remembered Camus making the above remark when the two men met in 1958 (see Lottman 1979, p. 626; Feraoun 2000).

9. On these estimates, see Todd (1996, p. 685). For details of Camus's interventions, see Morisi (2011).

10. Sartre in Fanon (1967, pp. 19–20). Sartre later notes: 'A fine sight they are too, the believers in non-violence, saying that they are neither victims nor executioners' (Sartre in Fanon (1967, p. 21; see also Sartre 1974, pp. 252–3)).

11. In 1973, Sartre told John Gerassi: '"There is a little falsehood in the obituary I wrote about Camus, when I say that even when he disagreed with us, we wanted to know what he thought. … He wasn't a boy who was made for all that he tried to do, he should have been a little crook from Algiers, a very funny one, who might have managed to write a few books, but mostly remain a crook. Instead of which you had the impression that civilisation had been stuck on top of him and he did what he could with it, which is to say, he did nothing"' (quoted in Todd 1996, p. 827; see also Todd 1998, pp. 415–6, revised translation).

12. These figures are quoted by Avishai Margalit (2003, p. 36). According to a report published in 2003 by the European Union, of the four million people who have died in wars since 1990, 90 % were civilians (Solana 2003, p. 29).

References

Alleg, H. (1958). *La Question*. Paris: Editions de minuit.

Aronson, R. (2004). *Camus and Sartre: The story of a friendship and the quarrel that ended it*. Chicago: Chicago University Press.

Brisville, J. C. (1970). *Camus*. Paris: Gallimard.

Bronner, S. (2009). *Camus—Portrait of a moralist* (2nd ed.). Chicago: University of Chicago Press.

Burnier, M.-A. (1988 [1973]). On Maoism: An interview with Jean-Paul Sartre. In R. Wilcocks (Ed.), *Critical essays on Jean-Paul Sartre* (pp. 34–45). Boston: G.K. Hall.

Camus, A. (1952, August). Lettre au directeur des Temps modernes. *Les Temps modernes*, 82, 317–333.

Camus, A. (1955 [1942]). *The myth of Sisyphus* (J. O'Brien, Trans.). London: Hamish Hamilton.

Camus, A. (1956 [1951]). *The rebel—An essay on man in revolt* (revised ed., A. Bower, Trans.). New York: Knopf.

Camus, A. (1957, June). M. Camus replies .... *Encounter*, 8(6), 68.

Camus, A. (1960). *Resistance, rebellion, and death* (J. O'Brien, Trans.). New York: Knopf.

Camus, A. (1965a). *Notebooks 1942–1951* (J. O'Brien, Trans.). New York: Knopf.

Camus, A. (1965b). Essais. In R. Quilliot, & L. Faucon (Eds.), *Bibliothèque de la Pléiade*. Paris: Gallimard/Pléiade.

Camus, A. (1987). *Albert Camus—éditorialiste à L'Express, mai 1955–février 1956*. Paris: Gallimard.

Camus, A. (1989). *Carnets III, mars 1951–décembre 1959*. Paris: Gallimard.

Camus, A. (2004). Correspondence between Camus and Jean Sénac. In H. Nacer-Khodja (Ed.), *Albert Camus, Jean Sénac ou le fils rebelle* (pp. 123–166). Paris: Paris-Méditerranée.

Camus, A. (2006a). In J. Lévi-Valensi (Ed.), *Camus at 'Combat': Writing 1944–1947* (foreword D. Carroll; A. Goldhammer Trans.). Princeton: Princeton University Press.

Camus, A. (2008). In R. Gay-Crosier et al. (Eds.), *Œuvres Complètes: Tome IV, 1957–1959*. Paris: Gallimard/Pléiade.

Camus, A. (2013 [1958]). *Algerian chronicles* (introduction A. Kaplan; A. Goldhammer, Trans.). Cambridge, MA: Harvard University Press.

Carroll, D. (2007). *Albert Camus, the Algerian: Colonialism, terrorism, justice*. New York: Columbia University Press.

Cruise O'Brien, C. (1970). *Camus*. Glasgow: Fontana/Collins.

d'Astier de la Vigerie, E. (1948, April). Arrachez la victime aux bourreaux. *Caliban*, 12–17.

Daniel, J. (1973). Malraux, Sartre, Camus et la Violence (entretiens). In J. Daniel (Ed.), *Le temps qui reste: essai d'autobiographie professionnelle* (pp. 243–259). Paris: Stock.

de Beauvoir, S. (1968). *Force of circumstance* (R. Howard, Trans.). Harmondsworth: Penguin.

Dunn, S. (1998). Albert Camus and the dubious politics of mercy. In R. English et al. (Eds.), *Ideas matter: Essays in honour of Conor Cruise O'Brien* (pp. 345–356). Dublin: Poolbeg.

Fanon, F. (1967). *The wretched of the earth* (introduction J.-P. Sartre; C. Farrington, Trans.). Harmondsworth: Penguin.

Feraoun, M. (2000). In J. D. le Sueur (Ed.), *Journal 1955–1962: Reflections on the French-Algerian war* (M. E. Wolf, & C. Fouillade, Trans.). Lincoln: University of Nebraska Press.

Hargreaves, A. (1986). Caught in the middle: The Liberal Dilemma in the Algerian war. *Nottingham French Studies*, 25(2), 73–82.

Jeanson, F. (1952a, May). Albert Camus ou l'âme révolté. *Les Temps modernes*, 79, 2070–2090.

Jeanson, F. (1952b, August). Pour tout vous dire .... *Les Temps modernes*, 82, 354–383.

Judt, T. (1998). *The burden of responsibility—Blum, Camus, Aron and the French twentieth century*. Chicago: University of Chicago Press.

Lebjaoui, M. (1970). *Vérités sur la révolution algérienne*. Paris: Gallimard.

Le Sueur, J. D. (2001). *Uncivil war: Intellectuals and identity politics during the decolonization of Algeria*. Philadelphia: University of Pennsylvania Press.

Lottman, H. (1979). *Camus—A biography*. London: Weidenfeld & Nicolson.

Marin, L. (Ed.). (2008). *Albert Camus et les Libertaires 1948–1960*. Marseille: Editions Egrégores.

Margalit, A. (2003, January 16). The suicide bombers (pp. 36–39). *New York Review of Books*.

McCarthy, P. (1982). *Camus*. New York: Random House.

Merleau-Ponty, M. (1969 [1947]). *Humanism and terror: An essay on the communist problem* (J. O'Neill, Trans.). Boston: Beacon Press.

Morisi, E. (Ed.). (2011). *Albert Camus contre la peine de mort*. Paris: Gallimard.

Ouzegane, A. (1962). *Le Meilleur combat*. Paris: Julliard.

Roblès, E. (1988). *Albert Camus et la trêve civile*. Philadelphia: Ceflan.

Roth, M. (1988). *Knowing and history: Appropriations of Hegel in twentieth-century France*. Ithaca: Cornell University Press.

Said, E. (1993). *Culture and imperialism*. London: Chatto & Windus.

Sartre, J.-P. (1952, August). Mon Cher Camus .... *Les Temps modernes*, 82, 334–353.

Sartre, J.-P. (1964). *Situations, IV—portraits*. Paris: Gallimard.

Sartre, J.-P. (1965). *Situations* (B. Eisler, Trans.). New York: George Braziller.

Sartre, J.-P. (1967). *What is literature?* (introduction D. Caute; B. Frechtman, Trans.). London: Methuen.

Sartre, J.-P. (1974). The writings of Jean-Paul Sartre. In M. Contat, & M. Rybalka (Eds.), *A bibliographical life* (Vol. 1, R. C. McCleary, Trans.). Evanston: Northwestern University Press.

Sartre, J.-P. (2001). To be hungry already means that you want to be free (A. van den Hoven, Trans.). *Sartre Studies International*, 7(2), 8–11.

Schalk, D. (2004). Was Algeria Camus's fall? *Journal of Contemporary European Studies*, 23(3), 339–354.

Solana, J. (2003). *A secure Europe in a better world: European security strategy*. Paris: European Union Institute for Security Studies.

Taleb Ibrahimi, A. (1966 [1959]). Lettre ouverte à Albert Camus. In A. Taleb Ibrahimi (Ed.), *Lettres de prison 1957–1961* (pp. 67–83). Alger: SNED.

Taleb Ibrahimi, A. (1973 [1967]). Albert Camus vu par un Algérien. In A. Taleb Ibrahimi (Ed.), *De la décolonisation à la revolution culturelle 1962–1972* (pp. 161–184). Alger: SNED.

Tillion, G. (1958). *Algeria—The realities* (R. Matthews, Trans.). New York: Knopf.

Tillion, G. (1961). *France and Algeria—Complementary enemies* (R. Howard, Trans.). New York: Knopf.

Todd, O. (1996). *Albert Camus—Une Vie*. Paris: Gallimard.

Todd, O. (1998). *Albert Camus—A life* (B. Ivry, Trans.). London: Vintage.

CHAPTER 13

Violence and Responsibility

Felix Ó Murchadha

Responsibility for acts of violence, even when accepted, is often displaced, passed on to another. My violence responds to his violence, their violence made our violence necessary, this small act of violence prevents much worse violence. Agency with respect to violence is complicated by the fact that the violent act, by interrupting the normality of the situation in which it takes place, overtakes the perpetrator as an event, not alone affecting, but also implicating all around it. Perpetrator, victim, and witness are not only three perspectives on a violent act, but are also three trajectories of the violent event itself, whereby each finds him or herself transformed. This transformation goes to the very roots of the fundamentally linguistic domain of human life, the domain of meaning seeking, of language directed towards understanding. Violence places this domain in a tail spin towards the evacuation of all meaning. Although this is sometimes understood as a descent into animality, or as an elevation to divine terror, violence seems rather to disclose something essentially human, namely, the groundlessness of rational discourse, its ultimate irresponsibility, and, in consequence, the abyss at the heart of that responsibility, and ultimately, of ethics and politics. This is so, because rational discourse is responsible to the extent to

F. Ó Murchadha
National University of Ireland, Galway, Republic of Ireland

© The Editor(s) (if applicable) and The Author(s) 2016
A. Fives, K. Breen (eds.), *Philosophy and Political Engagement*,
DOI 10.1057/978-1-137-44587-2_13

which it supplies grounds, while violence marks the refusal of grounds, the affirmation of force against the linguistic tendency to persuasion and agreement. Yet violence depends on language and reason, it is embedded in discourses of justification and condemnation; the violent event places perpetrator, victim, and witness in dilemmas of responsibility. Language and reason are bound together as *logos*, as *logon didonai*, because in both is to be found that giving and taking of responsibility rooted in a vision, which sees in terms of that which cannot be seen, that which ought to be, the ideas and values against which the real is understood.

Philosophers from Husserl to Derrida (but these are simply calling on an ancient tradition) have continually shown the manner in which philosophy is rooted in responsibility. If this is so, it is because the philosopher, by reading the real in the light of the ideal and the ideal in terms of the real, is responsible to the source of all intelligibility. Whether we think from the ideal or from the real or from the interweaving of ideal and real, philosophy is always concerned with the way in which the ideal (if only as the image of the real) exposes the contingency and ephemerality of the real. The ideas expressed as 'justice', 'truth', 'freedom', and 'goodness' are not simply concepts, but manifest an invisible source of humanity beyond or before the present structures of real societies and economies. The responsibility of philosophy is to be true to such invisible and 'ideal' sources. While such a responsibility would clearly appear to be non-violent in its intent and execution, if it can be shown, as will be attempted below, that violence stems from those very relations of ideal and real, invisible and visible, then philosophy in its own self-responsibility is implicated in violence.[1]

This chapter is framed by three paradoxes of violence stemming from this situation. The first three sections of this chapter address these three paradoxes respectively, before going on to suggest a way beyond them.

The first paradox of violence: violence arises precisely out of the disjunction human rationality brings between the real and the ideal, whereby the ideal by its nature seems to be a domain of peace and harmony.

A man punches his partner, a teenager's classmate posts an abusive message about him on social media, gunmen attack vulnerable targets in a big city, a caregiver degrades a patient. In each case, an act is committed, but the act once committed becomes detached from the agent. In one sense, this is common to all acts: once committed an act cannot be undone, its consequences are often unforeseeable for the agent, and the very reality of the act for those who experience it is not fully within the agent's purview. In this sense, all acts have an event-like quality; they form, so to speak, mini epicentres out of which emerge meanings which affect the situation in which they emerge. Situations have norms that set up boundaries with respect to the relations of self and other, and, in accordance with those norms, acts are carried out without perceived violation.[2] The violent act disturbs that situation; it transforms those within that situation into perpetrators, victims, and witnesses. The boundaries of self and other are no longer being negotiated in reciprocal terms; they are being violated.

Such violation has to be experienced. To experience an event as violent means to experience it as violating boundaries (Waldenfels 2006, pp. 80–81). What is perceived to be such a violation depends in part on the present recognition of those boundaries, or rather, the present recognition of the claim to respect those boundaries. That perception may vary and may, in particular, vary for the perpetrator, victim, or witness with respect to herself, but once she perceives a violation, she perceives the event as violent. Such awareness of violence may be a retrospective awareness of what at the time was perceived as non-violent.

The recognition involved here is not simply the physical experience of pain or harm: it involves a sense that the pain or harm experienced *ought not* to have occurred. In that sense, while irreducibly political and ethical in its context and manifestation, violence is metaphysical (in a Kantian sense) in origin: it concerns the fundamental differences of 'is' and 'ought', 'fact' and 'value', 'real' and 'ideal'. This is so because violence happens only as violation, and only a being which can make a claim against the real can be violated. Such a claim against the real—a claim which always contains within itself a negation, declared or undeclared—posits a truth to which the real is subject and against which it can be judged. It is precisely in this difference of real and ideal, of facts and values, of is and ought, that metaphysics functions and it is this difference that first makes violence possible. That initial translation of the real into the ideal responds to a pre-philosophical intuition of the difference of idea, expressed as word or symbol or concept, and the material reality which can be touched, laboured on, and which in the end marks mortality. The ethical claim is metaphysical in the sense of demanding that flesh and blood be recognized as more than their material reality; such a claim is vulnerable in locating itself within material reality.[3] Furthermore, such a claim understands itself as non-arbitrary, that is, as rooted in a rational nature which exceeds the individual, the group, even humanity as such. This claim, which Kant famously formulates as that to be respected as an end not simply as a means, both limits and provokes violence: limits it morally, while giving the conditions for its actual exercise in the violation of those very claims which form the basis of ethics (see Levinas 1969, p. 198; Derrida 1978, p. 147). Violence is first possible in this difference, not only because such a being which exists in and through that difference can endure violence, but also because only such a being can provoke violence. Furthermore, only a being which can perceive an unreal possibility can witness violence, and only a being which recognizes a claim that transcends the real can perpetrate violence.[4]

One of the earliest accounts of violence, fratricidal violence, is a story of conflict over recognition. The story appears in the Book of Genesis The New Jerusalem Bible (1994), 4: 3–8:

> Now Abel became a shepherd and kept flocks, was a keeper of sheep, while Cain tilled the soil. Time passed and Cain brought some of the produce of the soil as an offering to Yahweh, while Abel for his part brought the first born of his flock and some of their fat as well. Yahweh looked with favour on Abel and his offering. But he did not look with favour on Cain and his offering, and Cain was very angry and downcast. Yahweh asked Cain, 'Why are you angry and downcast? If you are doing right, surely you ought to hold your head high! But if you are not doing right, Sin is crouching at the door hungry to get you. You can still master him'. Cain said to his brother Abel, 'Let us go out'; and while they were in the open country, Cain set on his brother Abel and killed him.

This account comes early in the Book of Genesis, immediately following the banishment from Eden. Although the story supposedly concerns the first offspring of Eve, it actually assumes an existing civilization with established forms of worship. As it is placed, it complements the first violation recorded in Genesis, namely of the boundary of god and human, with a second fraternal violation. The two fundamental commandments of the Torah, to love god and to love your neighbour as yourself, in fact respond to prior violations of those commandments, those of Adam and Eve and of Cain. But the chronological priority is only superficial: as the story goes, Adam, Eve, and Cain recognized their sin prior to the commandments. The commandments simply give propositional form to that which is already evident. This is seen first and foremost in hiding, deception, and avoidance, all meant to elide the feeling of guilt. The structure of both stories is similar. A situation exists which is set in place by god, a situation which produces an emotion, in the one case of greed, in this case of anger. That greed and anger are both played upon by a tempter. The violation occurs, the perpetrator attempts to hide the crime, but the all-seeing eye of god sees through this deception and punishment follows.

The specifics of the story of Cain are interesting, however. Cain's violence does not originate in any material loss. Cain has lost nothing in material terms, but he feels his claim to respect to be violated. His offerings are the fruit of his labour, with these fruits he invests himself, and in offering them he is offering of himself.[5] In relation to Abel, his loss was one of respect: Abel saw him humiliated, while Abel himself was exalted. Cain was jealous of the higher favour shown to Abel, not in tangible, material terms but in terms which precisely are not visible or tangible, but are traced in the visible: the regard shown to him and his offering of himself.

Cain is provoked against his brother not by any injury directly or indirectly inflicted on him by his brother, but because he felt his brother to have been granted a higher ethical worth than he. His anger has no other horizon than that of justice: Cain feels himself unjustly slighted, his self-regard violated. Despite the fact that Cain is the criminal in this story, that he committed the ultimate violence of murder, it is also in the heart of Cain that the idea of justice emerges. Abel signifies his competition for recognition. The claim to recognition is one which can be made in the context of competing claims: the ethical claim is one which puts brothers in competition and, indeed, in conflict with one another.

The ethical claim interrupts the real, brings to the real a demand which nothing real can justify. Abel's offering was perfect only in the sense that it came from a humble and good heart, but a heart which only god could see; similarly, only through an insight into the heart of Cain can god's rejection of Cain's offering seem anything but arbitrary.[6] The ethical claim both places an obligation on another and does so in the name of that which he cannot see, which remains beyond all worldly claims, namely, the heart which seeks in the world that which is a sign for it, but which in so exposing itself can be deemed unworthy. This investment of the heart in the world opens up a domain of infinite ambition and infinite pain, because it is a domain not limited by the finite reality of worldly things. The ethical claim, while a claim to justice and peace, provokes violence by placing the real under the bar of a perception of a just peace.

The second paradox of violence: violence disrupts the order of reasons that retrospectively gives it meaning.

While the origin of violence lies in the heart of the perpetrator, a heart responding not to the simply real but to the real perceived in terms of metaphysical claims and 'insights', the event of violence is there for all to see. It is manifest in the world, in pain and suffering as violations in the body of the victim. Furthermore, such events are not simply observed, they are witnessed: the recognition of violation is constituted by a perception of injustice and the consequent sense of responsibility to right the wrong of the violation. The awareness of violence is already an injunction to act. As such, awareness is witnessing. Witnessing violence brings with it the responsibility to intervene in the violent event itself. Such a responsibility disallows any claim to distance from the event, or at least makes such a claim to distance a retreat from responsibility.

However, it is precisely the retreat from the responsibility of the witness which is necessary for a philosophical investigation of violence. This is so because the philosopher's concern is fundamentally a concern with truth before justice, even if it is the truth of justice. As such the philosopher—to put the case quite simply—does not undo injustice, but *thinks* (and perhaps writes, speaks) about justice. Nor is the philosophical account a bearing witness to violence, because such a bearing witness demands an acknowledgment and acceptance of the authority of that forum in which testimony is given, whereas the philosopher only accepts the forum of reason, which is a dialogue of the self with itself (see Ó Murchadha 2012). The phenomenological and transcendental reductions simply radicalize and make explicit the philosophical relation to the world. They require a loosening of 'those intentional threads that connect us to the world', a stepping back from those bounds and relationships which tie the empirical self of the philosopher to her community, to others, and, in the case of violence, to the normal obligations of witnessing (Merleau-Ponty 2013, p. xxvii). This is not to deny that philosophers have been concerned with justice, indeed with the coming to be of justice, but this concern has, in most instances, been one which seeks not so much to further the striving for justice within the community, but rather to develop in greater depth and detail the account of that ideal state of justice, which in a more fragmentary and ambiguous manner informs the common horror, but also selective insensitivity to the horror, of violence.

Once this step is taken, violence can then appear in a disinterested mode. But in allowing violence to appear in this way, we must be aware philosophically of a certain complicity, despite and through our disinterest. This complicity centres on the relation of thought to violence: reason and language seem innocent of violence, because reason is the articulation of grounds in facilitating understanding, while violence tends to destroy any common ground. But in articulating rationally the deficiencies in the real, philosophy reinforces the ethical sense of justice, which stokes Cain's anger, but further understands the real as that which needs justification or, if unjustified, needs to be augmented. Such augmentation, lacking any justification in the real itself, can only be imposed from without by that which in giving reasons justifies itself as its own cause, its own reason. But this amounts to a violence against the real, understood as a making good of its inherent deficiencies. In some accounts, this is itself simply a natural process, a violence made necessary by the *polemos* of the real. But such a view can only begin from that metaphysical gesture which interrogates the real from the vantage of the ideal. While in its rationality, philosophy may seem to be immune from violence, yet precisely as the articulation of human beings' metaphysical condition, philosophy provides oxygen for violence. The disinterested relation to the violent event mirrors the distance to material nature that makes violence possible.

It is revealing in this context how much violence is embedded in discourse, discourse of justification, understanding, and condemnation. Often, we can pinpoint when a violent event begins—the first shot, the first punch thrown, the first missile fired—but the violent act hardly ever stands alone; it is almost immediately spoken of, explained, condemned, and justified. And even when the trauma of violence makes it impossible for the victim to narrate it, it bursts into speech incoherently, symptomatically. What such discourses point to are the origins of specific violent events, which are deeply rooted and which are traced in the actual violent act. Such discourses may justify or condemn, but they give voice to an order of reasons which violence itself interrupts.

The order of reasons, as given in a discourse of justification, requires a certain patience: patience in the speaker, who cannot give all the reasons at once and must allow herself to slowly speak to each reason in turn, and the patience of the listener who, sometimes painfully, must wait to hear the account before responding. This patience involves both a stilling of the will and an acceptance of a logic of discourse which is subject to certain norms of consistency, truth, and intelligibility. Yet, it is precisely this patience which the violent act betrays, and often, the discourse of justification will acknowledge this with reference to provocation or the weariness of oppression. Precisely at this point, however, the discourse of justification breaks down, or rather shows through its failure that place out of which violence emerges. In telling a tale of violence we tell a story, but nothing in that story explains the violence, simply because violence testifies to a loss of patience with the order of explanation. In seeking the origin of violence, what we are seeking is not an ultimate reason, but rather that which breaks with the rational and normative order. We are seeking that which does not speak in the plethora of voices which speak of violence; we are seeking the unspeakable and unthinkable at the very core of speech and thought.

'Unspeakable' and 'unthinkable' are usually words we use to designate extreme acts of violence, but the latter merely bring into the open something essential to violence itself: in violating boundaries, it first and foremost violates the boundaries of speech, it refuses speech in its most fundamental mode, namely, that of coming to understanding. The question then is how such interruptions can be understood and, indeed, what their ontological status is.

To reiterate, violence has its source in the metaphysical gap between the real and the ideal, opening up an infinite domain of the ethical demand for justice. If it is the case, as Pascal says, that '"justice without force is impotent"' (quoted in Derrida 2002, p. 238), the ethical demand is fundamentally impotent in this way, or makes its claims precisely on the basis of such impotence. The ethical demand is for justice beyond the realm of law. Such a demand for justice leads us, as Derrida has shown, into an experience of aporia (Derrida 2002, pp. 251–254). The demand for justice is a demand for that which cannot be measured, that which opens up an infinite domain which law necessarily and repeatedly closes off. While rules and norms are general, justice always concerns singular being, individuals or groups in a unique situation (Derrida 2002, pp. 252–253). Implicitly, Derrida is appealing to the uniqueness of the individual (itself unspeakable, ineffable in its singularity), which Leibniz (1989) expressed as the 'indiscernibility of the identical'. Yet, Leibniz does not recognize the aporia of which Derrida speaks and does not do so, because he generalizes justice as a fundamental metaphysical concept. In doing so, he sets justice—in a manner as radical as Anaximander and Plato—as the ultimate metaphysical horizon and, in so doing, radically relativizes the problem of violence.

Fundamental to Leibniz's account of the monadological order of the universe is the principle that every monad is unique and that its identity rests on this uniqueness. Each monad has a reason sufficient for its own being and, furthermore, for the world as whole, so the totality of all monads has a reason sufficient for its being. These two demands to respect both, the singular and the general, are fulfilled in the divine being, which places each creature in a relation of pre-established harmony. But if the divine being can unify these two claims and thereby overcome all aporias, we are left with an apparent conflict between reason and experience. We experience evils which seem to contradict the creation of things by a good and just god, but reason commands that everything is for a reason sufficient to it and that that reason is found ultimately in the creator of the world, who could rationally only create the best possible world. The theology of this does not interest us here, but rather the inherent conflict between the rational real and experienced reality, in our case, between the claims of reason to find sufficient cause and the reality of violence, a conflict which can find concrete expression in the problem of violence. If violence interrupts the order of reasons, of reasoning, is this an interruption which appears only on the surface, which can be understood more profoundly in terms of an order which remains constant throughout?

The question here concerns ultimately the world and its comprehensiveness. Leibniz defines the world as follows: 'I call "World" the whole succession and the whole agglomeration of all existent things' (Leibniz 1985, p. 128). Within the world so understood, all things have a place, and where there are faults, these faults are happy, as Leibniz quotes the Easter service: '*O felix culpa, quae talem ac tantum meruit habere Redemptorem* (O happy fault, which has gained so great a redeemer)' (Leibniz 1985, p. 129). In such a view, all violence and all breaks in the rational order are redeemed rationally, serve a greater end. Here we find the roots of the notion of a 'hidden hand of history'. As Leibniz puts it: 'God wills order and good; but it happens sometimes that what is disorder in the part is order in the whole' (Leibniz 1985, p. 201). The point here is that all the apparent evils in the world do not amount to faults in the whole. Rather, seen in terms of the world as a whole, they can be understood to serve a greater good. We do not see this or we see it only imperfectly, because we do not see the world as such. Our view on the world is always partial, always perspectival. Only an absolute viewpoint, the viewpoint of god namely, can see the world as such and the greater good to which specific evils contribute: 'the very nature of things implies that this order in the Divine city, which we see not yet here on earth, should be an object of our faith, of our hope, of our confidence in God' (Leibniz 1985, p. 207).

The basic intuition here is that ground—groundedness—is all pervasive: everything has a ground, and all grounds are united in a ground giver. There is in such a view, a fundamental responsibility for the world: the world is as it is for reasons which can be given, everything can be accounted for, all things can be redeemed. The influence of these ideas does not depend on theism; they feed into the philosophy of history in Hegel and later in Marx (Elster 1985, pp. 107–109). In Hegel and Marx, we find the idea that history redeems the past, and that in consequence violence, though causing short-term harm, can function to bring about a greater good. The horizon of justice in this view is all encompassing, and through a certain ruse of reason, great violence serves an ultimately just end.

The third paradox of violence: opened up by the difference of real and ideal, violence reaches its apogee precisely in closing down that difference, in removing the vestiges of the ideal, of the ethical, from the world. The paradox points to an inner logic of the relation of violence and reason: violence in interrupting the order of reason does so as anomalous, as exceptional. Where, however, the exception becomes the law, where the appeal to reason is reduced to senselessness, then violence ceases to be an interruption and replaces the order of reasons with an order of pure contingency, where the arbitrary becomes the order of things.

Leibniz already knew that experience speaks against reason's theodicies, and Kant pointed out that we cannot know the purpose or aims of god, and, as such, we cannot read such aims in nature, at most, we read them into nature (Kant 1996a). On the basis of experience alone, we cannot know such a goal. To the extent to which the philosophies of history are rooted in secularizations of such theodicies, the same objection applies to such accounts: in giving an ultimate purpose to historical events, such philosophies seem at variance with the often painful experience of violence without end and with hardly remembered purpose. If experience is limited, as Kant argued, to sense experience, then the rational accounts of history can be no more than more or less rational acts of faith. Yet these very philosophies of history, in proclaiming a future which will end all violence, function in terms of the logic we have noted: the ideal (rational account) feedbacks on the real (lived experience) and justifies horrors on the level of the real, in terms of an ideal more real than the particularities of individual experience (Popper 1989). Theodicy justifies violence through an appeal to historical process: history understood in its totality can justify the use of (some) violence. It does so in the name of that justice which is being served by the use of violence. Violence finds its redemption in the historical process it serves. The metaphysical order of material reality and ideal reason is governed by a harmony which is apparent to reason, if not to experience. But if this very difference of ideal and real lies at the origins of violence, then it would seem that we are moving in a circle: that which makes violence possible is in turn that which re-inscribes it in the order of reason. However, if we begin from experience, another reality emerges.

Violence permeates the temporality of human existence and, in so doing, is structured in relation to experience. Violence expresses memories of past wrongs, aims at hoped for futures, and indulges in cruelty in the present. Above all, violence is real to our experience. Yet violence threatens to undermine the very structures of experience: closing off the future as the means destroy the very ends which gave rise to them; failing to allow the past to pass by, locking us in cycles of revenge; tempting us to the destructive orgy of the present where past and future have no sense. Experience in the mode of hope, memory, and perception, in its directedness towards future, past, and present, structures those modes of justification which attempt to make violence meaningful, while violence threatens the very possibility of experience.

In hope, violence serves an instrumental role. According to Hannah Arendt, violence can be justified only in terms of the future, only as a means, and only if it is likely to bring about something worthwhile. Violence, in this understanding, depends on that end to which it is directed; it 'stands in need of guidance and justification through the end it pursues' (Arendt 1970, p. 51). In this sense, violence may be justified, but is never legitimate: justification appeals to an end which is to be achieved and, as such, is future-directed; legitimacy appeals to a past, the, as Arendt puts it, 'initial getting together' of a group of people acting in concert (Arendt 1970, p. 52). Violence can never create power (is indeed in itself without any creative capacity), although power without violence is vulnerable to destruction, if faced by violence. Arendt goes on to comment on the theodical manoeuvre I have been tracing, although without reference to Leibniz. She points out that Hegel and Marx share a trust in the dialectical power of negation, which she says is rooted in the understanding of evil as privative of good, such that good can and, indeed ultimately, does come out of evil because evil is a 'temporary manifestation of a still hidden good' (Arendt 1970, p. 56). The illusion of violence, then, is centred on its presumed capacity to create, but without power it is, Arendt claims, fundamentally destructive. In other words, violence depends for its constructive capacity on power which grants it legitimacy.

However, such appeals to ends do not always characterize the justificatory discourses surrounding violence. Rather, the discourse on violence can often concern memories of past injustices suffered. Perpetrators and their defenders attempt to justify violence, not so much in terms of its function to achieve an end, but as a restoration of self, as a reaffirmation of the ethical claim of a wronged community. Such appeals to the past understand violence as responsive, as a response which aims to restore the ethical balance (Fanon 1990, p. 74). Violence responds to a perceived denial of the ethical respect owed to the perpetrator and the community he represents and, in this sense, does not simply serve to bring grievances to public attention; it responds to those injuries, to those denials of ethical claims (Ó Murchadha 2006; Enns 2012, pp. 37–63). Such violence is often powerless (as in the case of a victim of abuse attacking her abuser), but it can also be the nexus around which the 'getting together' of power can happen, as with resistance groups in occupied or colonized lands. The claim to legitimacy is in the ethical claim itself, which in such circumstances only violence can proclaim.

Finally, violence can be justified by reference to the present. But in fact, here it only superficially aims at justification. Such a view of violence is characteristic of fascism. The fascist cannot justify violence in terms of past or future, because to do so is implicitly to understand violence as ideally anomalous—the violent act needing a justification in terms of injustice done and/or justice to be achieved—while fascism glorifies in the violent event which is valued for its own sake, aesthetically, indeed as an art work, *das Gesamtkunstwerk*.

While the justification of violence in terms of past and future not only appeals metaphysically to an ethical claim for justice, but also finds violence in need of justification—that is, as in some sense evil, even if a necessary evil—to 'justify' violence in terms of the present is to undermine the very conditions of experience itself. Violence, however, threatens to render impossible all purpose, all possibility of good arising from evil. Appeal to past and future can at least give some appearance of insulating experience from violence through its focus on past goods robbed and future goods to be gained. Fascism, by contrast, can be understood as an experiment in rendering such insulation impossible and pointless. In the concentration camps, it would appear that the evil which Kant thought as impossible for human beings, namely diabolical evil, evil maxims pursued precisely as evil, is evident (Kant 1996b; Agamben 1999). The concentration camps aestheticized violence in the sense of destroying time: those imprisoned in the camps were stripped of their pasts and closed off from any future. They were reduced simply to beings persisting in a now, with no meaning and no purpose. To the extent to which they were given choices, as for example to become members of the *Sonderkommando*, these were choices between evils. Examples can be multiplied, such as those in the genocide in Rwanda who had to choose between death and joining the genocide, or, in a domestic setting, a wife who can only escape a life of abuse through killing the abuser whom she loves.

The question here amounts to a complete inversion of the place where we began. We began by asking whether philosophy and violence share a common origin, namely, in the difference between the real and the ideal, between is and ought. Now, we must ask whether the ultimate violence is one which closes off all reference to the ideal, which reduces experience to a fundamental positivism in which no reference to the good is any longer possible and where nothing is left but the choice of evils, which in being vacated of all good no longer can appear as evil. In such a situation, violence becomes the norm.

I have in the course of the above discussion listed three paradoxes of violence: firstly, that it arises precisely in the disjunction between the real and the ideal; secondly, that it disrupts the order of reasons which retrospectively attempts to give it meaning; thirdly, that while opened up by the difference of real and ideal, violence reaches its apogee precisely in closing down that difference and thereby becoming normalized. Violence emerges in the response to the difference of real and ideal, both in the sense that only through this difference is it possible, but also that the ethical claim rooted in this metaphysical difference provokes violence. The awareness of an ideal in critiquing the real opens up the hope of an end which justifies violence. But violence as a means can overwhelm the ends it serves, the reaffirmation of self can become an orgy of revenge, with past and future being closed off and violence becoming normalized. The space between the ideal and the real is closed through, literally, the creation of *u-topia*, a non-place without time, the radical positivism of a law beyond good and evil.

Philosophy, even as a discourse of non-violence, is implicated in the provocation of violence, and through its continual questioning of the difference of real and ideal, it anticipates the final violence of the annihilation of that very difference. But if violence in the end threatens to undermine the very structure of experience itself, then it threatens the very possibility of philosophy. In the face of violence, then, philosophy cannot simply fall back on its responsibility to justice and truth, cannot simply insist on rationality in response to violence, because to do so is to fail to perceive the implication of philosophy in the violence it opposes. Rather, the task is to find a way of retrieving the possibility of experience itself, as that which violence threatens ultimately to undermine.

The clue here is with respect to language: while violence originates in the linguistic capacity to transcend the real, its ultimate end is to block all recourse to linguistic articulation and in so doing, dissolve human experience itself. To name something is already to transcend it in its mere positivity, and it is that transcending which violence threatens through a silencing of all discourse in the dull monotony of its violation, to the point where the very awareness of violation fades away. Jean Améry, a 'survivor' of Auschwitz, puts the situation very well:

> I recall a winter evening when after work we were dragging ourselves, out of step, from the IG-Farben site back into the camp to the accompaniment of the Kapo's unnerving 'left, two, three, four' when – for God-knows-what reason – a flag waving in front of a half-finished building caught my eye. 'The walls stand speechless and cold, the flags clank in the wind' [from Hölderlin's poem 'Life's Middle'], I muttered to myself … and [I] expected that the emotional and mental response that for years this Hölderlin poem had awakened in me would emerge. But nothing happened. The poem no longer transcended reality (Améry 1980, p. 7).

By making violence the norm, fascism blocks any transcendence of reality by closing off the temporal structures of possibility, and thereby, excluding both the responses of non-violence and the justifications of violence. It blocks the way to the latter, because justifications are rooted in appeals to justice which the fascist state refuses, as all that that state decrees is just; it blocks the way to non-violence, because this response to violence is only possible where violence is not the norm and the oppressor sees his own better part in the non-violent protestor.[7]

A possible strategy, then, is to remain with the present, the moment of violence, and to think through its structure. Violence is unspeakable, it reduces us momentarily to infancy—*infantia*: inability to speak. As Agamben points out, the human being is not 'by nature' linguistic, because if he were he would not have an infancy, he would not need to be brought to language by his society and culture (Agamben 2007, pp. 59–60). The learning of language is a learning of culture, a social becoming, a finding of that community of fellow beings which makes human life possible. The unspeakability of violence is the unravelling of those ties that not only bind human beings, but also, make them who and what they are. But in unravelling those ties, it discloses the fundamental tension in human experience between the transcendence of the moment in speech and the desire for the infantial immediacy within the moment.[8] If violence discloses the unspeakable, the ineffable, it is this, too, which is sought in mystical ecstasy. For all the philosophical critiques of such immediacy, it continually recurs, showing the loss of the immediate, the singular, in the coming to speech. It is precisely this singularity which Derrida (2002) points to as the aporia of law and justice: the universality of law by seeking equity blocks off the way to the singularity of the person, the situation. The horror of fascist violence is that it blocks the linguistic move to the universal not to reveal the singular, but to annihilate its singularity before taking its life.

But the unspeakability of violence, its refusal of transcendence, the ineffable in violence, shows up the fault line between language and infancy. This points to the interruptive quality of violence: violence interrupts the transcending movement of thought and speech. It is this interruptive moment which Benjamin and Levinas, precisely in the name of an eschatological peace, call 'another violence' (Benjamin 1996) or a 'good violence' (Levinas 1969). Benjamin, as later Arendt, speaks of violence as a means, but seeks then to critique it (in a quasi-Kantian sense), not in terms of the justice or otherwise of the ends pursued, but in its own terms, as a means (Benjamin 1996, p. 247). Justifications of violence understand just ends as reachable through justified means and means as justified if employed for just ends. What, Benjamin asks, if justified means and just ends were not harmonized in this way, but rather were in conflict? In other words, what if the just ends tend to justify means which are not justifiable and justifiable means do not reach just ends? This, he thinks, is precisely what the cycle of revolution and oppression teaches us. In such a case, he argues, we need to think of another kind of violence. The clue he takes for this is violence as 'manifestation' (Benjamin 1996, p. 248). Someone impelled by anger, for example, can engage in violence without any preconceived end (and indeed may immediately regret an end which his violence achieves). This, he thinks, points towards something essential about the authority of law: the law-enforcing state requires violence to manifest its own power. In opposition to this, which Benjamin calls 'mythic violence', he opposes 'divine violence', which is not law-making but law-destroying, not setting up boundaries but destroying them (Benjamin 1996, pp. 249–250).

As already suggested, such an account has a strongly eschatological tone. But such eschatology simply makes manifest that characteristic of the now, the moment, which allows it to open up the reserves of the present, singular and ineffable though they may be, in which boundaries are destroyed not for the sake of an unrealized future, not to avenge an unpassed past, not as an aestheticisation (and eroticization) of cruelty in the present, but rather in order to interrupt and suspend norms, set aside boundaries, and release self and other to the vulnerability of their own being. Philosophy can in this way echo violence, but in so doing subvert it, not by giving conceptual weight to justifications, but by demonstrating in its own practice the modes of interruptive speech which suspend the norms of discourse. Philosophy does this in its singular, verging on infantial, pursuit of the rich and complex idealities of justice, truth, freedom, and goodness as they emerge in the coming to expression of things to which all human experience is responsible.

NOTES

1. It is always dangerous to speak of philosophy in the singular, and clearly the history of philosophy in relation to violence is varied. We need only think here of Heraclitus, Plato, Augustine, Hobbes, Spinoza, Kant, Hegel, Marx, and Levinas, to see these variations. My claim, however, is that the source of violence is the same as the source of philosophy (in the difference of the ideal and the real), and that philosophical reflection cannot escape that implication and, nonetheless, remain philosophy. Implication, of course, does not necessarily mean advocating, and does not mean justification (indeed, it can mean the opposite).

2. Violence is not simply a matter of perception, but is always in relation to perception on the part of perpetrator, victim, and witness. Violence disturbs the normality of a situation and is violent precisely in the context of that normality. This is not to say that norms are free of violence, but rather that violence can only be perceived in terms of norms and normality. To see certain norms as violent is implicitly to deny their normativity; to perceive the normal as an exercise in violence is implicitly to deny its normality.

3. See Pascal (1999, p. 231): 'the human being is only a reed, the weakest in nature, but he is a thinking reed'.

4. Violence is ascribed to animals and, more clearly, to natural phenomena such as storms only through a metonymic shift of meaning. The lion attacking a gazelle is not violent because the gazelle makes no ethical claim and, *a fortiori*, cannot have its ethical claim violated.

5. Commentators point out that the text in emphasizing that Abel brought the first born and the best suggests that Cain's offering was less than the best, perhaps keeping the best for himself (see Speiser 1964, p. 30). So Cain's distress and anger at God's rejection of his offering may also reflect his own guilt.

6. This emphasis on the heart is not simply a Biblical one; for Kant, too, only God can judge the heart of the moral agent (Kant 1996b, p. 85).

7. The appeal to the heart and moral sense of the oppressor is essential to the Gandhian approach of satyagaghra (Sharma 2008, p. 17). On the rule of law and 'opening to the adversary', see Balibar (2012, pp. 12, 14).

8. I coin this word, as—revealingly—the word 'infantile' is inescapably derogatory.

REFERENCES

Agamben, G. (1999). *Remnants of Auschwitz*. New York: Zone Books.
Agamben, G. (2007). *Infancy and history*. London: Verso.
Améry, J. (1980). *At the mind's limits. Contemplations by a survivor on Auschwitz and its realities*. Bloomington: Indiana University Press.
Arendt, H. (1970). *On violence*. London: Harcourt.
Balibar, E. (2012). Lenin and Gandhi: A missed encounter?. Satyagraha Foundation for Nonviolence Studies. http://www.satyagrahafoundation.org/pdf/balibar_leninandgandhi.pdf. Accessed 20 July 2015.
Benjamin, W. (1996). Critique of violence. In M. Bullock & M. W. Jennings (Eds.), *Selected Writings. Vol. 1: 1913–1926* (pp. 236–252). Cambridge, MA: Belkamp Press.
Derrida, J. (1978). Violence and metaphysics. In J. Derrida (Ed.), *Writing and difference* (A. Bass, Trans., pp. 79–153). Chicago: University of Chicago Press.
Derrida, J. (2002). The force of law: The "Mystical Foundation of Authority". In G. Anidjar (Ed.), *Acts of religion* (pp. 228–298). London: Routledge.
Elster, J. (1985). *Making sense of Marx*. Cambridge: Cambridge University Press.
Enns, D. (2012). *The violence of victimhood*. University Park, PA: Penn State University Press.
Fanon, F. (1990). *The wretched of the Earth*. London: Penguin.
Kant, I. (1996a). On the miscarriage of all philosophical trials in theodicy. In A. Wood & G. Di Giovanni (Eds.), *Religion and rational theology* (pp. 19–28). Cambridge: Cambridge University Press.
Kant, I. (1996b). Religion within the bounds of mere reason. In A. Wood & G. Di Giovanni (Eds.), *Religion and rational theology* (pp. 39–216). Cambridge: Cambridge University Press.
Leibniz, G. (1985). *Theodicy*. La Salle: Open Court.
Leibniz, G. (1989). Discourse on metaphysics. In R. Ariew & D. Garber (Eds.), *Philosophical essays* (pp. 35–68). Indianapolis: Hackett.
Levinas, E. (1969). *Totality and infinity: An essay on exteriority* (A. Lingis, Trans.). Dordrecht: Kluwer.
Merleau-Ponty, M. (2013). *Phenomenology of perception* (D. Landes, Trans.). London: Routledge.
Ó Murchadha, F. (2006). On provocation: Violence as response. In F. Ó Murchadha (Ed.), *Violence, victims, justifications: Philosophical approaches* (pp. 201–218). Oxford: Peter Lang.
Ó Murchadha, F. (2012). The political and ethical significance of waiting: Heidegger and the legacy of thinking. In F. Halsall, J. Jansen, & S. Murphy (Eds.), *Critical communities and aesthetic practices: Dialogues with Tony O'Connor on Society, Art and friendship* (pp. 139–150). Dordrecht: Springer.
Pascal, B. (1999). *Pensées and other writings* (H. Levi, Trans.). Oxford: Oxford University Press.

Popper, K. (1989). Utopia and violence. In K. Popper (Ed.), *Conjectures and refutations* (5th ed., pp. 477–488). London: Routledge.

Sharma, J. N. (2008). *Rediscovering Gandhi*. New Delhi: Concept Publishing Company.

Speiser, E. (1964). *Genesis*. New York: Doubleday.

Waldenfels, B. (2006). Violence as violation. In F. Ó Murchadha (Ed.), *Violence, victims, justifications: Philosophical approaches* (pp. 73–94). Oxford: Peter Lang.

(1994). *The New Jerusalem Bible*. London: Darton, Longman and Todd.

INDEX

Printed by Printforce, the Netherlands